Disorientations

Disorientations

Eastern Europe in Transition

Text by Pavel Kohout

Captions by Alexander Smoltczyk

Afterword by Hanns Joachim Friedrichs

With 89 colour plates

selected from the work of 13 Bilderberg photographers

Thames and Hudson

Translated from the German **Der Wilde Osten**
by Karen Williams

Printed and bound in Switzerland

CONTENTS

THE WILD EAST

The Story of a Relapse and a Recovery

Pavel Kohout

The East is where the sun rises. Thus ran one of the first revelations which grown-ups confidently disclosed to me. It seemed credible enough: a city like Vienna, for example, undoubtedly lay east of my birthplace, Prague, as every atlas would confirm.

Much later, having been forcibly expelled from my native country and shipped off to that very same Vienna, one of the things awaiting me there was the news that my future home now very definitely belonged to the West. Prague, on the other hand, was now in the East. The globe of my schooldays was obsolete.

Admittedly, I had already slowly come to realize that no magic potion would help the inhabitants of Soviet Vladivostok, geographically speaking America's western neighbours, escape their fate: namely to be the easternmost outpost of the political East. In Central Europe, this confusion of the cardinal points was nevertheless disconcerting.

But that was the way it stayed. Whereas, a century ago, the word East meant the Orient and was scented with Indian spices, Chinese tea and Japanese incense, from 1917 onwards it served as a synonym for what was seen – both then and for a long time afterwards – as the greatest and most just of all revolutions.

Millions of people, profoundly disillusioned with the Tsars, utterly exhausted by poverty and war, hopelessly confused and demoralized by civil war and unpractised in the exercise of elementary civil rights, represented a malleable explosive for the group of intellectuals who promised them definitive historical justice.

Instead, in-depth scientific analyses of the sorry state of the Capitalist society of the day were soon subordinated to a new ideology in which anything unsuitable was first deleted, later suitably rewritten. Within a few years, Party bureaucrats had taken over the power of the soviets, and the adjective 'revolutionary' was tagged on to the word justice, which was administered by secret police who considered themselves to be above the law.

While the centripetal force of hope won more and more hearts for the glorious October Revolution all over the world, and workers from China to Austria attempted similar uprisings, the centrifuge of cleverly veiled power had long since started spinning out its waste matter – and in particular those idealists calling for the implementation of the original aims of 'their' Revolution – on to the dungheap of history.

As alleged traitors to the workers' holy cause, victims were liquidated first individually and then *en masse* by the real traitors, who first forced them, often with purely psychological pressure, to admit publicly to horrific crimes. This effective ploy further endorsed the necessity of the revolutionary Terror. Thus the greatest political fraud in history took its course, one whose agents – as perverse as they were successful – legitimized their crimes with 'noble' thoughts.

It was a task made easier for them by the inexorable rise of Fascism. In view both of the danger represented by the Nazis and of the impotence of the bourgeois democracies of the thirties, the leading Soviet Communists appeared to many as the only hope. Faith in this illusion was briefly shaken by the Hitler–Stalin pact, which let the masks slip, but only burned more strongly when the USSR, on the side of the Allies, bore the brunt of the Second World War.

The end of the war brought with it a tragic contradiction: the liberators of the countries east of the Elbe previously enslaved by the Germans now became their new occupiers. Upon their arrival, geometrical longitudes ceased to hold and were replaced instead by political ones. Be it Berlin, Prague or Vienna – everything was now the East, where the sun of Communism would rise.

The paradox of this devastating development was that the Wild East was spawned with substantial support from the mild West. First through the world depression, which threw the entire Capitalist system into question, and later through the fatal sell-out by the British and French governments at Munich in 1938, which shattered the trust of those threatened peoples of Europe in Western democracy. The situation was compounded by America's traditional ignorance of the Old World, which led in Yalta and Potsdam to a misjudgment of Soviet expansionism.

The stage was set, and the Cold War provided the new absolute ruler in the Kremlin with a welcome excuse to lower the Iron Curtain. From Cheb in western Bohemia to Sakhalin in the Sea of Okhotsk there fell an artificial polar night which was to defeat all attempts at illumination for decades to come.

People treated with particular brutality by the Wild East tend to compare it with the Hitler regime; many observers in the Western world are tempted to do the same. But one question continues to baffle: how, after their experience with the Nazis, was it possible for entire nations to keep alive a criminal system of government?

Anyone who took the trouble to read Hitler's *Mein Kampf* can have been left in no doubt as to what strategies his principles implied; factory-line killing was no more than their logical conclusion. National Socialism was the compound of envy and hatred nurtured by the eternal lumpenproletariat, forged by degenerate brains into a deadly ideology which pretended to be both national and social. That, too, was a fruit of the world-wide crisis afflicting Capitalism.

Only one suffering from Orwellian amnesia would deny that our own era opened with something of a Wild West, and not just in the sense of territory civilized – often barbarically – by American pioneers. The Wild West of the twentieth century flourished in the many places where the Industrial Revolution had led a still unbridled Capitalism to put aside all considerations of human welfare.

Tales of the lives of the working masses, even in enlightened countries such as England and the USA, read a hundred years later like horror stories from today's Third World. Thus European women and children, too, once laboured in the mines for up to twelve hours a day. The rise of Socialism promised an end to such modern-day slavery.

The mechanism of social development leads to model situations. The individual of the genus man continuously seeks to surmount every newly installed control and defence mechanism in order to dominate other men. Nothing is too sacred to be employed, however pervertedly, in this personal bid for power.

Even that bulwark of European morality and culture, the Roman Catholic Church, once degenerated into a mere instrument of power, giving its blessing to anything it deemed expedient to its ends, even if that included sending the innocent to the stake. It took a vigorous reform movement instigated by Protestantism to inspire the old Church to repentance and renewal.

Socialism assumed a comparable task in showing Capitalism where the limits lay. By organizing the defenceless and teaching them solidarity, it forced Capitalism to curb its excesses, to abandon its methods of total exploitation and to exercise moderation. It is to early Socialism that we owe the 'Capitalism with a human face' of today.

But the ideas, the history, the symbols and solutions and even the saints of Socialism, from the martyrs of the Paris Commune to the heroes of the anti-Fascist Resistance, were then suddenly requisitioned by the Communists. In established tradition, they declared the former Social Democracy to be the traitor of the working classes and themselves to be the sole legitimate heirs of the revolutionary legacy. As self-proclaimed 'proletarian internationalists', they simultaneously revealed their global ambitions.

This historical theft, as sophisticated as it was cynical, was the reason why grown-up, often highly intelligent, people at first swallowed the lie. They became the stooges of a new system of injustice in the firm conviction that they were continuing the work of their Socialist predecessors, whose numbers included many outstanding figures from the sciences and arts – something inconceivable in the ranks of the Nazi Party.

It is, above all, this malfunction of the intellect that we have to 'thank' for the fact that the Stalinism camouflaged as 'Marxism–Leninism' maintained its credibility as the perfection of Socialism for so long. For most of the worshippers, missionary activity for the devil and his hell came to an end no later than the mid-fifties with Khrushchev's speech to the Twentieth Congress of the Soviet Communist Party (February 1956). Many of the deceived committed suicide. The deceivers, on the other hand, completed a rapid exercise in self-criticism and declared themselves the sole legitimate restorers of order.

Before these events (as well as the Second World War) had led to the birth of the Wild East, officially known as the 'Camp of Peace and Socialism', the easterly parts of Central Europe had composed a very colourful mixture. With the exception of Czechoslovakia, which represented an unparalleled haven of democracy for its day, the entire region teemed with totalitarian regimes.

Among these were Germany (which had already been encouraged by many Austrians into effecting a sisterly invasion), Poland, Hungary, Yugoslavia, Romania and Bulgaria – all of them politico-military juntas headed by 'leaders', marshals, even admirals – in land-locked Hungary of all places! – or monarchs with a bent for absolutism. With the exception of Czechoslovakia and the German Reich, all of them countries we would today describe as underdeveloped.

Since, in the only legal elections held in the newly emerging East, even the comparatively free and prosperous Czechoslovakia gave its left-wing parties a parliamentary majority, and thereby enabled them to pre-programme future events, the ease with which the Communists rose to power in other, less liberal, countries may be well imagined.

Communism may have been beaten, but it is still far from being dead; its spirit lurks not simply amongst the political *Nomenklatura* – the self-serving privileged élite – but seeks fresh, unsuspecting converts all over the world. It is high time for an objective analysis of its genesis. Any further historical lies, even where circulated by its victims with the worthy intention of finally discrediting the nightmare, will only lead to the birth of a dangerous legend.

The Communists were supported in their successful series of putsches not only by the Soviet imperialists but by a goodly part – sometimes even the majority – of the nation concerned. The poor and the oppressed had long been waiting in vain for liberation by the rich and democratic West. They then turned to those who succeeded in shaping a jumble of beggar nations into a world power which could stand up to, indeed strike fear into, even America.

The Soviet Union of the twenties and thirties undoubtedly made enormous strides, leaping from the Dark Ages to the threshold of the modern age. Its fiendishly staged political farces were convincingly acted, and had the victims playing the culprits who sought to foil the triumph of the proletarians of the earth. Victory in the war, in which the USSR had both fought heroically and suffered unspeakably before the eyes of the world, ensured the optical illusion was complete. Many Stalinist murders were attributed to the Nazis.

An eternity passed before, in 1956, the giant screen which had flickered solely with images of happiness and pride finally cracked to reveal the blood and filth behind. For a short while the fate of the murderers hung in the balance; some were even hastily executed. But that simply enabled the accomplices to pull off another trick: they laid the blame not on the 'auspicious System' but on a small number of evil-doers, thereby smearing some of the leaders and many of the brightest hopes for the future with abominable crimes. Damnable as this was, the Revolution soldiered on.

Millions who had previously supported it, often of their own free will, were suddenly faced with a dilemma. Had their long years of struggle and grind, had perhaps even their whole lives, been meaningless because, like utter idiots, they had supported the wrong cause? Or was it a just cause after all, and was it perfectly sufficient to punish a handful of wicked sinners in order to bring their yearned-for Communism into closer reach? The individual of the genus man has a tendency to find solace in self-deception.

The thieves of the Revolution got off one more time.

But the Revolution was condemned.

There were already a host of people who had recognized the truth of the situation and who wanted to compensate for their blunder. Seeking to prevent intellectual error from becoming moral failure, some were driven by their despair to the barricades, to pay for the damage with their own blood.

East Germans, Poles and Hungarians staged uprisings in the fifties, tried to liberate themselves with the force of their anger alone, to flee to the West in their territorial entirety, so to speak. But every such escape bid ended beneath the crushing tracks of tanks, in a warning lesson to others: the same end awaited anyone attempting to leave the holy kingdom of Peace and Socialism.

The Czechs and Slovaks therefore adopted a different tactic. Rather than banging their heads fruitlessly against the walls of the regime, they conceived the idea of a thrust from within. It was a course of action possible only in a country where the Communist Party still had hundreds of thousands of members, inherited from its pre-war tradition, who remained loyal to its original ideals. They continued to hold many of the important posts within the Party, and now began to open up Czechoslovakian politics, unobtrusively but deliberately, to non-Communists.

With the natural instinct of the Central European, the cleverest among them immediately recognized the opportunity this represented for the country as a whole. Instead of launching noisy recriminations and internal battles, they seized their chance. The loosely knit allies now quietly set about preparing the ground for future structural changes.

'Democratic Socialism' was their initial goal, to be replaced as the pace quickened by 'Socialism with a human face' – and not simply to reassure Big Brother. While admirers of pre-war policies envisaged the country's future transformation into a 'simple' democracy with a 'normal' market economy, reformists still true to Communism believed in a 'third path' which would combine the advantages of both systems. Just how far their utopian ideas could have been made reality is a question which will remain for ever unanswered.

For the guarantor of world Socialism and guardian of the finest revolutionary traditions of the workers sent in the tanks to crush this peaceful process, too. The armies commanded to invade Czechoslovakia on 21 August 1968 included those of earlier fellow rebels. The West reacted with outrage, issued stern warnings to the occupying forces and surpassed itself with declarations of solidarity with the occupied, no doubt knowing it could do no more. After a few weeks the matter was dropped, and it was back to business as usual. The conservatives argued for unsettling the Soviet regime with the carrot and stick of trade and military might; the progressives for policies of détente.

As a 'Biafra of the spirit', as the Communist Louis Aragon described it, and as a 'cultural graveyard', according to Heinrich Böll, Czechoslovakia was definitively exiled to the Wild East. An exile which for many years seemed permanent. The extreme right breathed freely again, relieved that the danger of a friendly, perhaps even functioning, Socialism had finally passed. The extreme left consoled themselves with the argument that it must indeed have been a counter-revolution put down by the true revolutionaries. 'Better a pragmatic Socialism than none at all' was the motto of the day.

The Wild East seemed firmly cemented in place. Knowing today how close it was to collapse, one can only ask:

What made it possible in the first place?

It is time to air another lie, and one with which the humiliated masses sought to explain their enduring impotence under Communist tutelage. Namely that those 'on top' sat so firmly in the saddle that all resistance spelled suicide, while those 'underneath' were lost for generations to come. The law of this state of national emergency was simple: every man for himself.

It is also time to divulge that, for many people, the more this so-called 'pragmatic' Socialism revealed itself a cynical confidence trick, the more acceptable it became. One consequence of living within a permanent gigantic fraud is the tendency to counteract it with swindling on a private level.

'If you don't steal, you're robbing your family!' became Czechoslovakia's most famous catchphrase – in a state built upon the philosophical legacy of dyed-in-the-wool humanist Tomáš Garrigue Masaryk.

It is time to admit too that this degenerate Socialism survived not just on Soviet bayonets, but on the gradual silent acquiescence of broad sections of the population as well. Despite rejecting all, or almost all, of its political tenets, they nevertheless took part in the hijacking of the masses and thereby infected the entire body of their own society.

And it is time to confess that this rotten Socialism also offered splendid advantages – for those neither willing to exert themselves nor to see others who did so bettering their lives as a result. The system offered reliable protection from any such confrontation by nipping private enterprise in the bud.

Only within this sham Socialism was it possible for the uneducated and unqualified to receive a considerably higher wage than graduates with long years of study behind them, simply because membership of the working class counted for more. Was it surprising that education soon became seen as a luxury, and intellectuals as nincompoops?

Only within this un-Socialism were the untalented also allowed to be lazy, without having to fear that their standard of living would be any lower than that of most of their fellows – not counting the grasping *Nomenklatura*, of course. They were not even required to work hard – it was sufficient simply not to disturb the wheels of power. When out for a drink, they might even mimic the popular Good Soldier Švejk, long recognized as a harmless safety valve and tolerated as such.

Only within this would-be Socialism could the regime afford to proceed almost civilly against its critics, whom it seldom mistreated and usually only harassed or at most imprisoned. As for disciplining the average citizen, the quiet threat of the loss of such modest privileges as a better job, a trip abroad or the admission of children to the career of their choice was usually quite sufficient.

Only within this non-Socialism could the former executioners take early retirement because the authorities had since learnt how to employ more effective means of indirect force, without upsetting the finer feelings of their spoilt West European neighbours.

In Alexander Solzhenitsyn's brilliant summary: 'They used to torture us with hot irons; now they use cold coins.'

Those responsible for the pseudo-Socialism which did not want to end included not simply the infamous manipulators, but also all those who were only too willing to be manipulated.

When, a few years back, the firm of Glasnost & Perestroika announced the 'grand reopening' of Socialism, past experience led most people in both East and West to expect another hoax – a particularly cunning reincarnation of Stalinism, perhaps. The lightning of Chernobyl, accompanied by thundering untruths, seemed to illuminate a familiar backstage scene.

This time, astonishingly, the feelings of the populace concurred with the convictions of the rulers in the Kremlin, who sought to preserve the East, from Mongolia to Czechoslovakia, in its same wild state. These bigwigs were soon watching paralysed, however, as their new chief comrade lifted one taboo after another – even if, on some occasions, with ill-concealed hesitation.

After a while it became possible to identify unmistakable similarities between the budding perestroika and the Prague Spring that had been pronounced officially dead. This time, too, reform had started from the centre of power: the Wild East was to be reclaimed with the aid of 'true' Socialism. But it was already too late: there was almost nothing left that could be reclaimed, and even less that could be called Socialist.

Only in the Hungarian Communist Party could figures still be found who enjoyed a certain degree of support among the general public. In the rest of the East, every former, or even potential, reformist had long since been removed from the ranks – half a million in Czechoslovakia alone. Entire Party leaderships were dominated by opportunists and cynics who had long since forfeited the trust of their peoples.

Then, suddenly, the clock struck. The hour had come for all those who – in a label which sounded no less suspicious to the many Western ears still bent to a system they did not have to live in themselves – were called 'dissidents': the men and women who, despite years, and in some cases decades, of harassment and intimidation, had stood up for elementary civil and human rights. Although they remained without access to the media, their message spread like wildfire. People shed their fear like old skin.

The flagging organs of power rallied themselves and sent their praetorian guards into the final fray. Batons and water cannon were brought out one last time, and there were even a few live bullets fired, all in the vain hope that, if the worst came to the worst, the tanks from Moscow would hurry to their neighbourly aid. But the strange man in the Kremlin only continued to do what earned him – deservedly, for all his mistakes – the Nobel Peace Prize: nothing.

'Life will punish those who don't move with the times', he informed his vassals, and simply left them to their fate. The small hole bored into the Iron Curtain by the brave Hungarians proved a fateful signal. The Berlin Wall – that hated symbol of the arbitrary division of Europe – fell just a few weeks later. And the domino effect toppled the last remaining bastions soon afterwards.

The miracle year of 1989 appeared to signify the end of the Wild East.

But it was to be otherwise.

Demons die hard. Over forty years – and over no less than seventy in the Soviet Union – a misguided Communism altered the thoughts and feelings of whole generations. For those countries with no, or only brief, past experience of democracy, the gulf separating them from the West and its scale of values grew ever deeper. Lies gradually became the accepted idiom, if not quite the truth; deception no longer represented even a petty offence, but simply a normal pattern of behaviour.

For those four or seven decades, any problems or conflicts threatening to cloud the bright picture of an all-conquering, all-embracing Communism were simply hushed up, swept under the red carpet which covered the vast area of the 'Camp of Peace' from wall to reformatory-style wall. Mass-media falsifications and artificial amnesia took their effect on the brain cells and genes of the people trapped within. The consequences can still be felt.

Used to tricks of all kinds, but unused to exercising their newly acquired civil rights, many people shrug off their unexpected freedom as just another ruse by the invincible authorities, whom they see playing the wolf in sheep's clothing simply to bite all the harder in the end. Stalin would be delighted by the numbers that pine after him, the strict father figure who nevertheless protected his children from the need to make decisions and thus to take responsibility.

People's uncertainty as to whether they will be able to run their own lives is now coupled with their disillusionment with a West which, worshipped only yesterday, is today not simply unwilling to share its riches with the poor, but is still calling upon them to keep their noses to the grindstone. That seems unfair: people want instant wealth, as in Capitalism, but they also want their peace and quiet, as in Socialism.

It is good at least to be able to let off political steam without risk. Why should the only people to have a say be the 'protestors', the ones who alienated themselves from the masses? Obedient slaves are suddenly discovering that they are born leaders eligible for higher orders. The red carpet has disappeared, and the unsolved problems it once hid now lie waiting to be used as battering rams with which to storm the palaces of power.

The 'Velvet Revolution' which took place amidst the peaceful jangling of key-rings in the autumn of 1989 has upset the plans of those it caught napping, memories of whose former passivity and even collaboration can only be erased by dramatic action. Every explosive left behind by the old regime is now being detonated in order to demonstrate to the new representatives their inability to cope. Regardless of the fact that the most important task – fundamental political and economic reform – is thereby being undermined and delayed.

Suffering particular turbulence as a result is the very country which set the reform process in motion. The sluggish democratization of the USSR has given its beleaguered *Nomenklatura* and military top brass time to recover from their initial shock and to close ranks. The still powerful centralized economy causes bottlenecks which it then immediately blames on the not yet fully established market economy.

Inexperienced democrats incite anarchy, which in turn sounds the call for restoration of order. Meanwhile, the 'internationalism' which once blurred regional distinctions has been replaced overnight by a national chauvinism which admits no common denominator. Instead of joining forces in order to make up the catastrophic delay all the faster, rusty hatchets are being disinterred and long-outdated enmities revived.

'*Divide et impera!*' – 'Divide and rule!' The trusty sword of the tyrant now being wielded by peoples so recently liberated spells certain self-destruction.

Revenge is suddenly on the agenda, and since previous allegiances were almost purely nominal, everyone is going for everyone else. One feeling nevertheless binds them all: hatred for those who refused to compromise and who now represent the righteous few. There is nothing the individual of the genus man can stand less, and nothing he suppresses more, than his own bad conscience.

The voice of reason, only recently declared the sole legal mouthpiece of the new era, goes unheard amidst the din, while the shattered economy sinks into deeper and deeper chaos and social tensions reach new explosive heights.

Meanwhile, the defeated Stalinists are laughing again – at the Pyrrhic victory scored by their vanquishers.

Thus the East remains wild!

But this horrifying picture, however appropriate it may be, is nevertheless deceptive. Microprocesses can be observed beneath the stormy surface which indicate that the insidious decline of the 'European psyche' in the former political East has been halted; new cells and genes are forming, albeit predominantly in young organisms.

It is both astonishing and encouraging to see the speed with which more and more people are accustoming themselves to freedoms of which they, and in some cases generations of their forebears, had not the slightest previous notion. After just a few months they already consider them as indispensable as the air they breathe. Full freedom of opinion and movement has already become part of their blood.

The omnipresent fear, so real that it stamped even the streetscape, vanished as quickly and completely as did the ghostly border installations with their instruments of death. Every day saw the suffocating lid which had stifled every initiative and dream lift another inch – a development deemed irreversible by virtually everyone who has had an opportunity to experience it.

The Wild East effectively deprived its citizens, whom it declared incapable of managing their own affairs by law, of all their rights; it thereby also released them from their obligations. The return of civil rights, as recently enshrined in new basic laws, paves the way for the rebirth of a sense of duty.

Lifting the Iron Curtain is like opening a floodgate: the volume of water represented by the higher-level civilizations threatens to overwhelm everything lying below. Happily, however, the lower water level rises to meet it and the law of liquids in communicating vessels comes inexorably into force.

Communities which, momentarily panicked, fail to close the floodgate half-way, or even fully, will – in view of past experience – surely survive this 'in-between period'. Such a transitional crisis is positively harmless compared to the bloody coups feared just a couple of years ago.

If no large-scale political earthquake occurs in the near future, if national conflicts do not escalate to civil-war proportions, and if the Soviet Union in particular halts its downhill slide and starts to integrate itself into the European security and economic system, then the days of the Wild East will be numbered, and soon it will haunt none but the pages of picture books.

Then the East can return to being simply a respectable geographical term, and the concentrated energy of the ancient continent of Europe can be used to revitalize the region which has for so long been languishing in abject poverty:

the Poor South.

Prague/Vienna, May 1991

P.S. Only a few months later, the tragedy of a disintegrating Yugoslavia, alongside the drama of a dissolving Soviet Union, demonstrates that the realization of this dream still remains a long way off.

The East seems, on the contrary, to be experiencing its wildest phase yet – but that changes little as far as its history and our hopes are concerned.

Vienna, November 1991

THE PLATES

With everything now permissible in the Wild East, everything has to be tried out. Without fear of kitsch or convention. 'Down with Socialist Sur-Realism' – thus the motto of Moscow painter-poet Vadik Moroe. Tulle and foam rubber generously compensate for the letter his own name lacks to turn him into a Monroe. Down with the ubiquitous icons of power, vampire eyes for Lenin, effeminate make-up for Gorby, and Marilyn for the Central Committee! (August 1990)

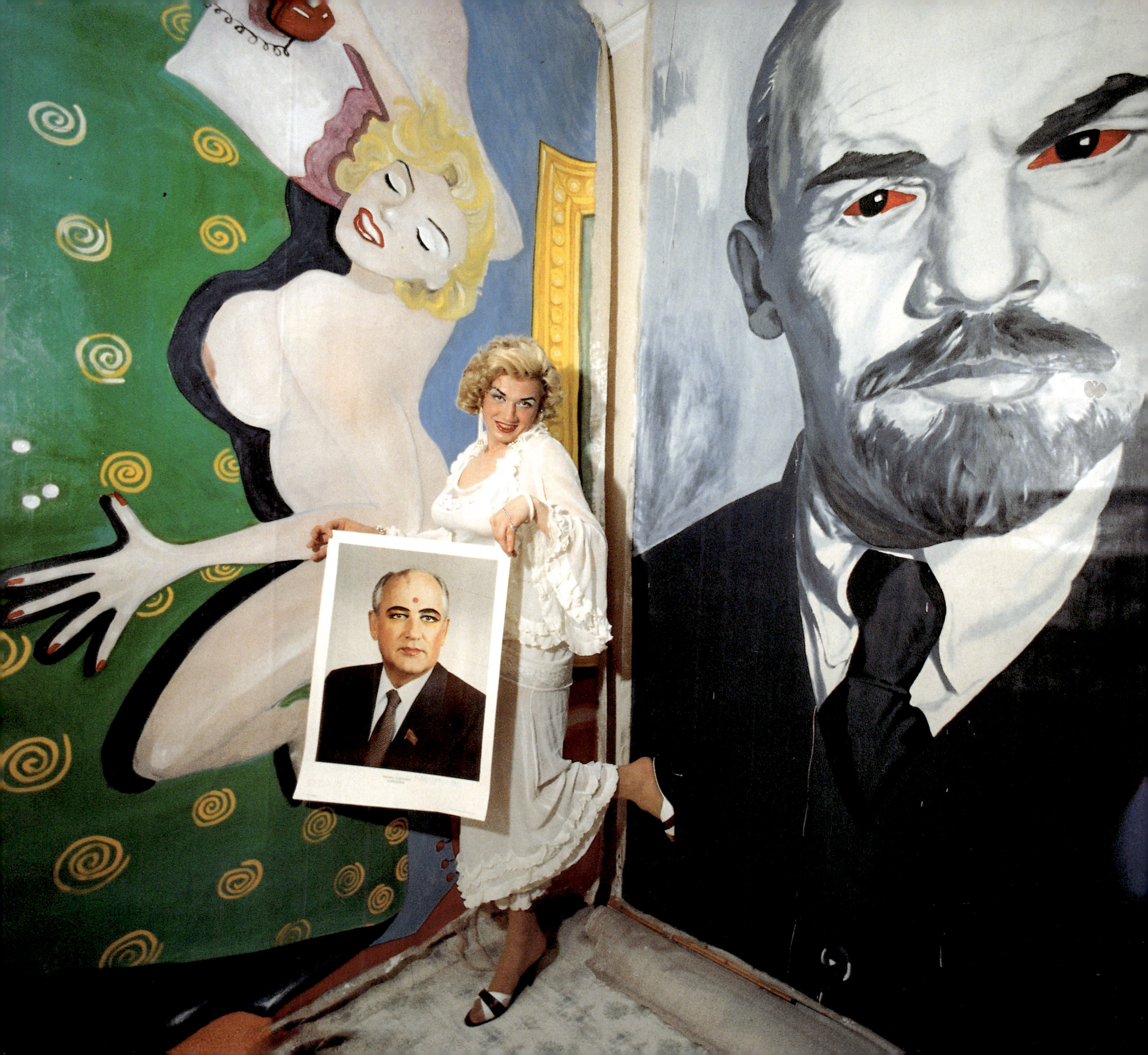

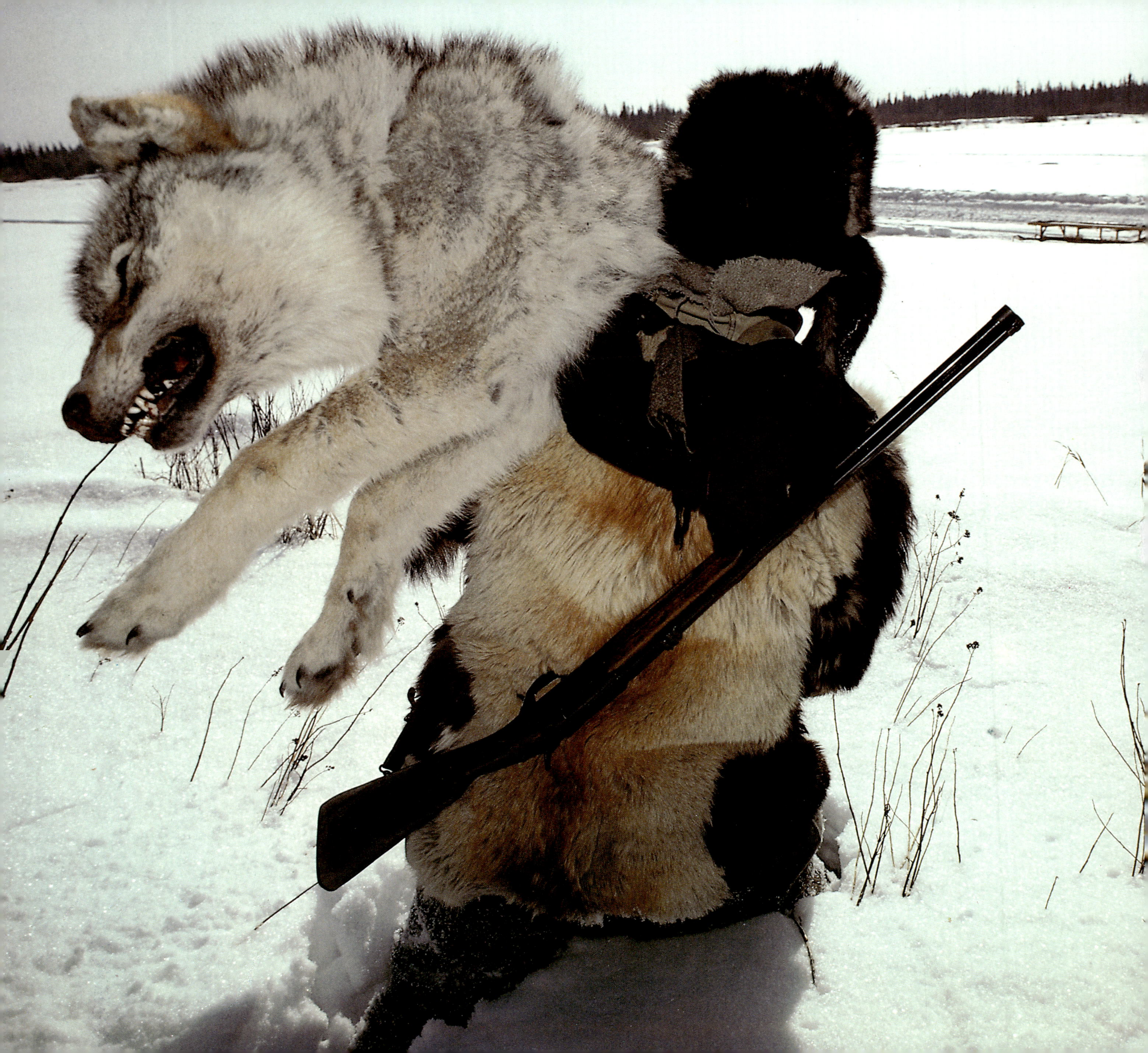

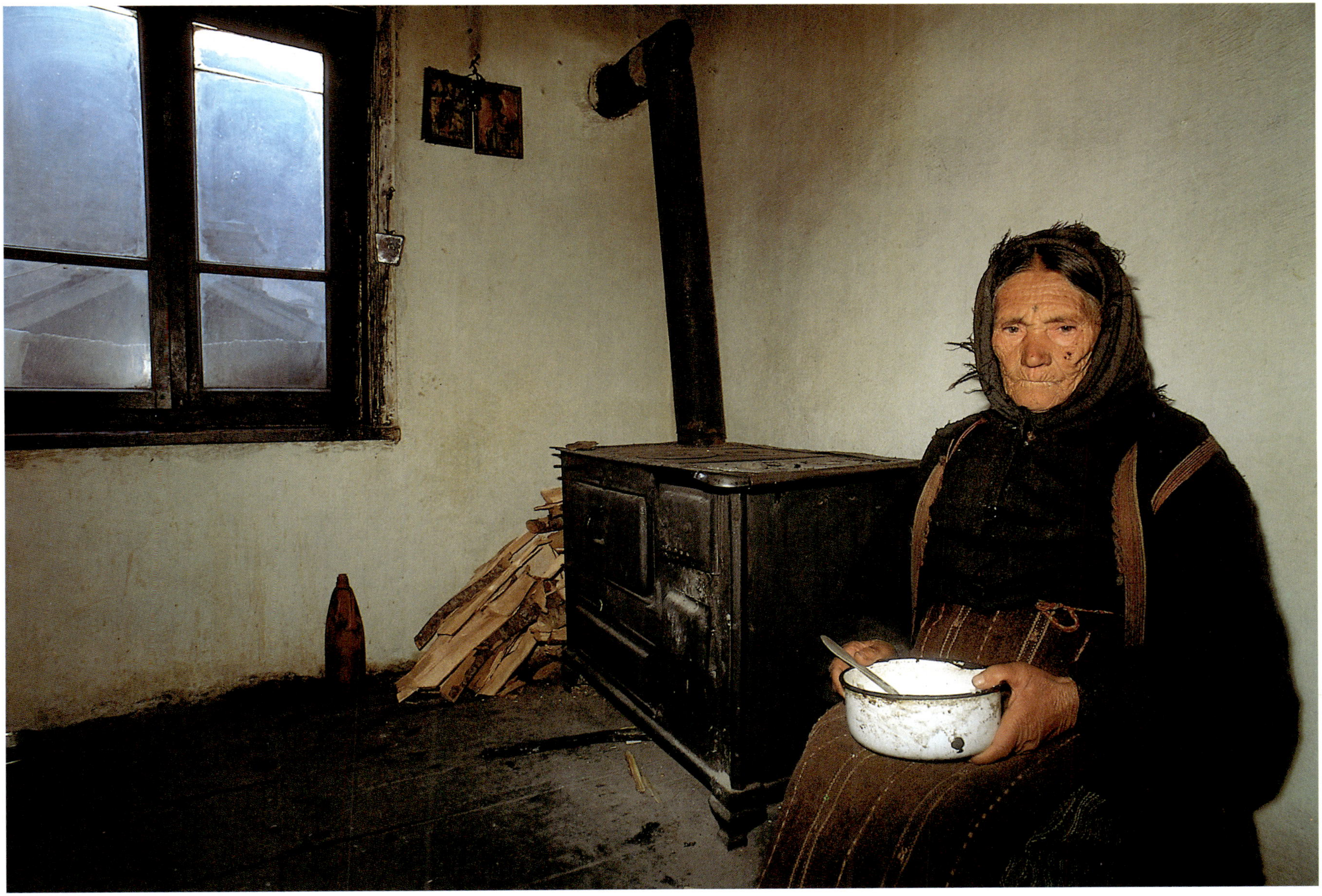

Facing page • Its inhabitants call Siberia the 'last country'. A country where they still hunt wolves and bears in temperatures of down to −60°C (−76°F). Fyodor Mikhailovich Toropov, known as Fedya, is used to it. He is one of the best hunters from Yerbogachon, a village in the Irkutsk region. In winter, alone with his dog, he roams for weeks on end through the taiga. For bagging a wolf he earns a special bonus of a hundred roubles, for an ermine fifteen. The central collection point in the village pays prices fixed by the State; even the remotest wilderness is part of the overall economic plan. (March 1988)

Above • The 'Land of the Centenarians' is what the Bulgarians call the Rhodope mountains on the border with Greece. Time has bypassed its villages, and its people live to a ripe old age. This farmer's wife from Pirin has worked all her life, performing the same chores, eating the same meals, seeing the same faces every day. But now she is alone. The young people have moved to the city, to the high-rise blocks of Sofia. There will soon be no centenarians to succeed her. (February 1989)

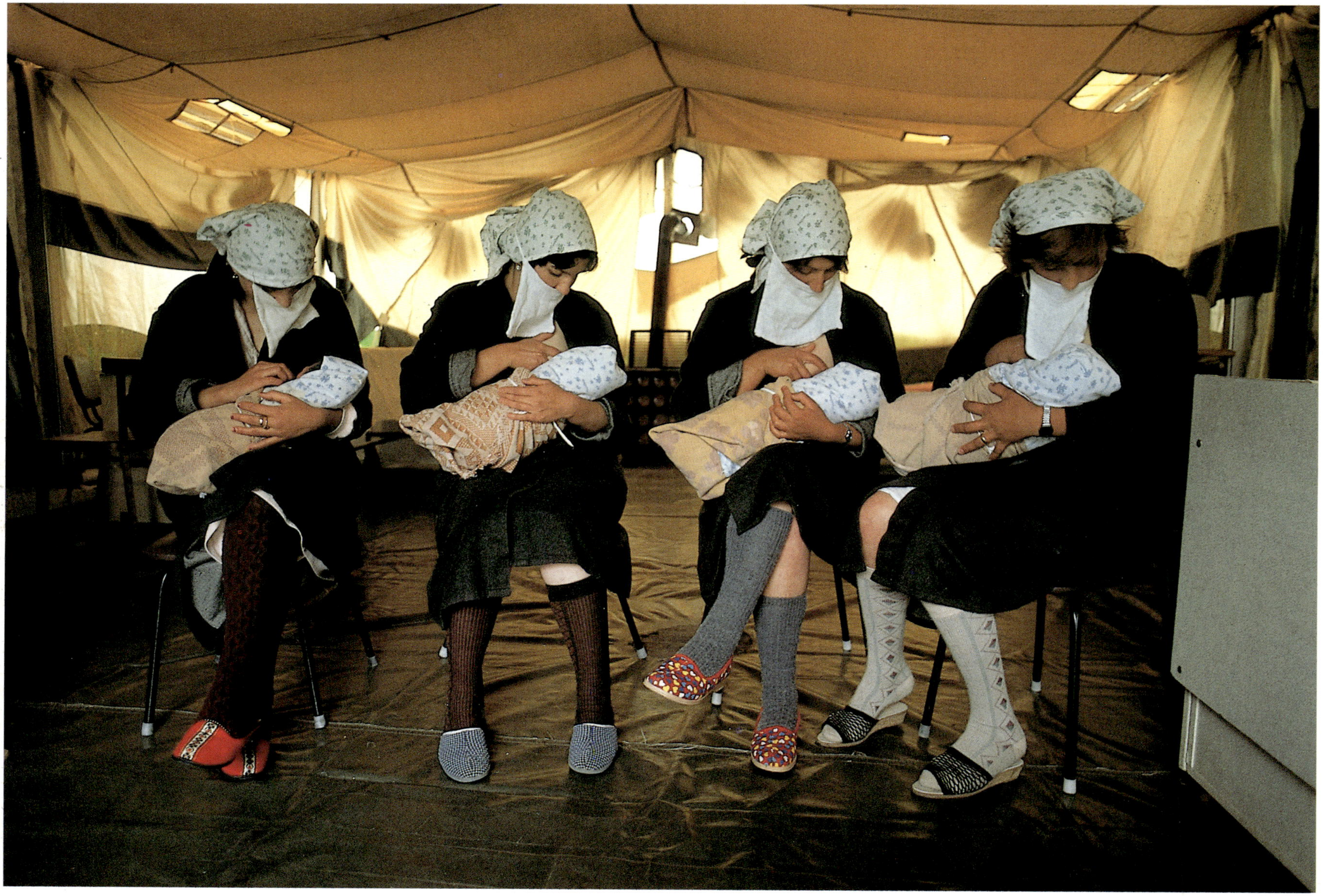

Above • Life carries on in Armenia. While, outside, bulldozers flatten the mounds of rubble left by the earthquake, babies are breast-fed in the maternity tent in Stepanavan. The delivery ward was one of the first to be set up in the emergency Red Cross hospital. For the victims, that was important: as long as there are mothers, life will somehow carry on. (December 1988)

Facing page • The youngest of the great and glorious Soviet navy. On the banks of the Neva, cadets from the Leningrad (now once again St Petersburg) naval school rehearse for the Revolution parade. Many are orphans; the oldest is sixteen. The élite of the Soviet fleet are trained here for three years. Alongside the normal school curriculum, 'Defence' is also on the timetable: a reflection of the new military doctrine. (January 1990)

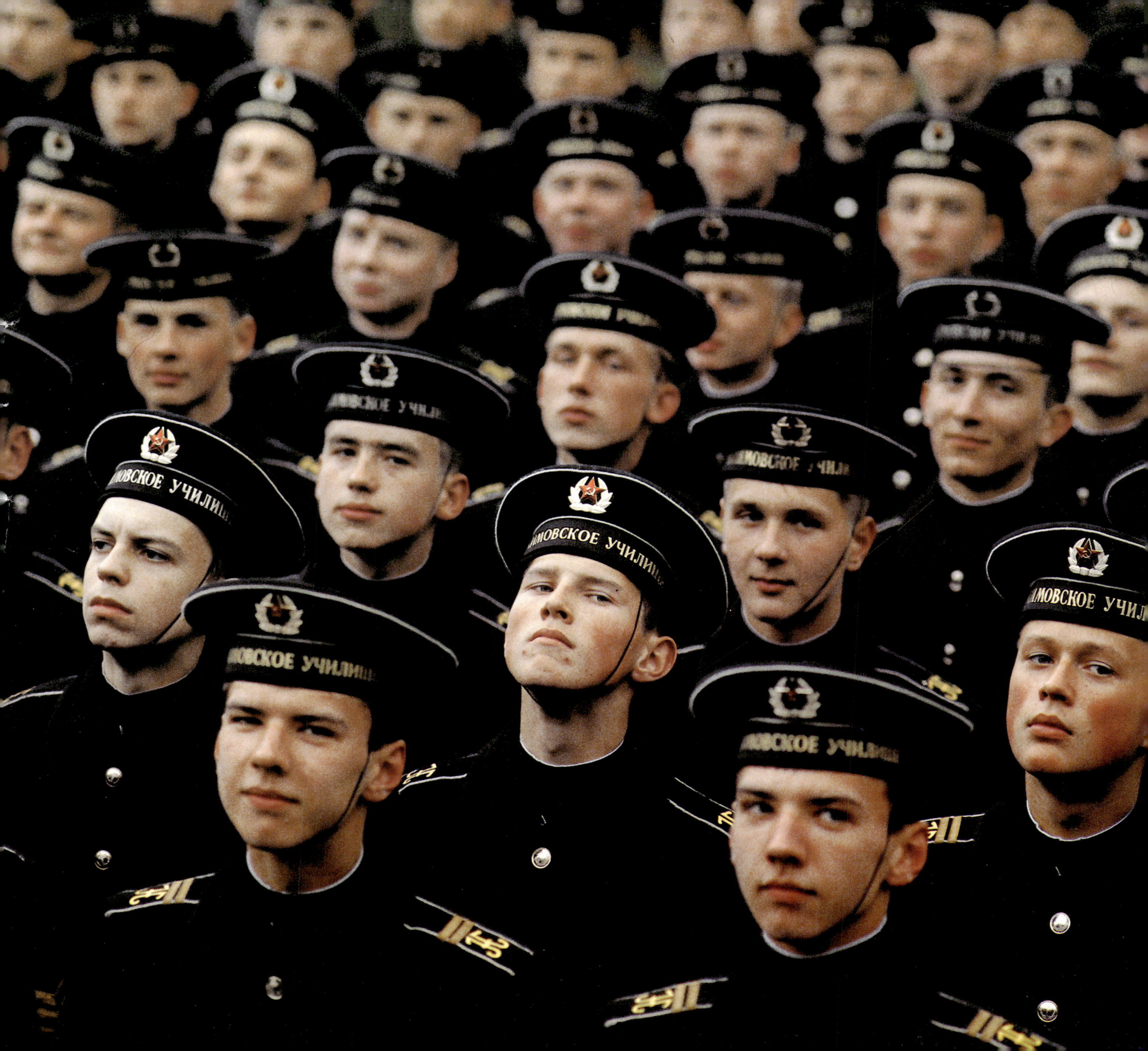
МОВСКОЕ УЧИЛИ
ИМОВСКОЕ УЧИЛИЩ
МОВСКОЕ УЧИЛИЩ
МОВСКОЕ УЧИЛ
МОВСКОЕ УЧИЛ

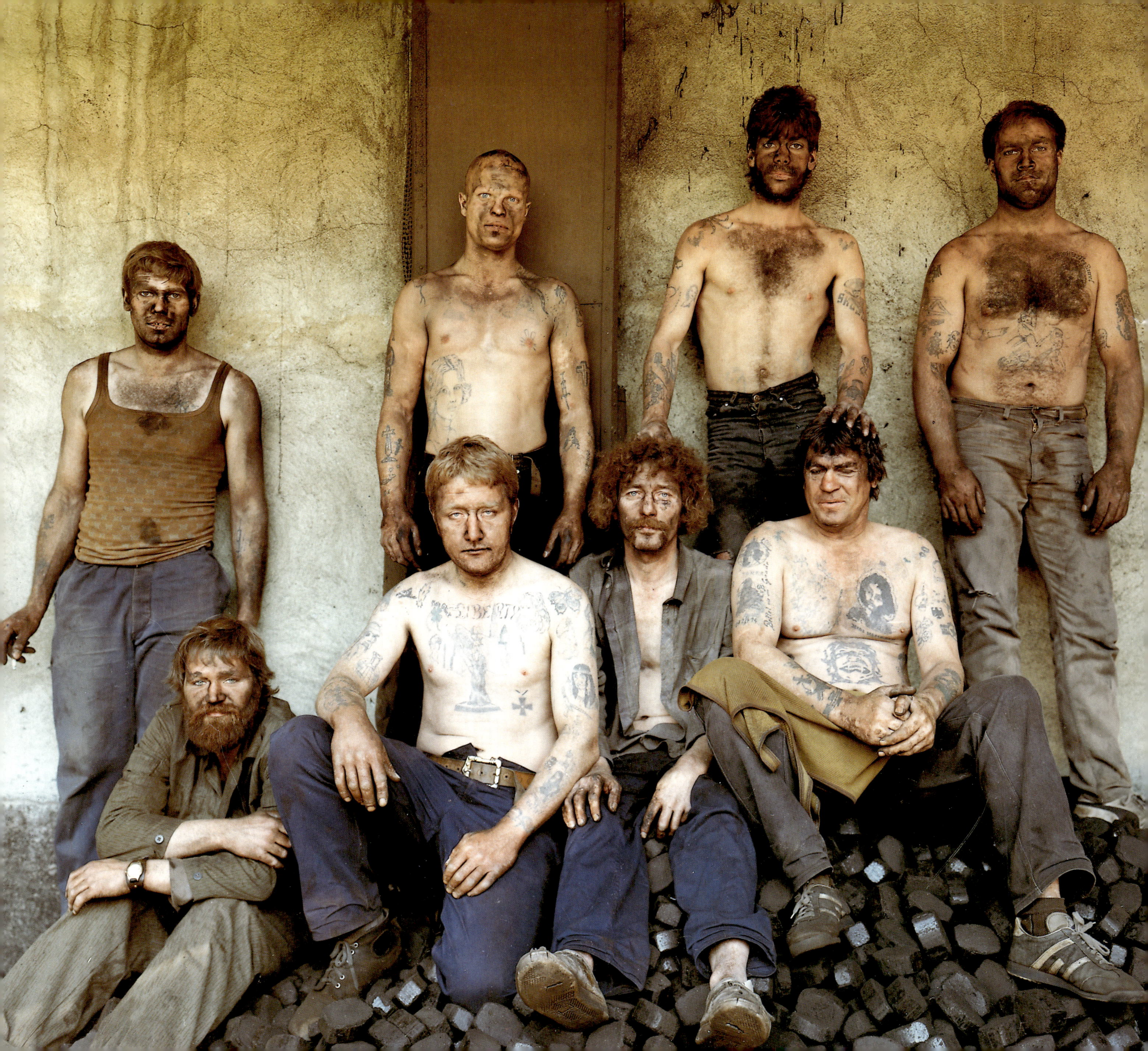

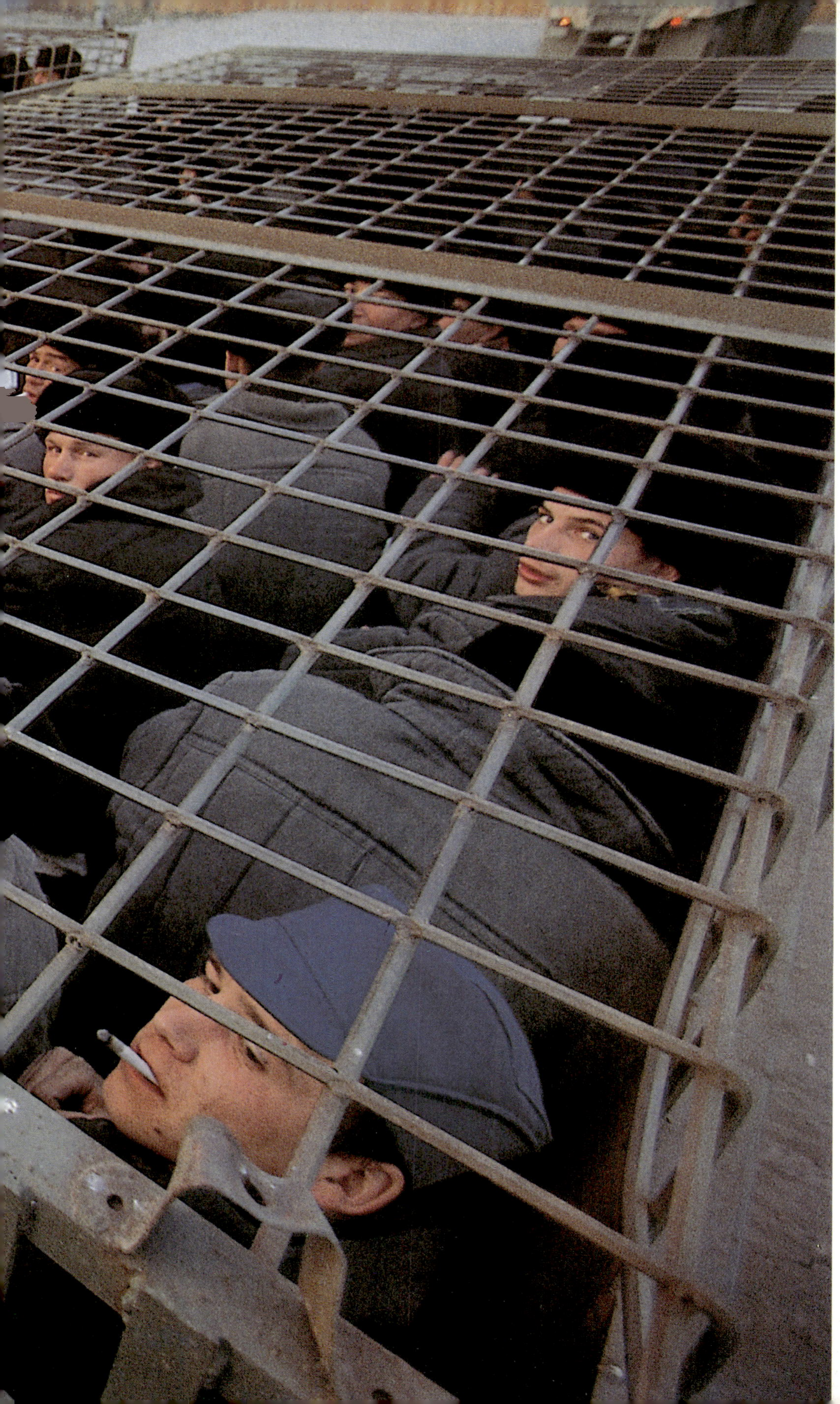

Siberia's human cages. Re-education in Camp 272/32, east of Lake Baikal, supposedly teaches prisoners 'increased Communist consciousness'. Each morning the men are taken in trucks to work in the chemical factory at Sayansk. The factory's vinyl chloride plant was supplied by a West German company, its workforce by the Soviet penal code. (March 1990)

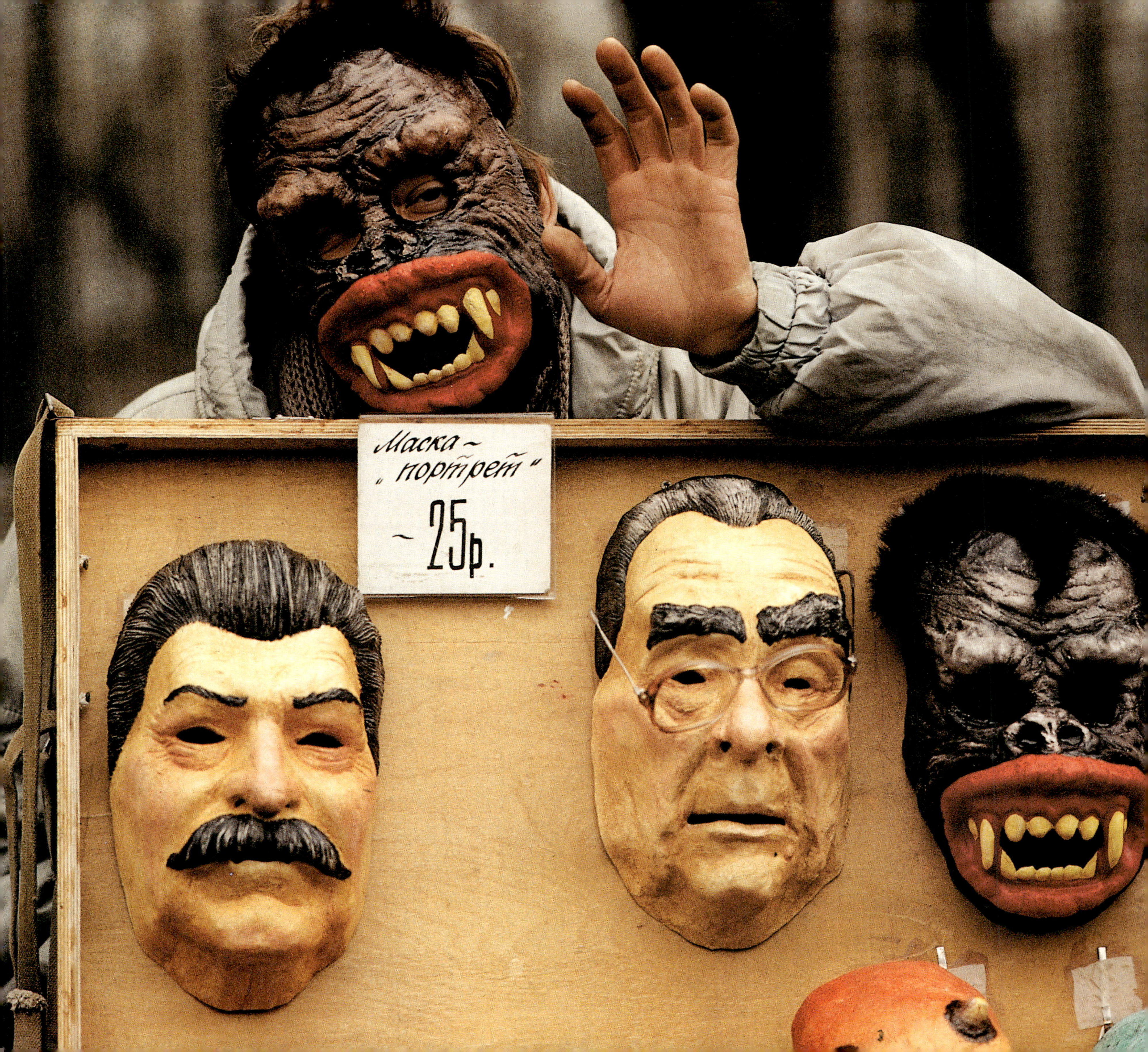
Маска –
„ портрет "
~ 25р.

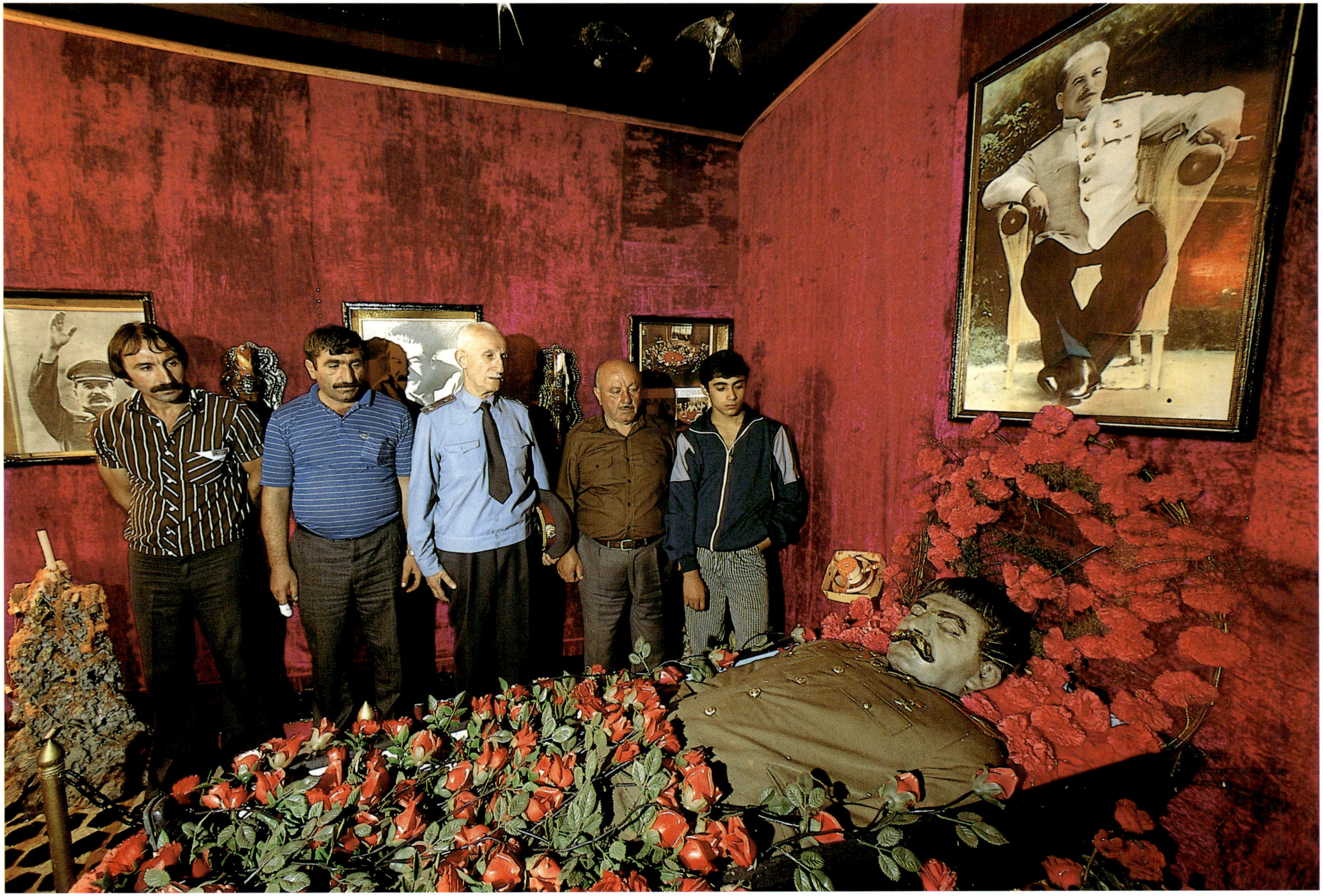

Facing page • Masks – because no one needs to hide any more. For just twenty-five roubles, Muscovites can play at being both monster and dictator: Stalin, Brezhnev and King Kong have long been all the same to the hawkers in Ismailovo Park. For objects of derision are no longer dangerous. (May 1989)

Above • Masks – because calls for the former all-powerful leader are being ever more loudly voiced. In a Georgian village near Tbilisi, the Kunelauri family have built a private mausoleum. The death mask is home-made, and the tape recorder plays Stalin's favourite air – 'Fly away, black swallow'. Up to forty bus-loads of visitors come every day, amongst them the retired militiaman from the 'Stalin Society'. 'At least under them there was something to eat', he says. (March 1990)

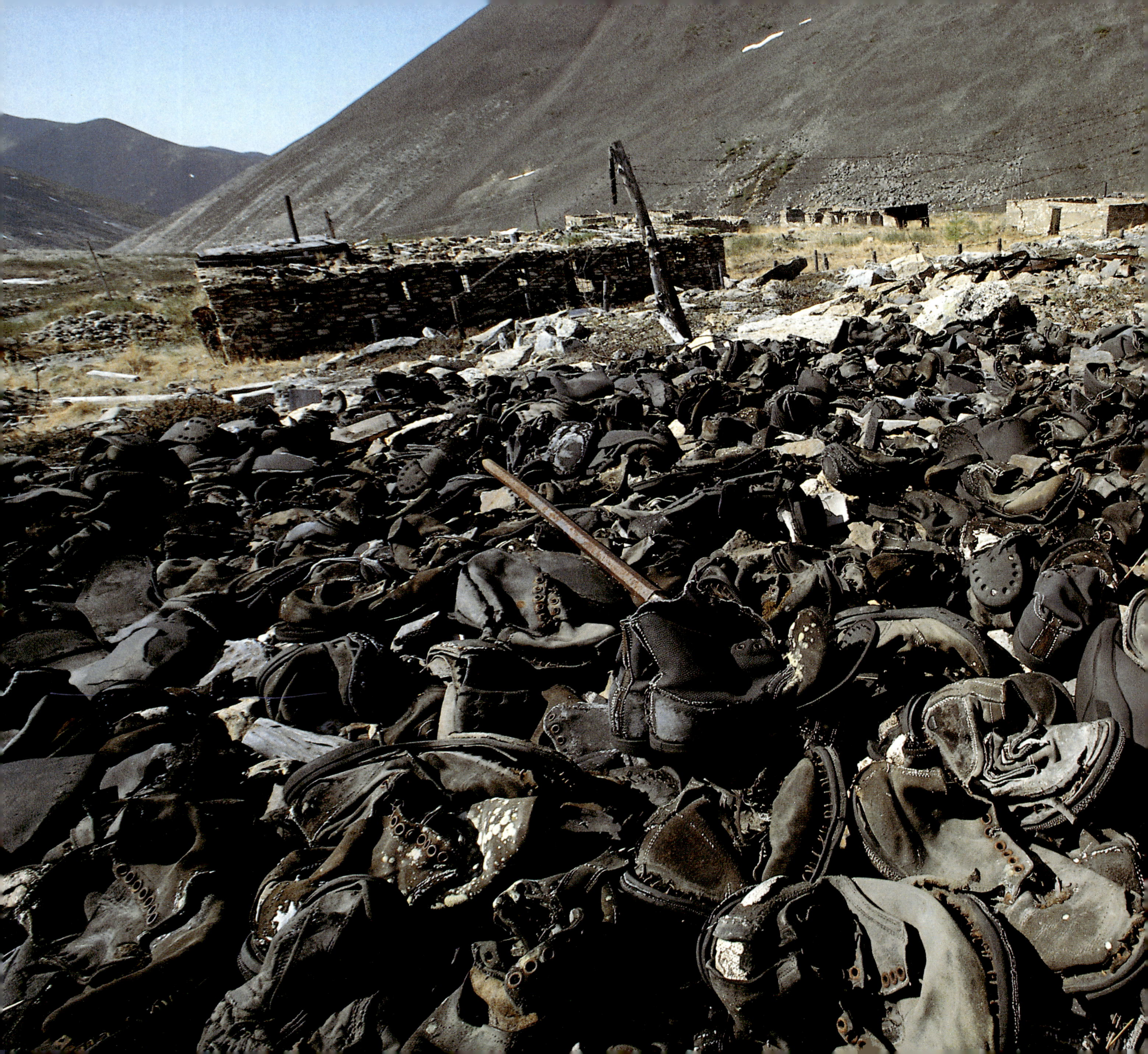

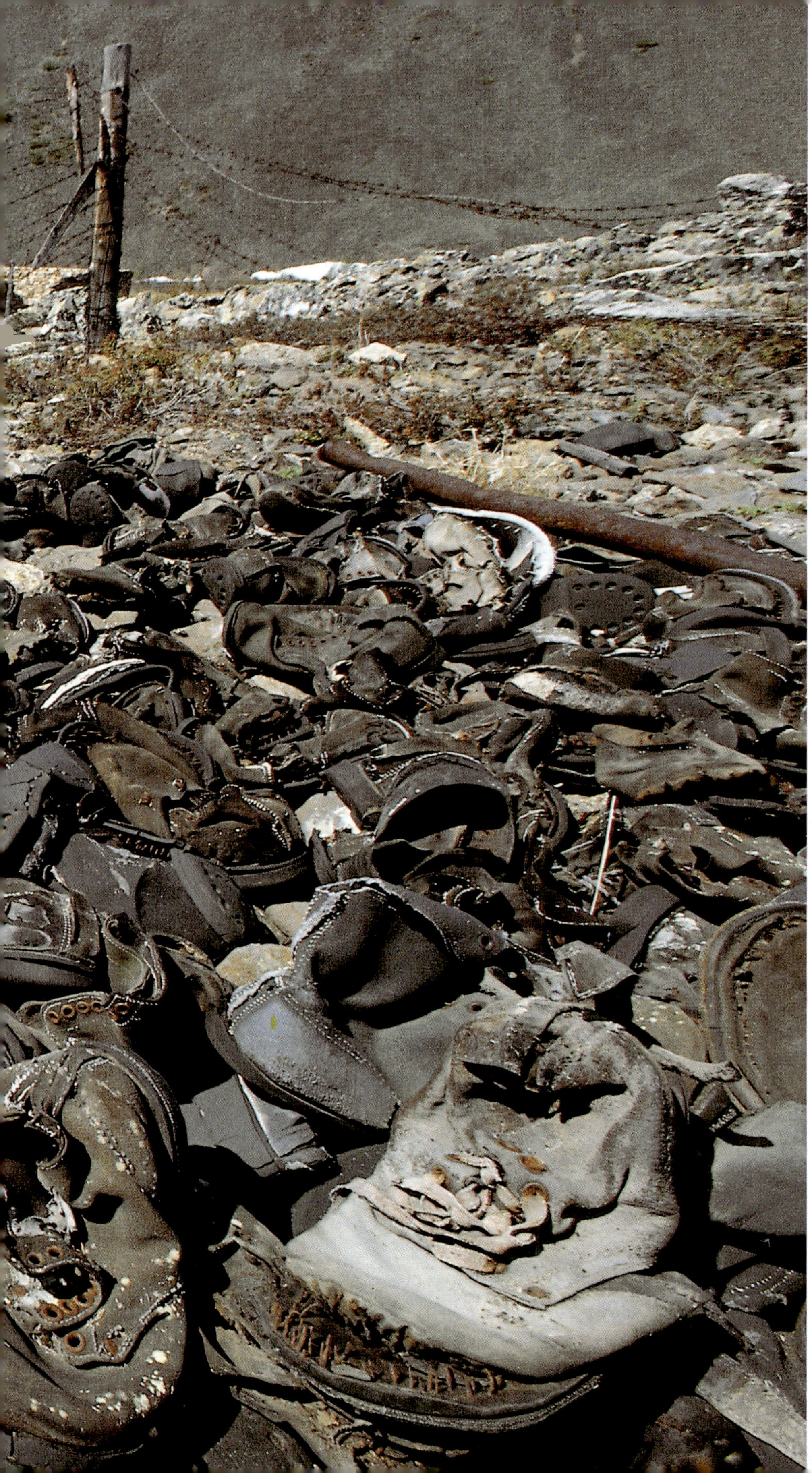

The forbidden land at the northeastern extremity of the Soviet Union: Kolyma. Prisoners in the Butugychag gulag clawed uranium out of the frozen ground with their bare hands. Fifty thousand forced labourers, and temperatures lower than −50°C (−58°F) for months on end. Anyone mentioning 'the metal' was shot on the spot and buried in the pits. The camp existed for twenty years; two million people lost their lives. The crimes of the culprits were statute-barred after ten years. What still remains is a mountain of shoes, together with fear, mistrust and paralysing resignation: Stalin's bequest to perestroika. (March 1990)

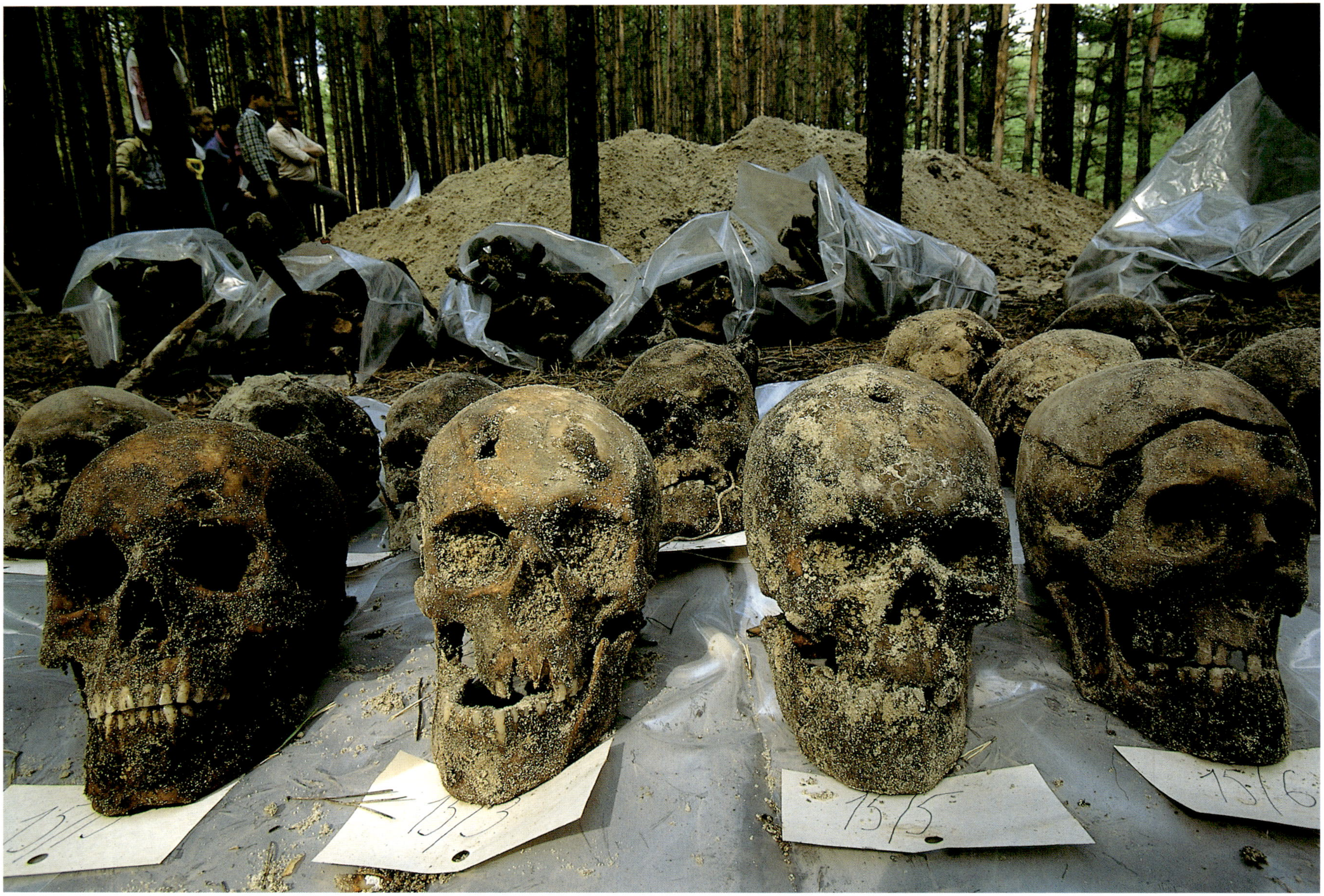

Pinewoods near the town of Voronezh, in the middle of Russia. The people of Voronezh call it 'Stalin's Wood'. Everyone knew how it got its name, but no one wanted to talk about it. Now the living are digging up the dead in order to make them speak. Four thousand skeletons have been found, hands tied behind their backs, bullet holes in their skulls. The 'Memorial' group has so far counted 169 mass graves. Every day brings new discoveries; the gulag was everywhere. Meanwhile, as the living are asking, what is to be done with the dead? (April 1990)

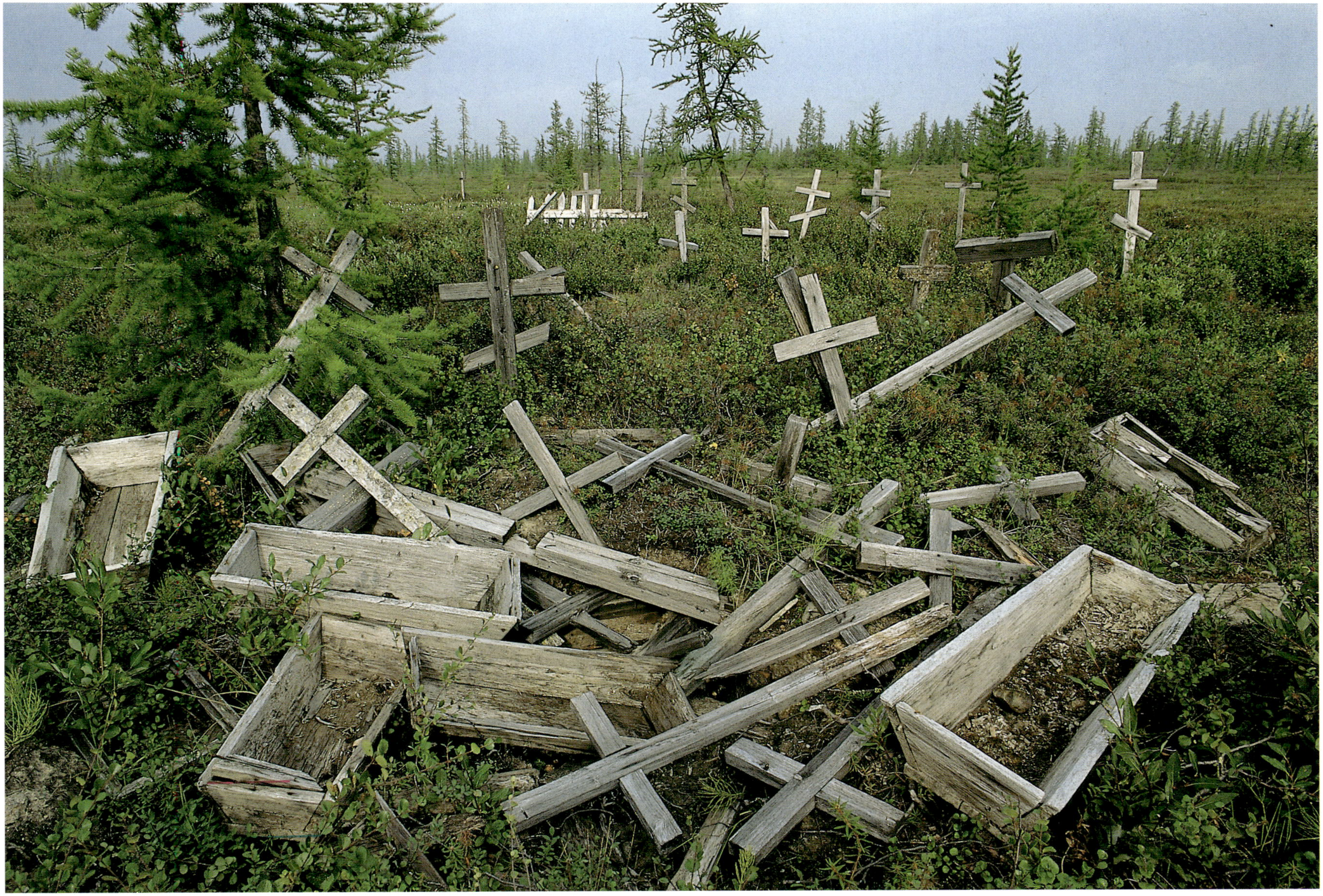

In the taiga, on the Arctic Ocean, a different wood. But the same story. The graves of women convicts and their children by the railway embankment of 'Section 501'. After the war, Stalin had ordered a railway to be built through northern Siberia from Moscow to America. The tracks did not withstand the Siberian frost for long. The people neither. In recent years the graves of the infant dead have been plundered. Ashtrays made from children's skulls are sold as 'gulag souvenirs' by grave-robbers. What is to be done with the dead? (April 1990)

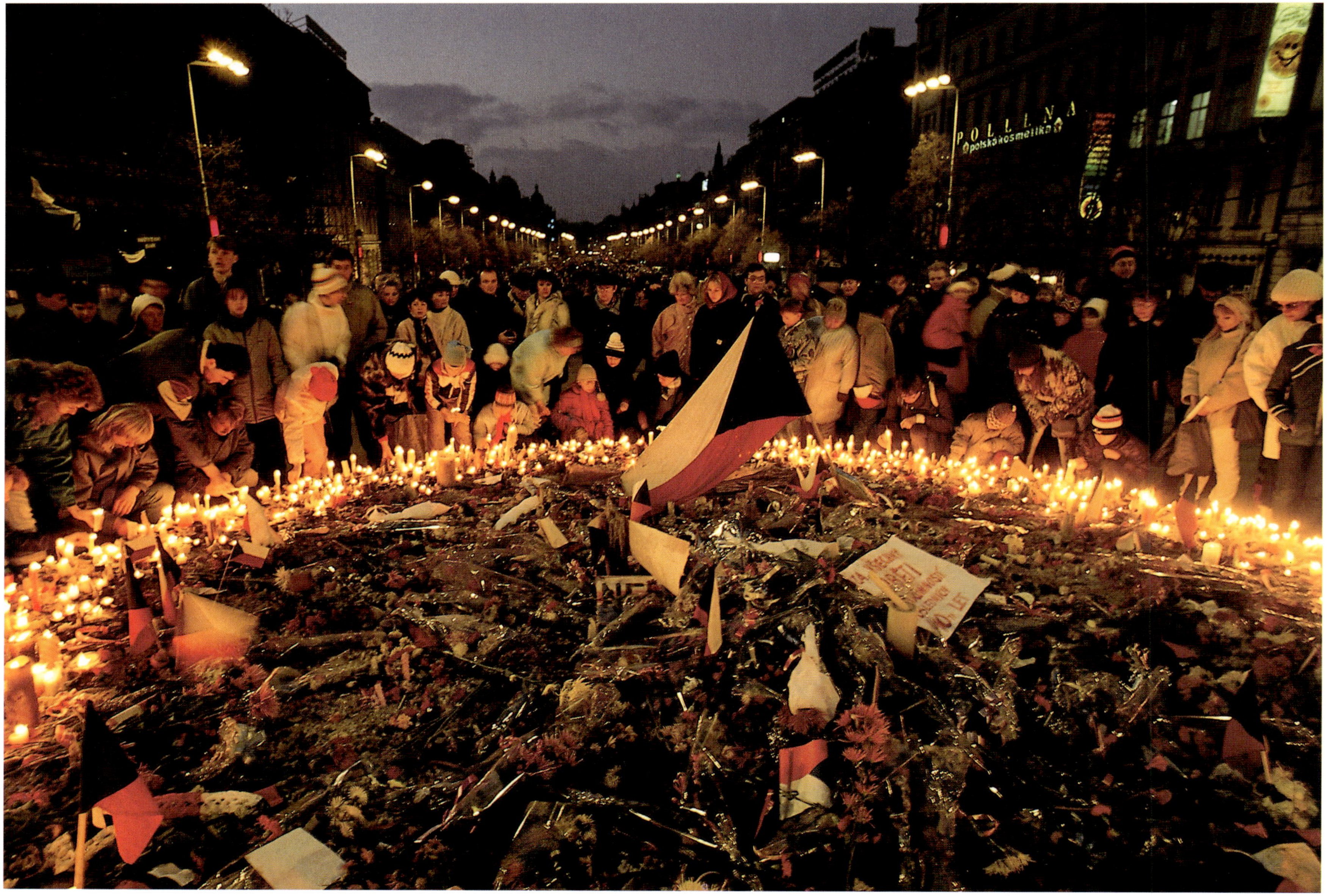

Spontaneous memorial for Jan Palach on Prague's Wenceslas Square. The student burned himself to death in protest against the 1968 invasion of Czechoslovakia by the armies of its 'sister nations'. During the 'Velvet Revolution', people bring bunches of flowers, flags and candles. An act of remembrance which manages without speeches or monuments. (November 1989)

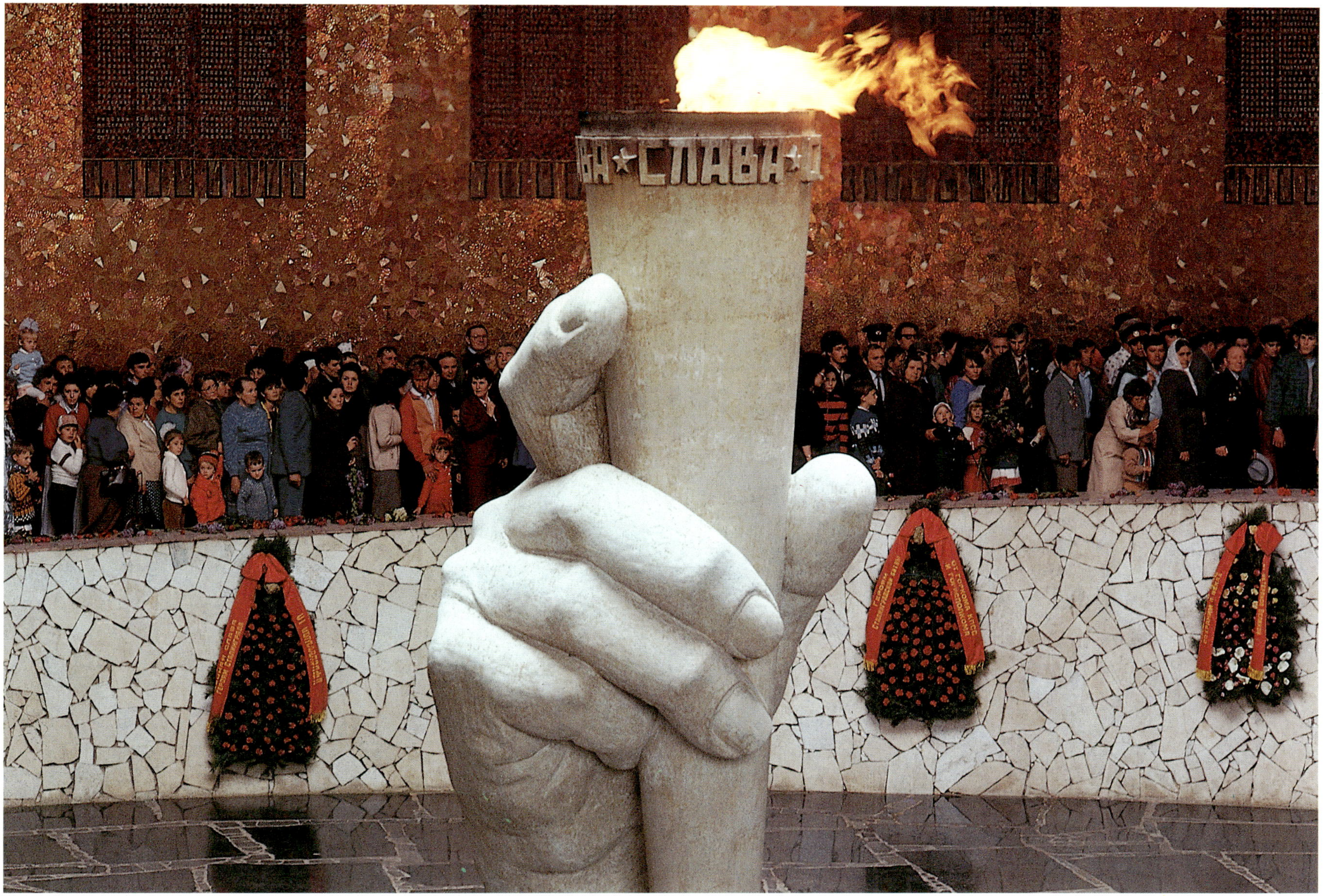

Memorial to the Second World War in Volgograd, the former Stalingrad. Twenty-six million Soviet citizens lost their lives in the war. It is a past that will not fade, a memory that cosmetic changes and the gigantic scale of the official monument fail to erase. (May 1988)

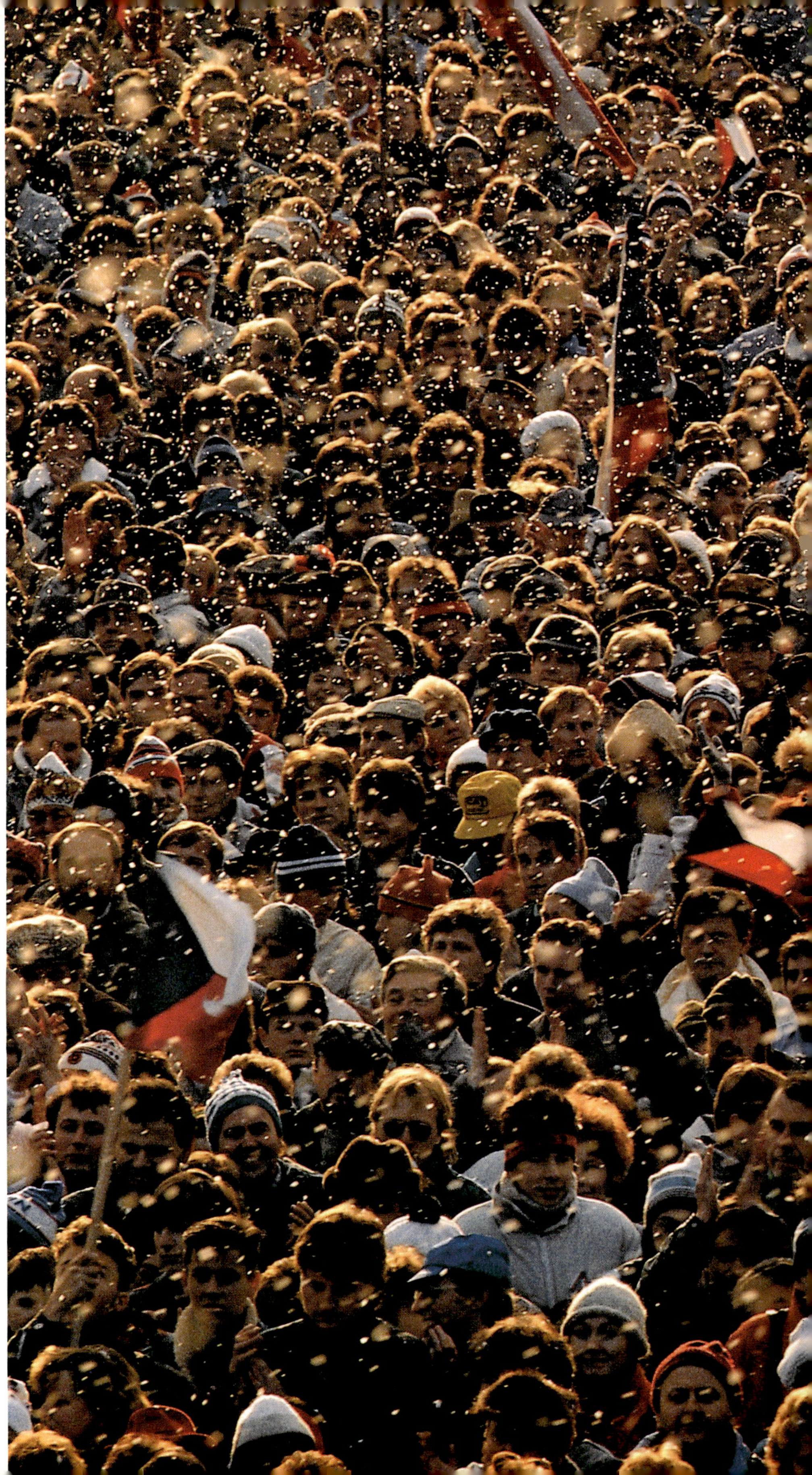

The people. Suddenly they were there, despite the snow and the ban by the municipal authorities. They occupied the streets and squares previously reserved for officially sanctioned processions, and trumpeted some simple truths until the walls collapsed. 'We workers of Kladno go with you' reads the banner in Prague's Letna Park. The climax of the 'Velvet Revolution' was reached when Vaclav Havel and Alexander Dubček appeared together in front of half a million people. 'The people' – a tired cliché had become a reality and was making history. (November 1989)

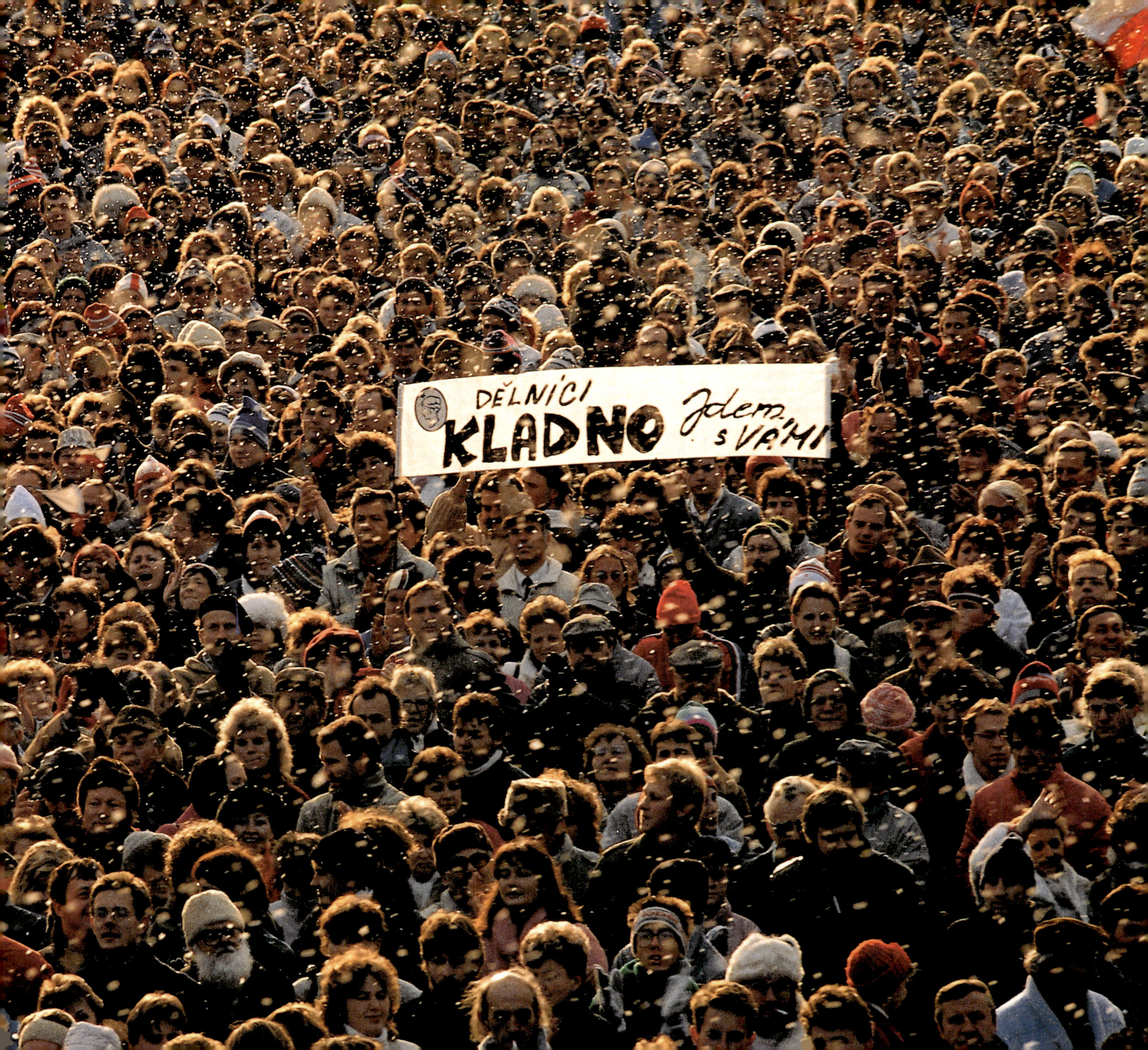
DĚLNÍCI
KLADNO
Jdem s VÁMI

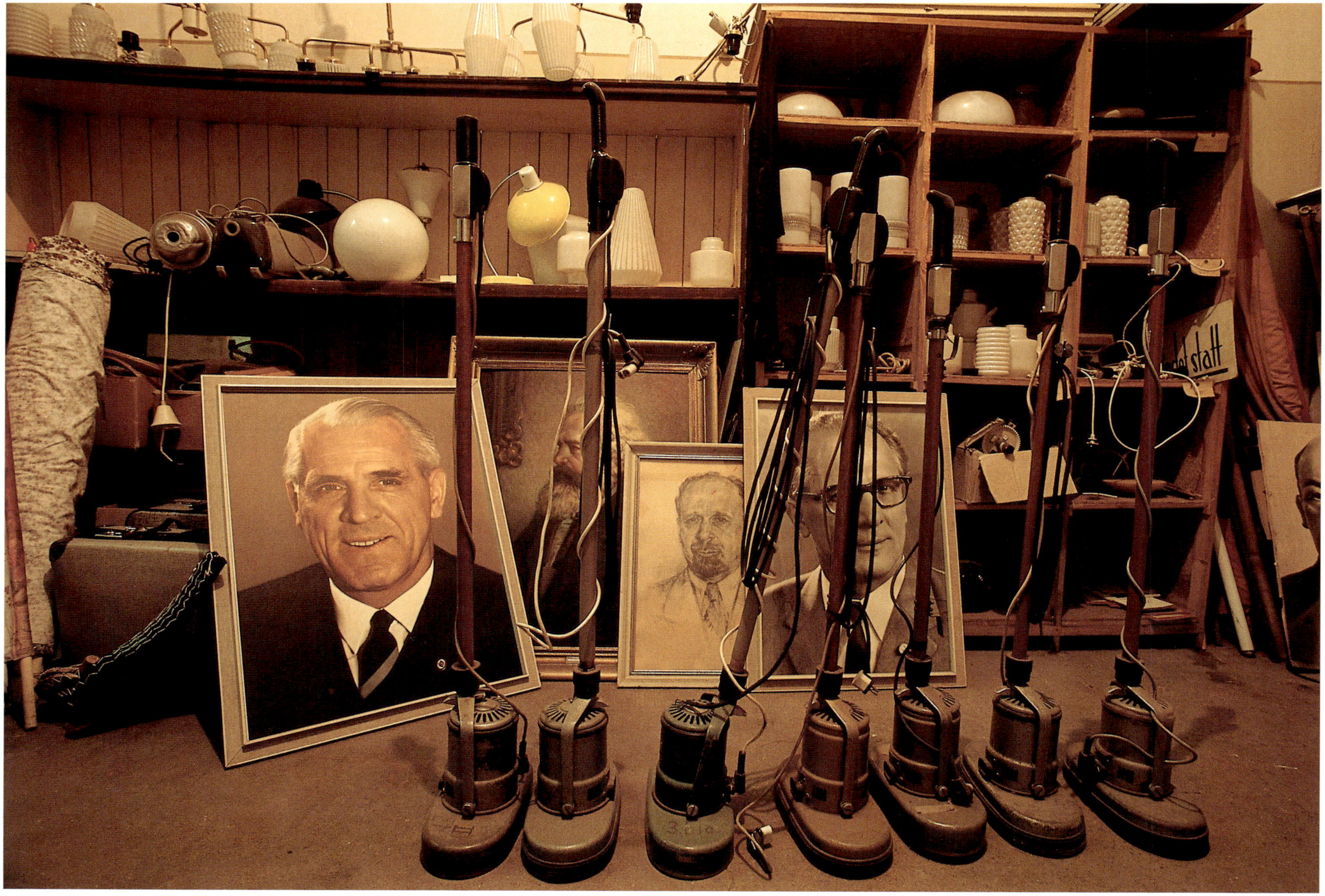

The broom cupboard at the Karl Marx Hof hotel in Bad Elster, Thuringia. The glorious heroes of the workers' and farmers' State are now gathering dust beside the broken table lamps. Only the floor polishers still stand stiffly to attention. (September 1989)

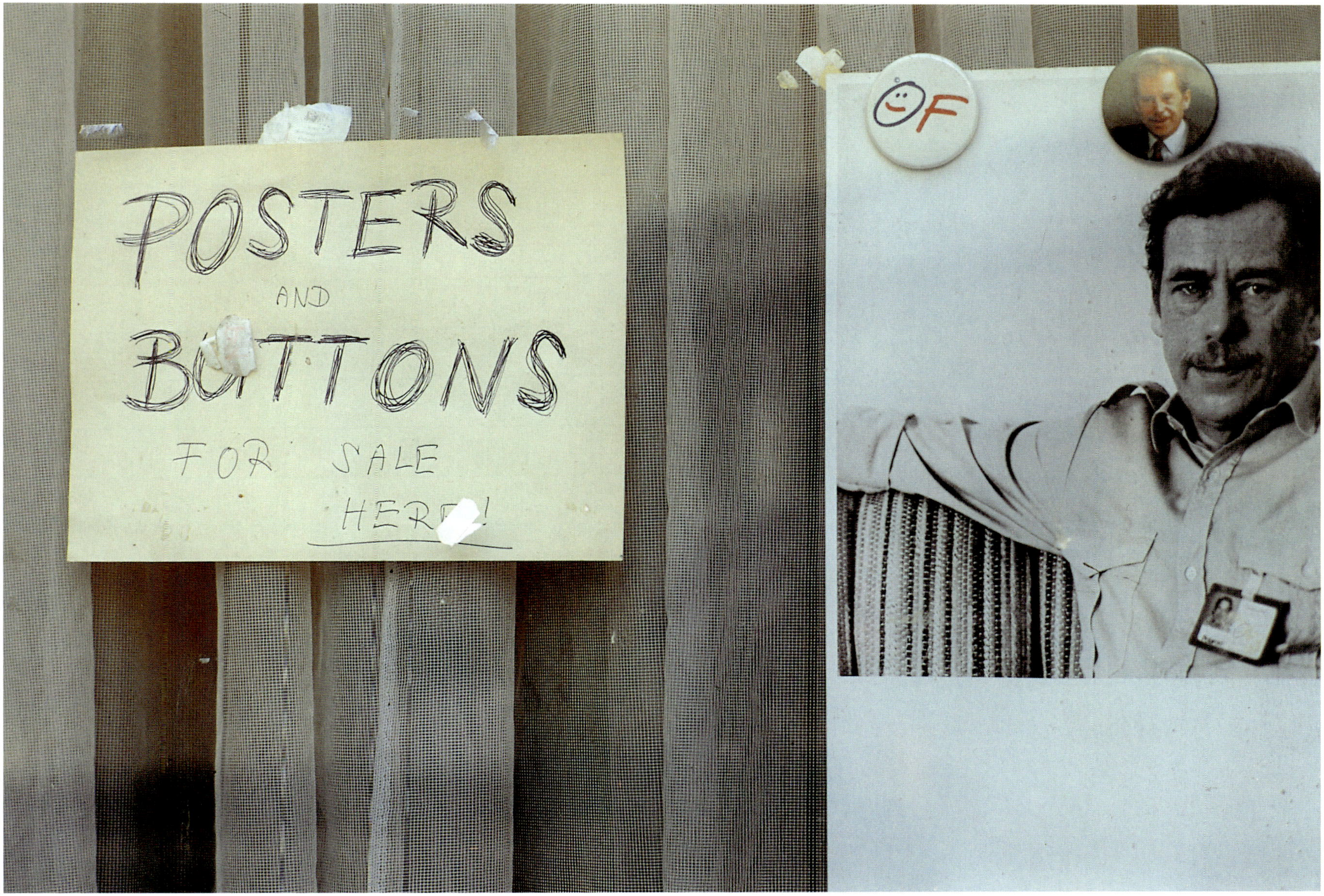

'I can't stand the sight of myself any more', said the new president, Vaclav Havel, as he passed through the streets of Prague. The portrait of the former non-person today hangs in every window of the city. The ministers of the new government have their own fan clubs and are worshipped like rock stars. Which, after office hours, some of them indeed are. (June 1990)

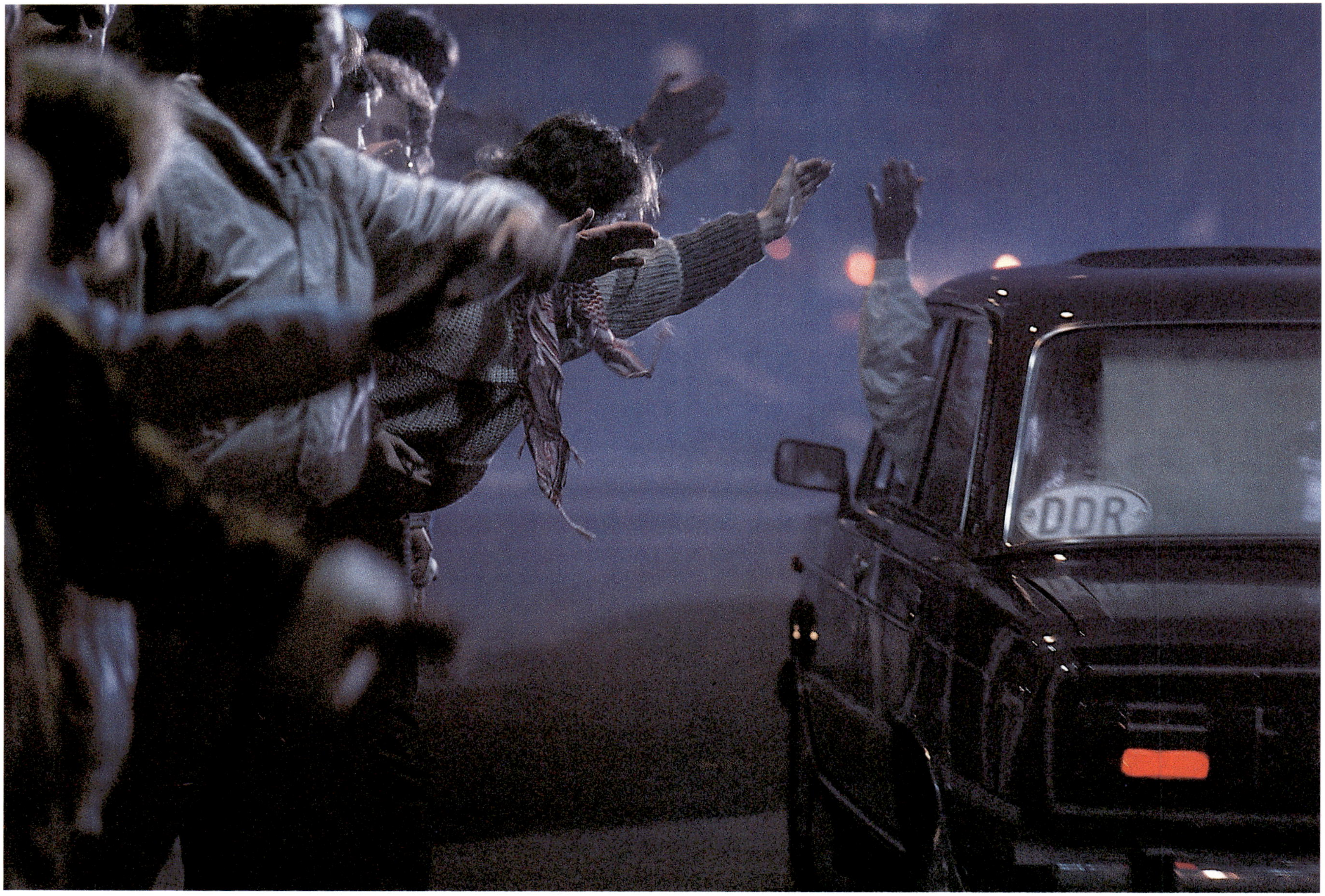

Berlin: the night of the Trabants. Those unreal hours between 9 and 10 November 1989 when, after twenty-eight years, a nightmare finally ended and no one wanted to sleep. Nobody knew where the journey would lead to. Nor, that night, did they care. '*Wahnsinn!*' – 'Incredible!' – they exulted, and pounded the passing Trabants on the roof. (November 1989)

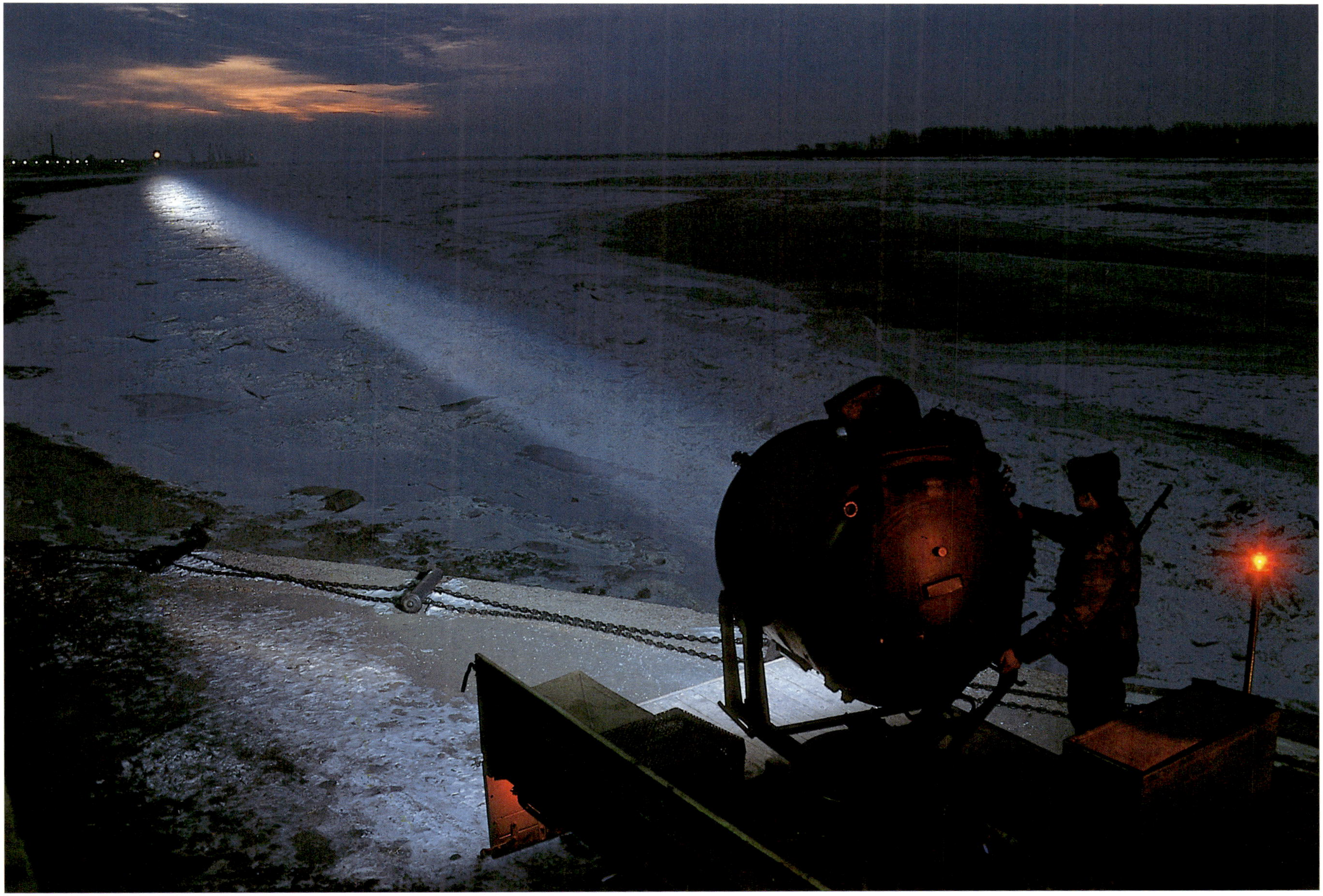

Six and a half thousand kilometres (four thousand miles) farther east lies the Amur, the river forming the boundary between the Soviet Union and China. It remains frozen. While the borders at the other end of the empire open up, KGB troops on the Amur stick to their guns. They used to have orders to shoot. Today, tourists and pedlars are permitted to cross the river. Dawn is breaking. It will soon be day. (January 1990)

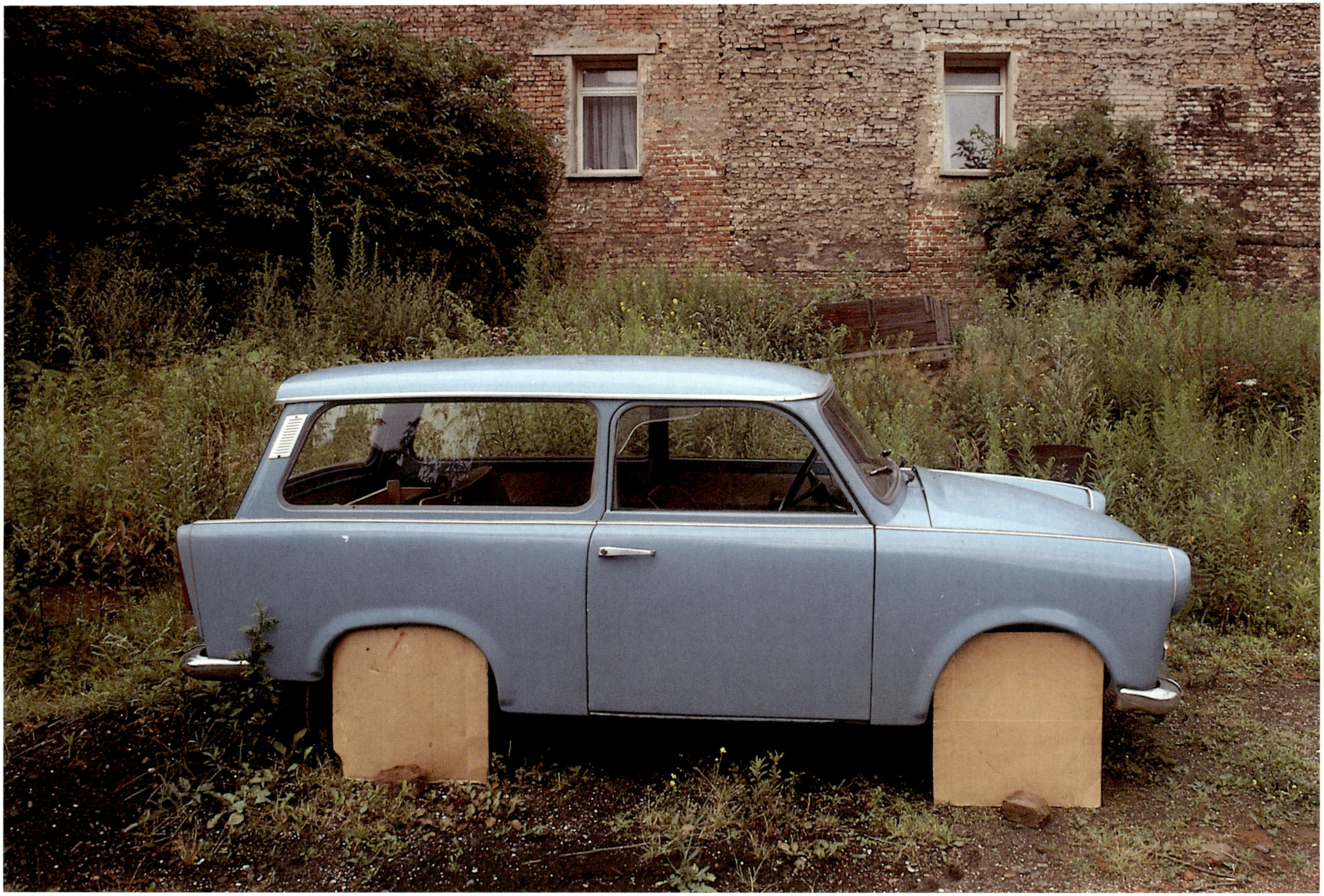

Above • Trabant on blocks. In the land of the Wall, the plastic car became the tool of private escapes. The 'Trabi' was awaited, nursed, washed and loved as tenderly as a child. Amidst the spluttering of its two-stroke engine, rattling down bumpy roads in a fug of steel-blue fumes, real-life East Germans sought to escape the misery of 'pragmatic' Socialism. Whether it was to be a trip out into the countryside or simply a spin round the block – the Trabi made up for a great deal. (June 1988)

Facing page • Trabant on legs. With the great exodus of summer 1989, these modest vehicles were transformed overnight into a symbol of freedom and adventure. Sculptor David Cerny called his work *Quo vadis?*. Today it stands in the garden of the German embassy in Prague – the city where it all began. *Quo vadis, Trabi?* (June 1990)

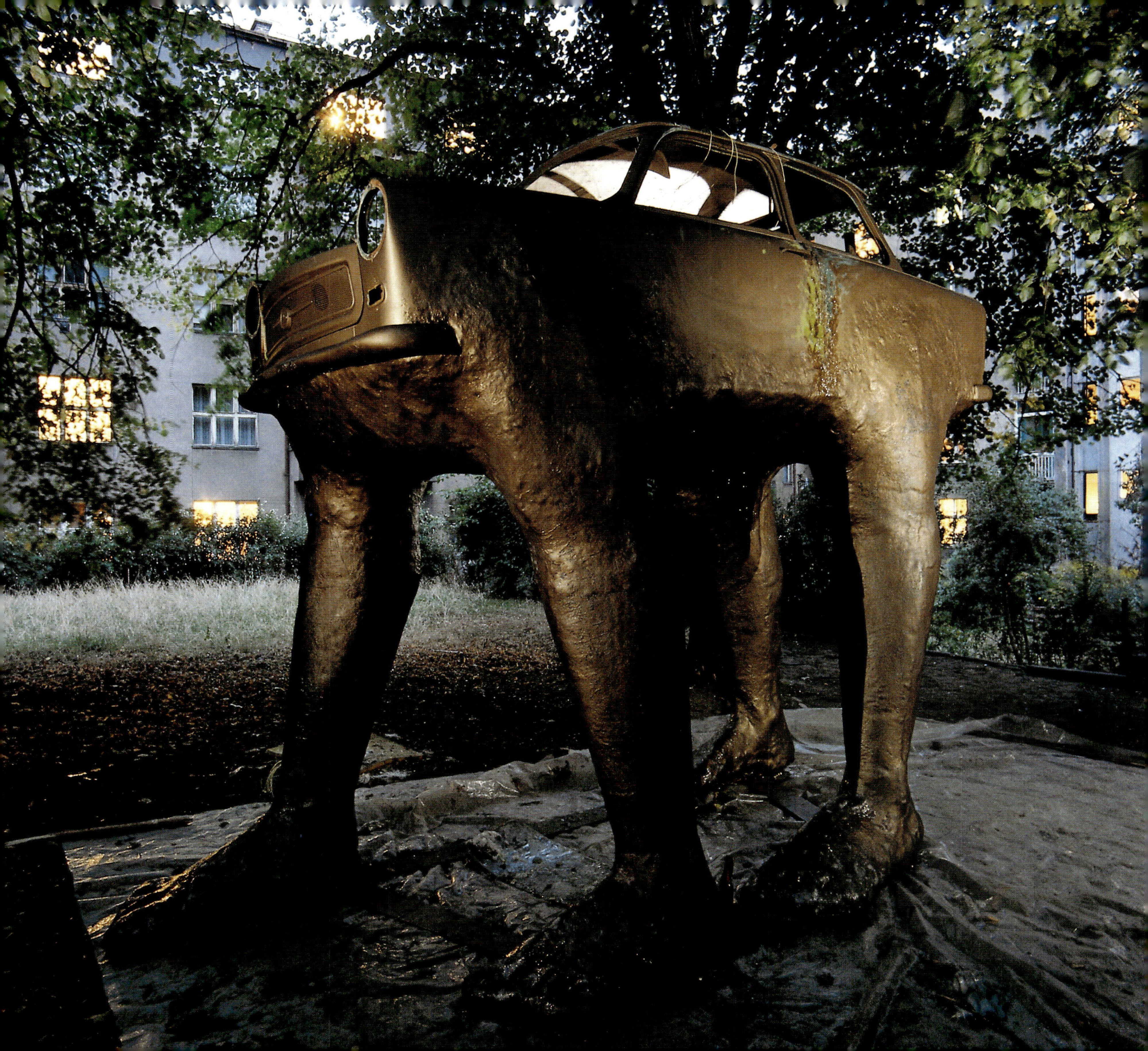

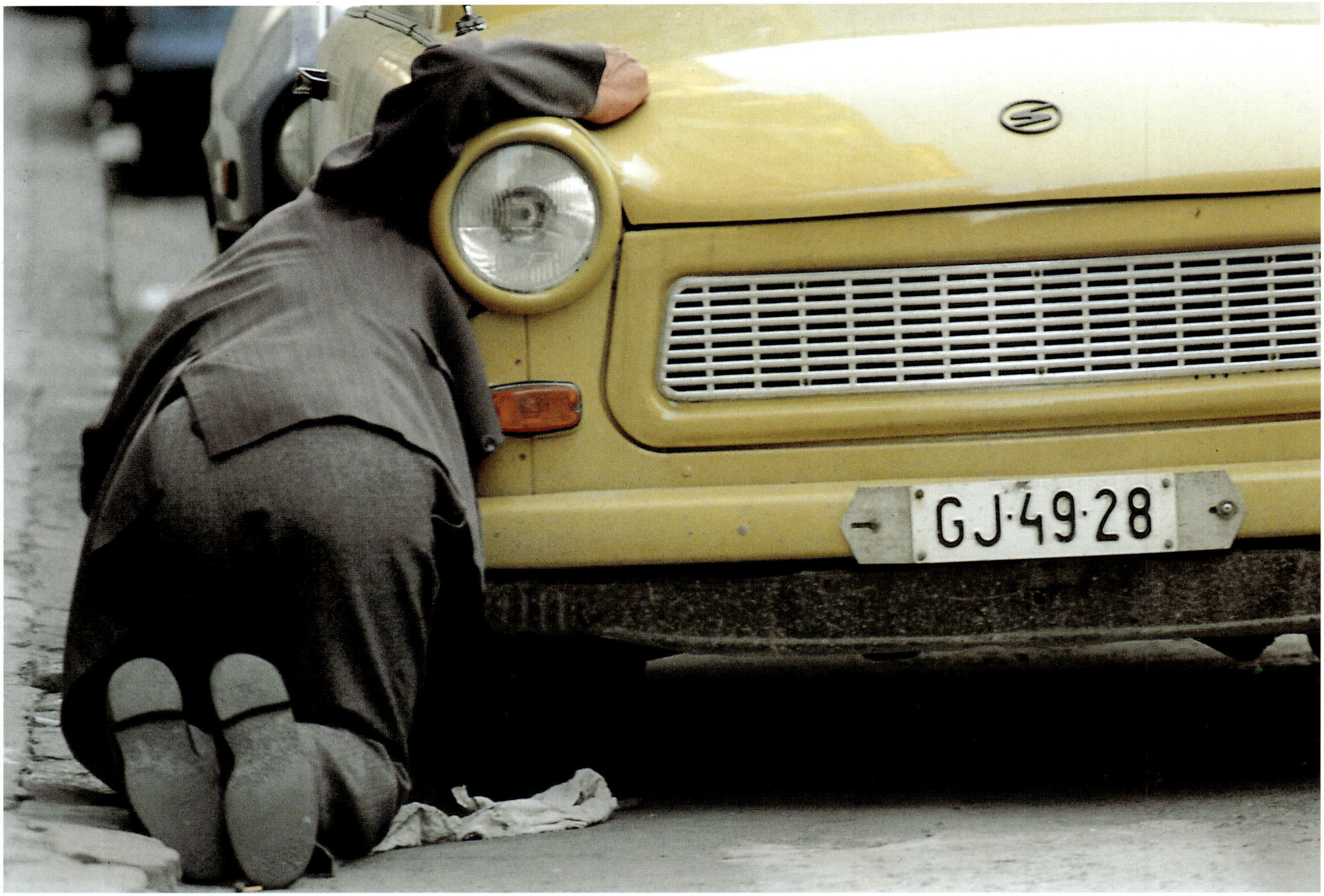

Running repairs were a fact of life for anyone wanting to keep their cherished product of State-owned manufacturing more or less on the road. Like this amateur mechanic in Budapest. There was no question of overtaking the class enemy on the motorway. Simply being there was enough. (May 1988)

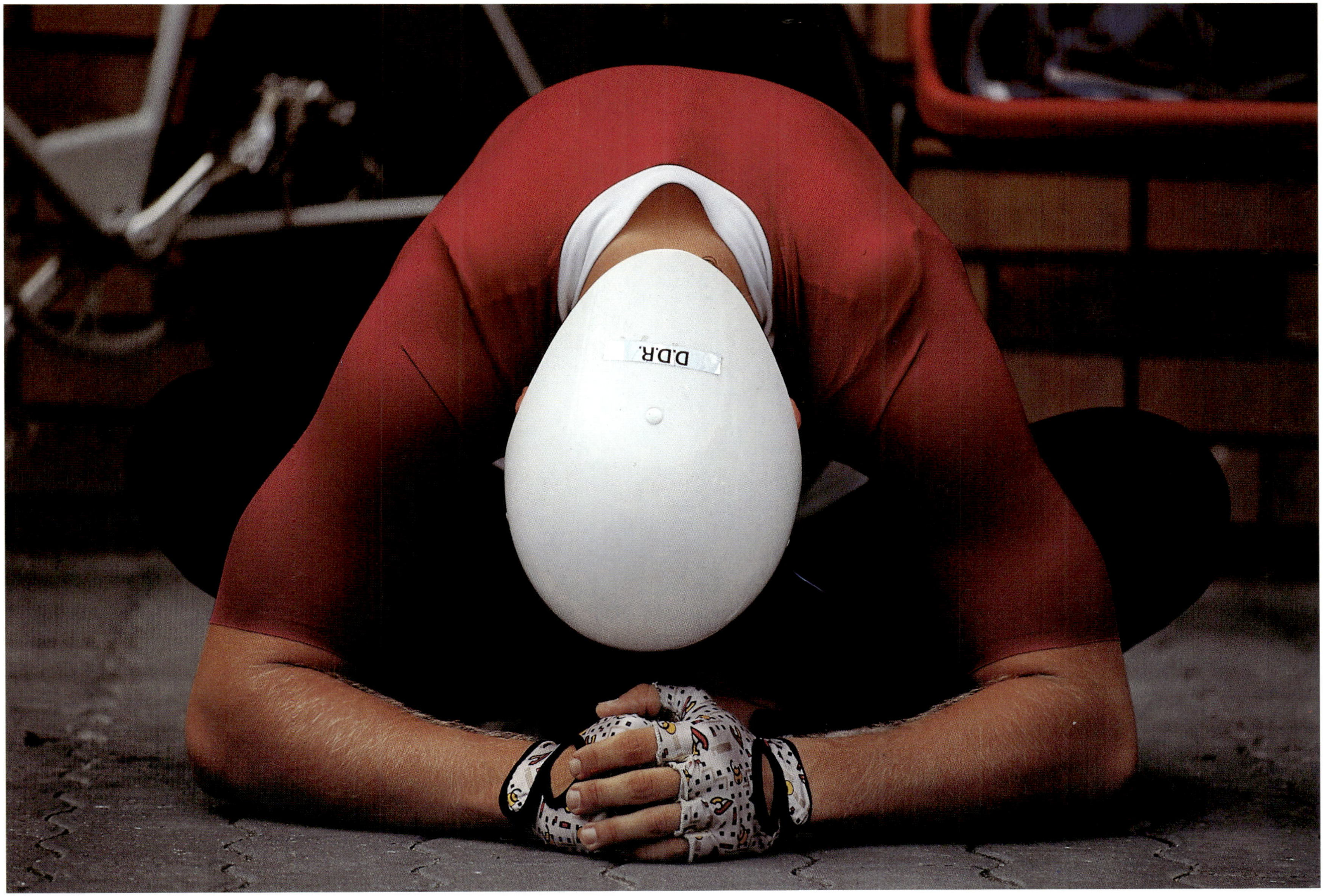

'Catch up with and overtake Capitalism!' That was the motto expounded by the party chiefs. But since the economy failed to stay the pace, it was left to East German sportsmen and -women to outstrip the West German competition. The top athletes in Leipzig had just one mission: the gold medal. A prize for which no price was too high. Drugs and physical breakdown were an accepted part of the system. (April 1988)

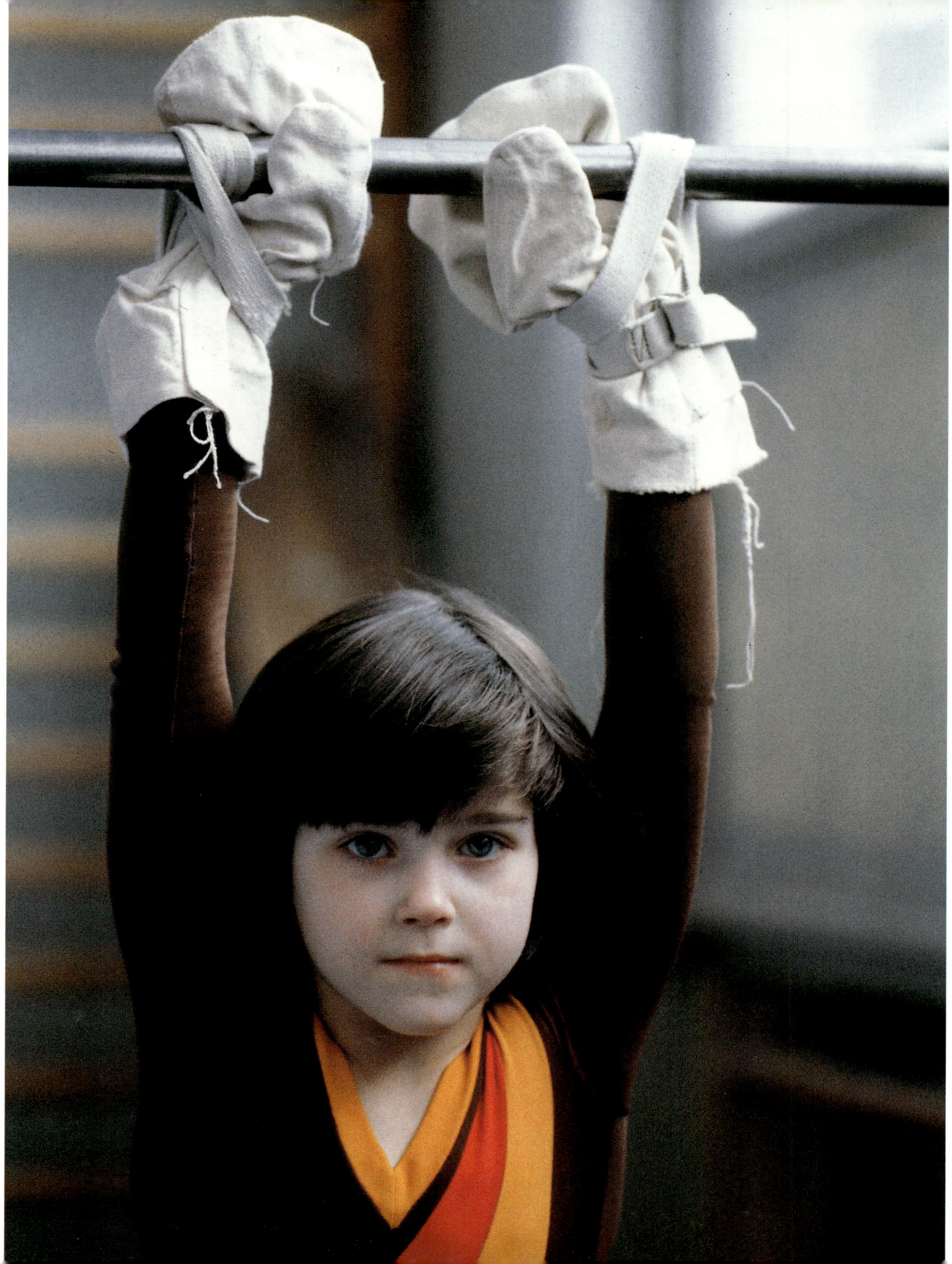

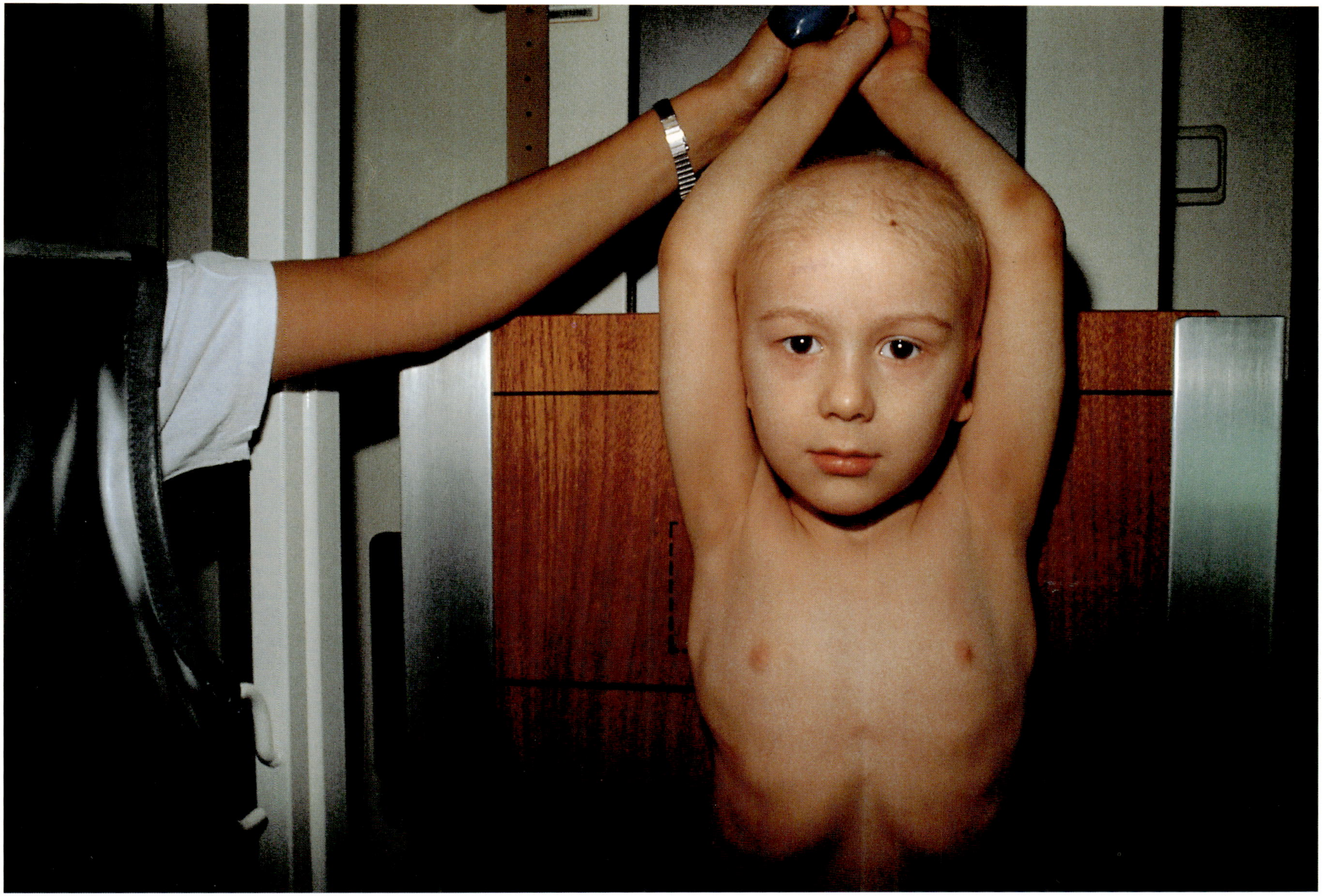

Facing page • Top Soviet gymnasts start young. In Moscow's Gymnastics School Number One, girls as young as six are trimmed into shape. Up to six hours of sport every day – just 'games', as the trainer would have it, or the abuse of a child's body? (June 1988)

Above • Sasha from the 'Zone'. The five-year-old orphan from Chernobyl is being X-rayed in Vienna's St Anna hospital. He has a tumour of the lung. When he was not yet old enough to talk, something happened near Sasha's home town of Gomel for which the people of Belorussia had no name. The Chernobyl flames lit a flare visible far beyond the Soviet Union. Radiation is perhaps the only aspect of Socialist practice which will survive the times. Even if Sasha does not live to see it. (September 1990)

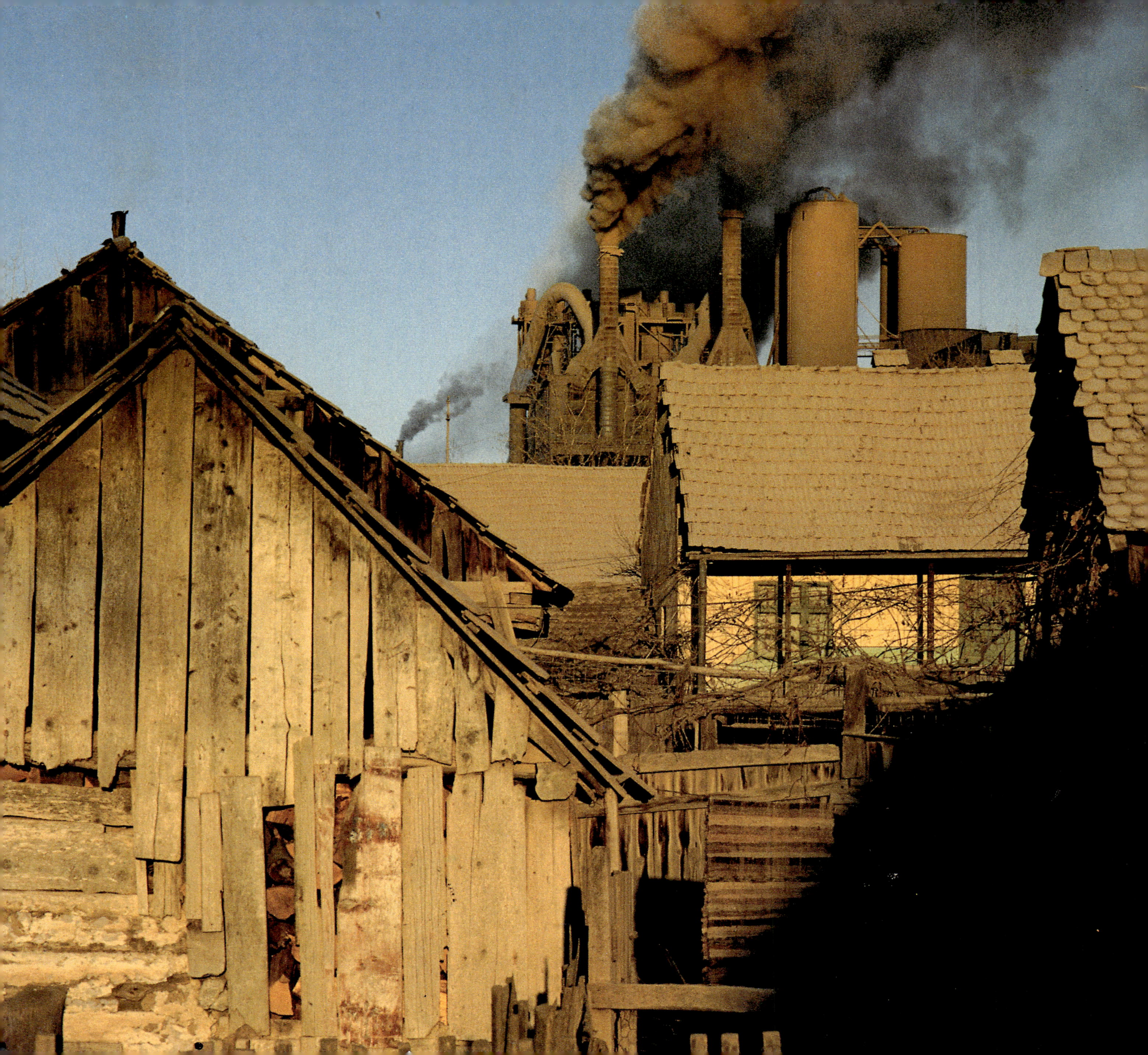

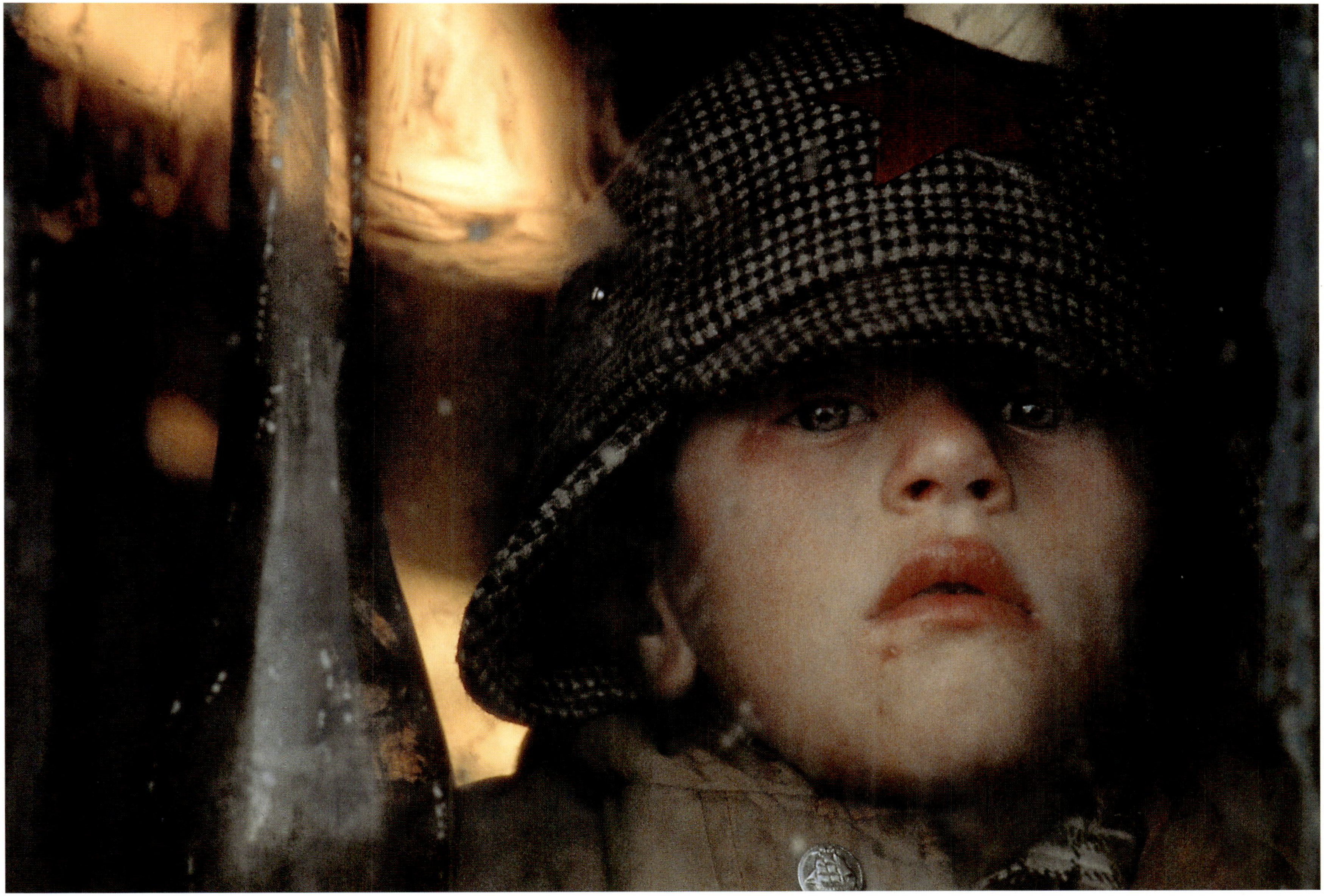

Facing page • A Romanian cement factory near Hoghiz in Transylvania. Smokestacks hoist their sooty pennants to celebrate the victory of the great *Conducator*, Nicolae Ceauşescu, over man and nature. The village is dusted with a powdery dirt which creeps through every slit in the wooden shacks and into mouth and nose and ears. There are no filter plants. The cement is used to make precast concrete slabs for new buildings. Thus the villages of Transylvania are being 'systematized into agro-industrial complexes'. As the *Conducator* wanted. (October 1990)

Above • Back to the future. After a long odyssey across the Ukraine, a boy is back home in the village of Gden, 17 kilometres (about 10 miles) from the Chernobyl reactor. His family has dwindled: one brother died two years after the accident. The state 'liquidators' washed the roofs of the houses and pronounced the village decontaminated. So where has his rash come from? The doctor puts it down to a weakness of the immune system. It might just be a common infection. Who knows? Life goes on as if Chernobyl had never happened. Under the red star. (October 1990)

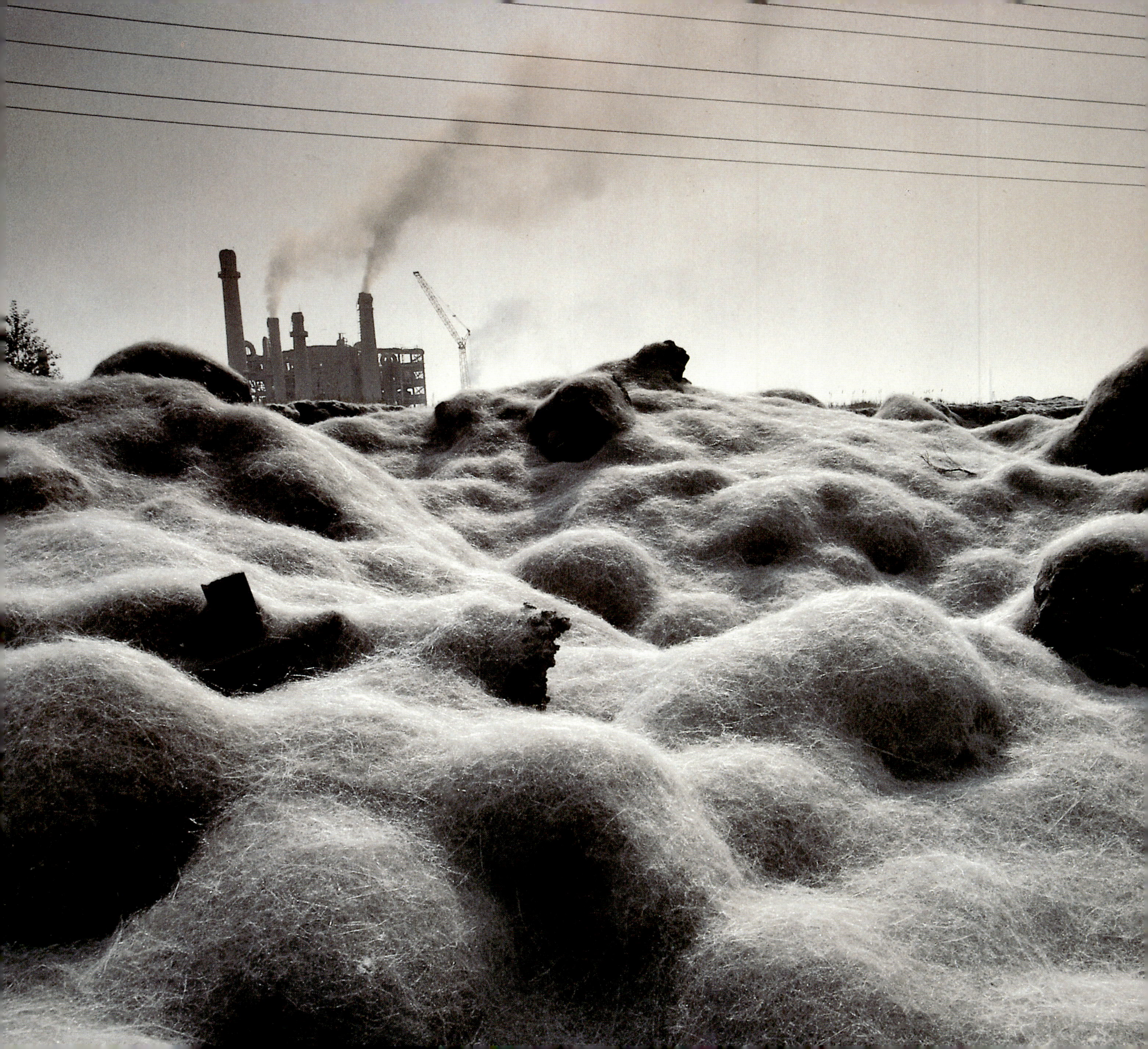

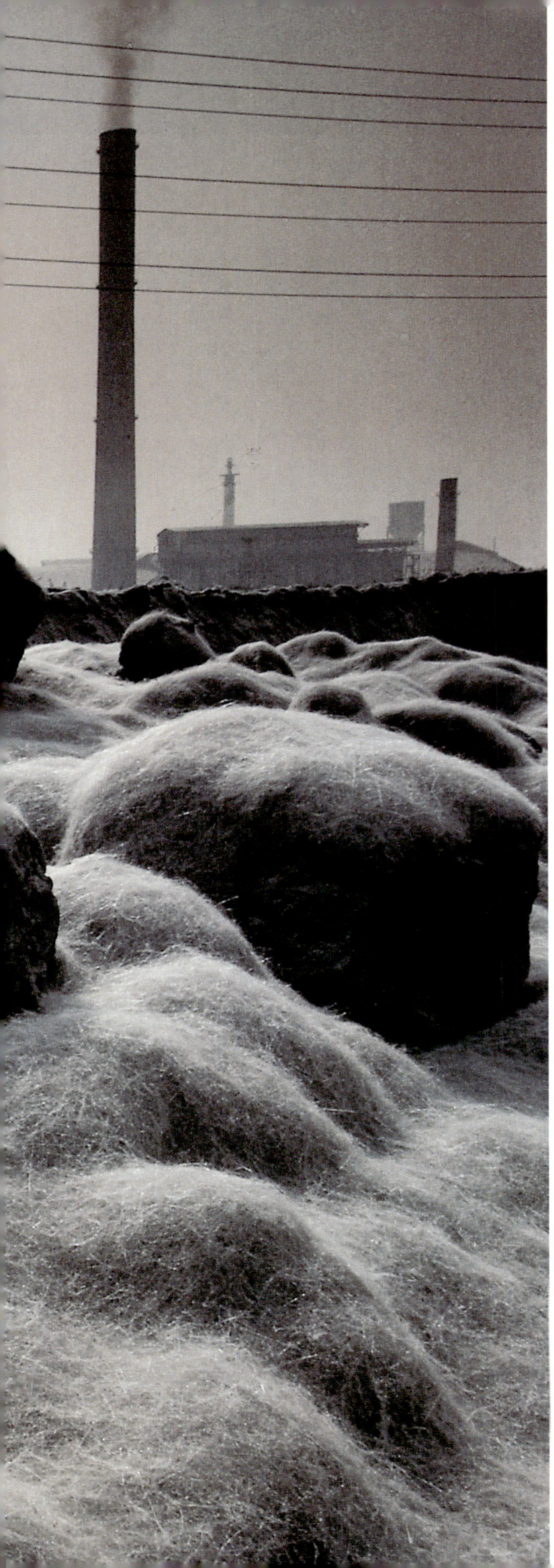

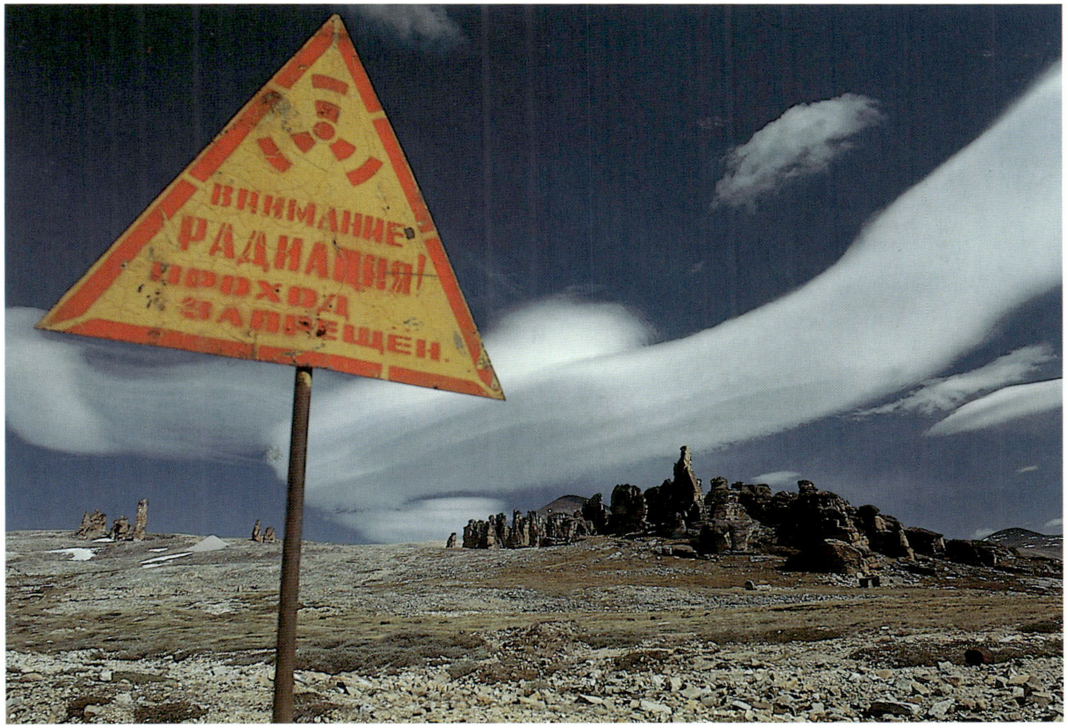

Above • 'Warning, Radiation!' cautions a sign near the former Pevek gulag in Siberia. Prisoners had to extract the ore from the uranium mines with their bare hands. How long is the half-life of Stalinism? (March 1990)

Facing page • The snow drifting down from the skies above the Novokuznetsk industrial zone does not come from Siberia. Nor only at Christmas. The white blanket which covers the countryside consists of toxic metal fibres released from the blast furnaces when the factory stacks cool. They also settle in human lungs. One million tons of poison are injected into the air every year – two tons per inhabitant, children and old people included. Not that there are many senior citizens in the Novokuznetsk basin: the life expectancy for men is fifty-four. (March 1990)

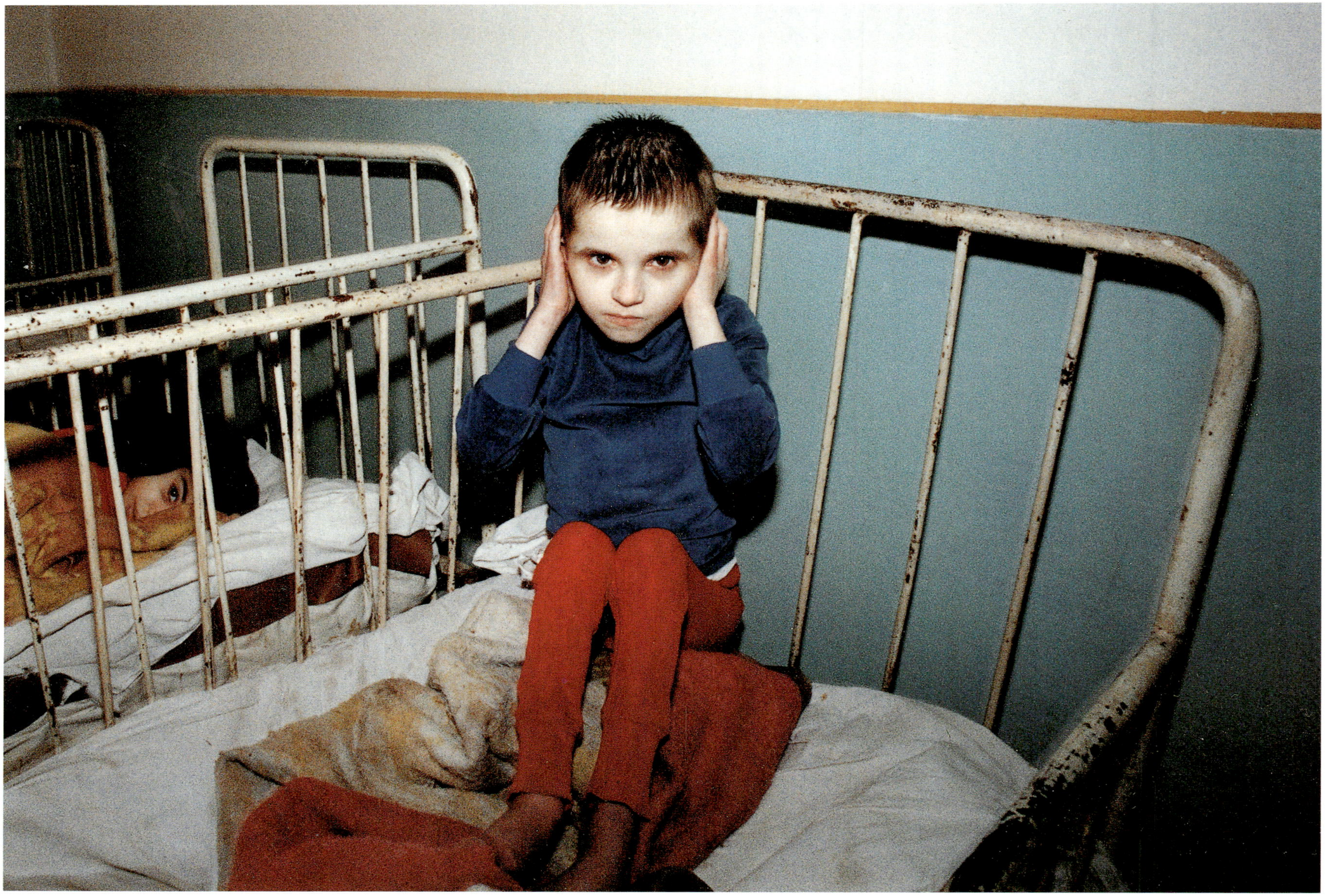

It is five past twelve in the Cighid orphanage. Romania's dictator has been overthrown and her iron gates are slowly opening – but in the homes and asylums it is far too late. This little girl refuses even to listen or speak. Her life consists of bare dormitories, metal cots, inadequate nourishment and the cold: even in winter, there is only cold water to wash in. Now she is suffering from hospitalism. (January 1990)

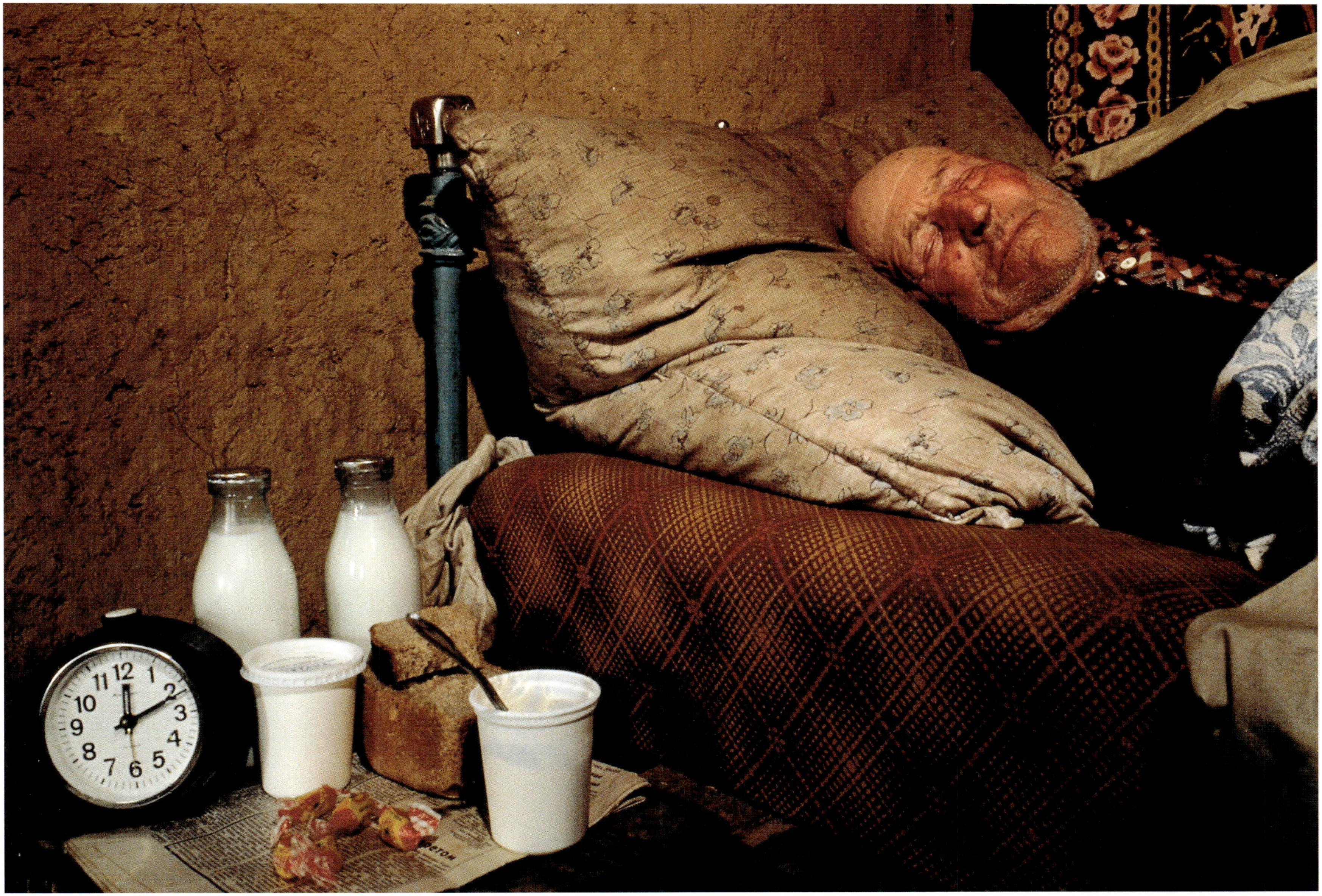

It is ten past twelve in Spierigye, 30 kilometres (19 miles) from reactor block number four. The old man has returned to his highly contaminated village. The authorities evacuated him after the Chernobyl catastrophe in 1986 without finding him a new apartment. For two years the man from Spierigye was forced to beg from door to door. Then he went back to the 'Zone'. To die in the place where his family is buried. In radioactive earth. (October 1990)

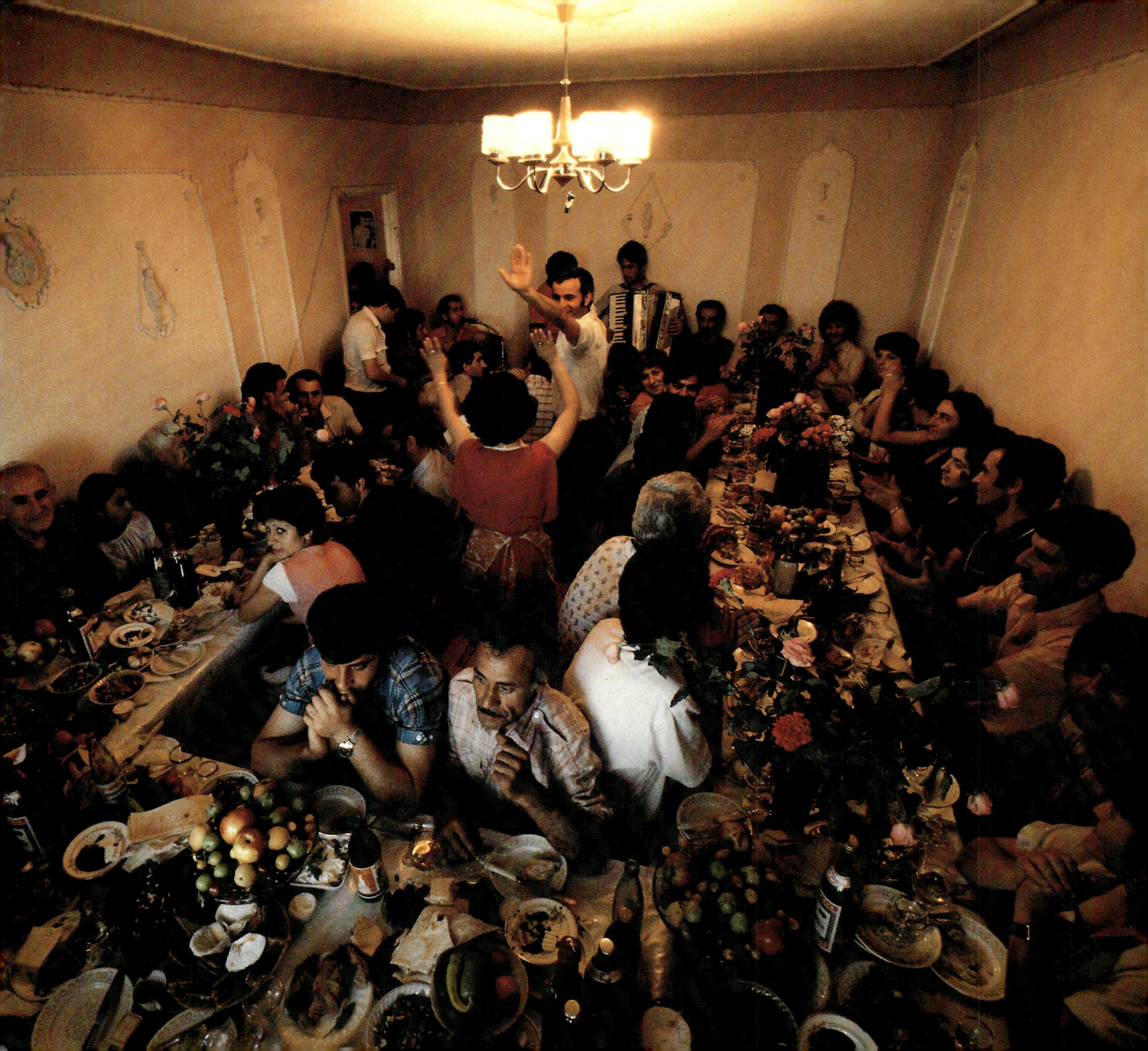

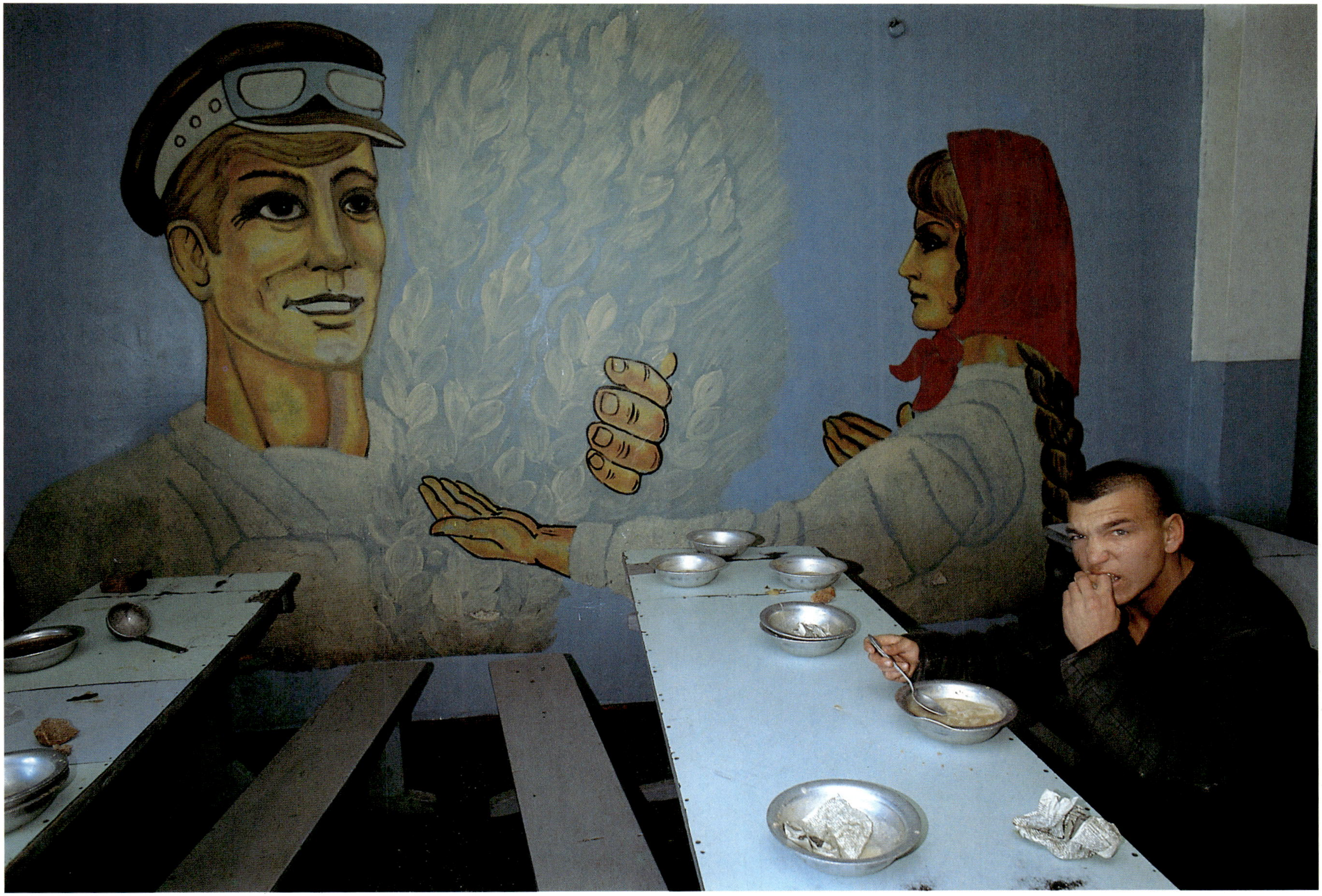

Facing page • Family festivity in the apartment. In Armenia, the oldest Christian state in the world, christenings are always occasions for celebration. There is dancing and singing, eating and drinking – and no one minds that the banqueting hall measures just 16 square metres (172 square feet). There is space for a party even in the smallest home, and Armenians have already survived much worse. (August 1986)

Above • Good and evil finely divided in Station Sima, a Siberian labour camp. Harsh correction measures are intended to re-educate jailed criminals in the proletarian ethos. The mural paints the New Man in glowing hues, but the soup in the tin bowl is as colourless as usual. (March 1990)

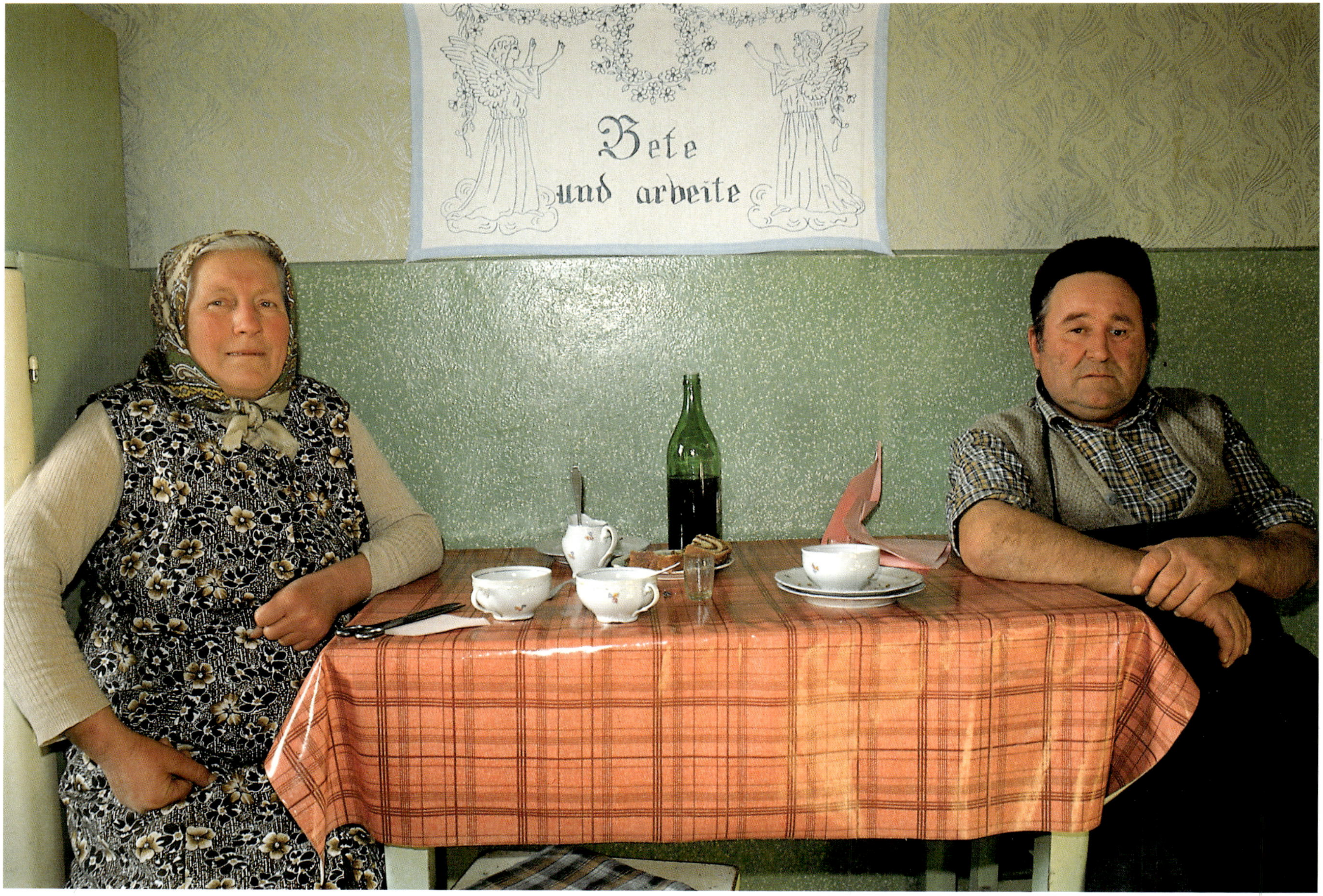

Above • '*Bete und arbeite*' – 'Pray and work'. Voluntary asceticism in an impoverished economy. Insulated from the changes in the West, Transylvania's Saxons have preserved a conservative Lutheran way of life. Some 200,000 Germans live in Romania, where they are seen as hard-working, clean and industrious. 'Our roots are here. But we've had enough', they say. Many now want to return to the '*Reich*', as they still call it. A home they have never seen and where their stubborn Protestantism would be viewed as an outdated affectation of Germanness. (August 1988)

Facing page • Enforced asceticism. A gypsy family in Transylvanian Betesti. Life under Ceauşescu was hard for everyone, but the gypsies were the poorest of the poor. Even after the 'liberation', they would continue to serve as scapegoats. In contrast to the country's other minorities, such as the Germans and Hungarians, the Romanies have no political organization in Romania. They, too, dream of a West – one which lies somewhere in the north, far beyond the Carpathian mountains. (December 1988)

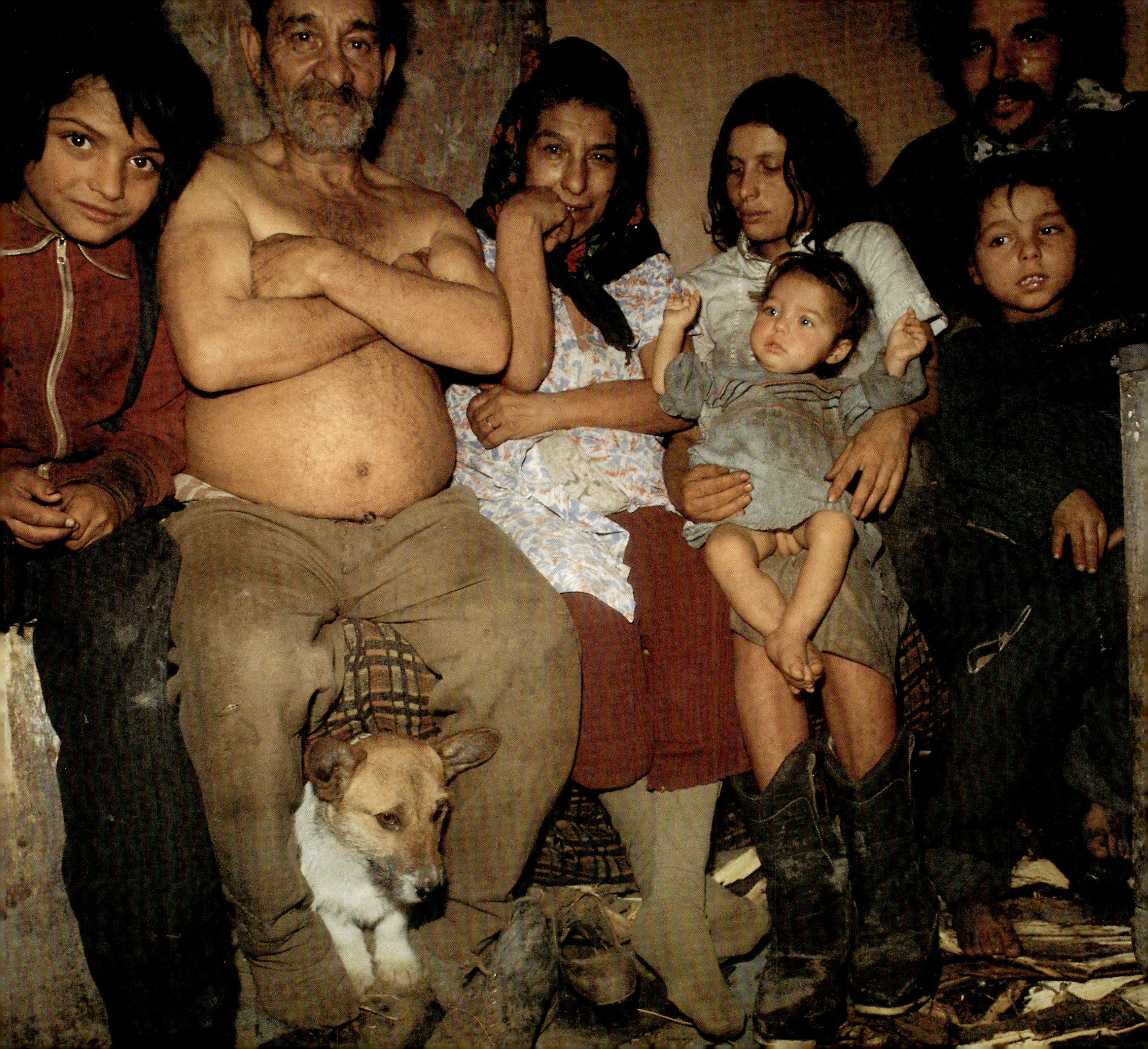

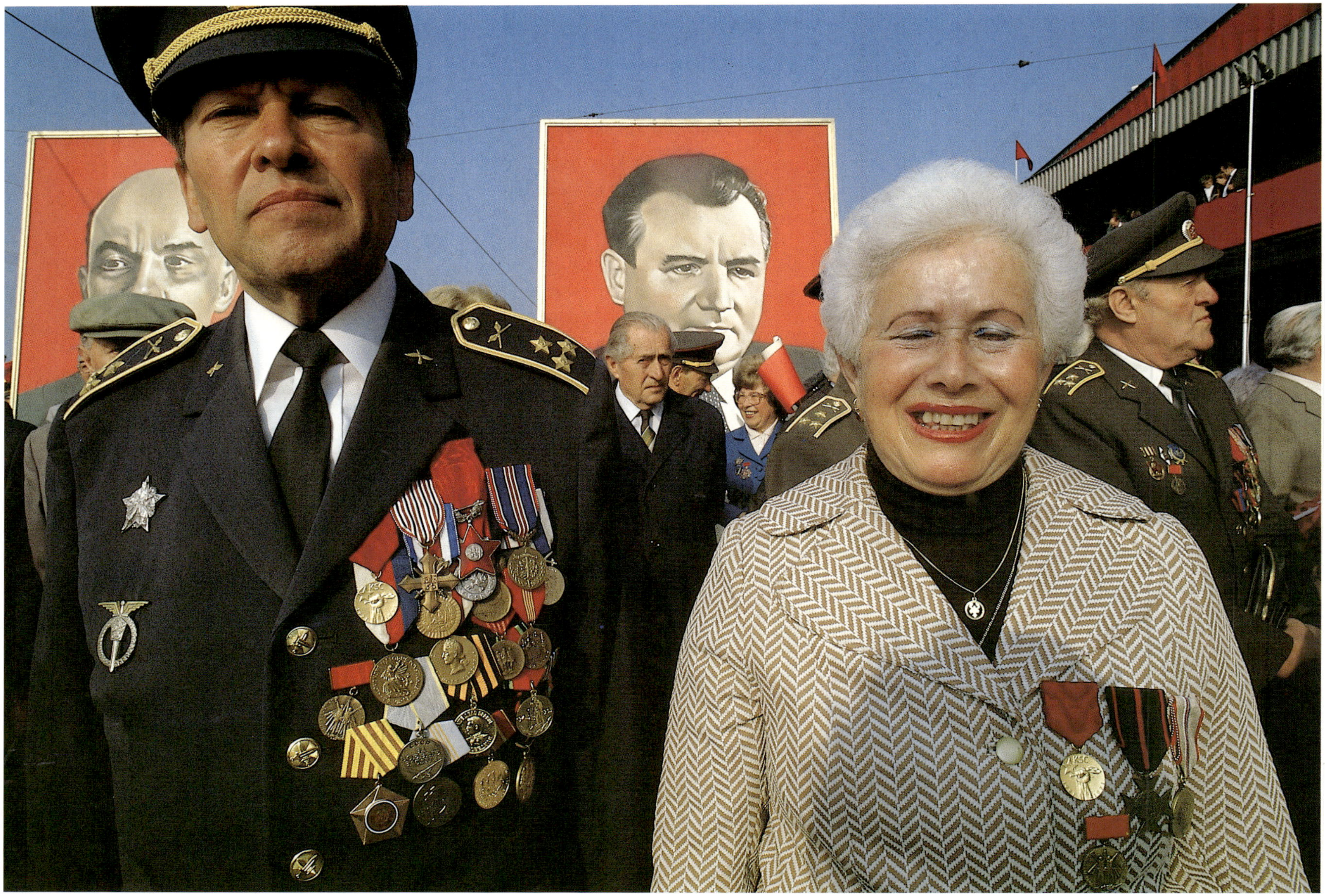

A last first of May in Prague's Letna Park. The Party watches its people – veterans and meritorious old Communists – march past just one more time, their breasts weighed down with medals. Even the leaders – Lenin and party chief Jakeš – mingle with the workers on May Day, albeit only on posters. No one dreams their decorations will soon be up for sale in the Prague flea market at knock-down prices. Nor that Letna Park will shortly be seeing Vaclav Havel and Alexander Dubček give their first public address. Should one laugh or cry? (May 1988)

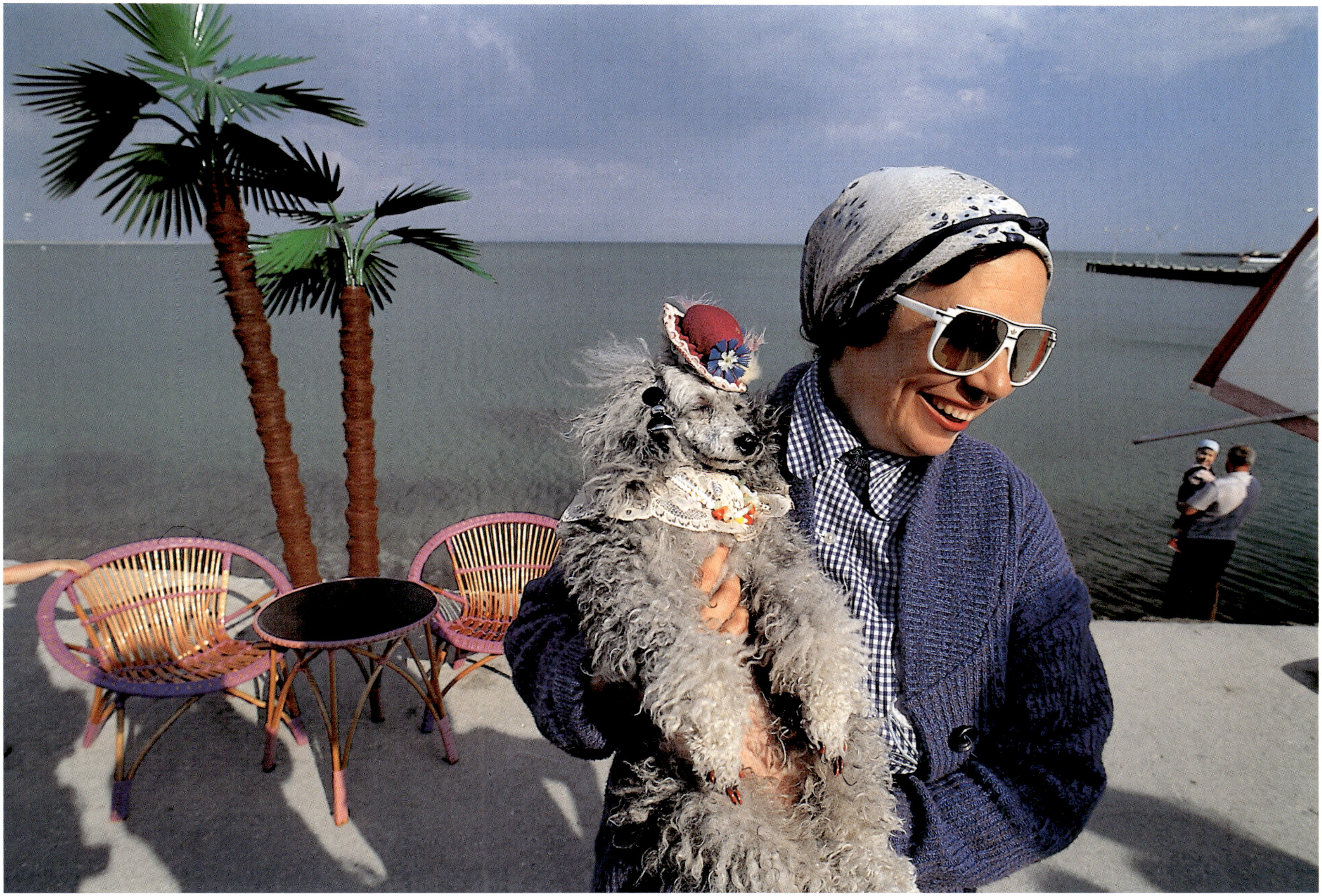

Here she is again, the 'Lady with the Little Dog' on the promenade at Yalta. But what in Chekhov's story was still a cosmopolitan haven for the aristocracy has, since the Revolution, become a centrally planned regeneration plant for working-class heroes and prominent party members. Vladimir Mayakovsky knew as much: 'People can be repaired quickly in the mighty forges of the Crimea.' (May 1988)

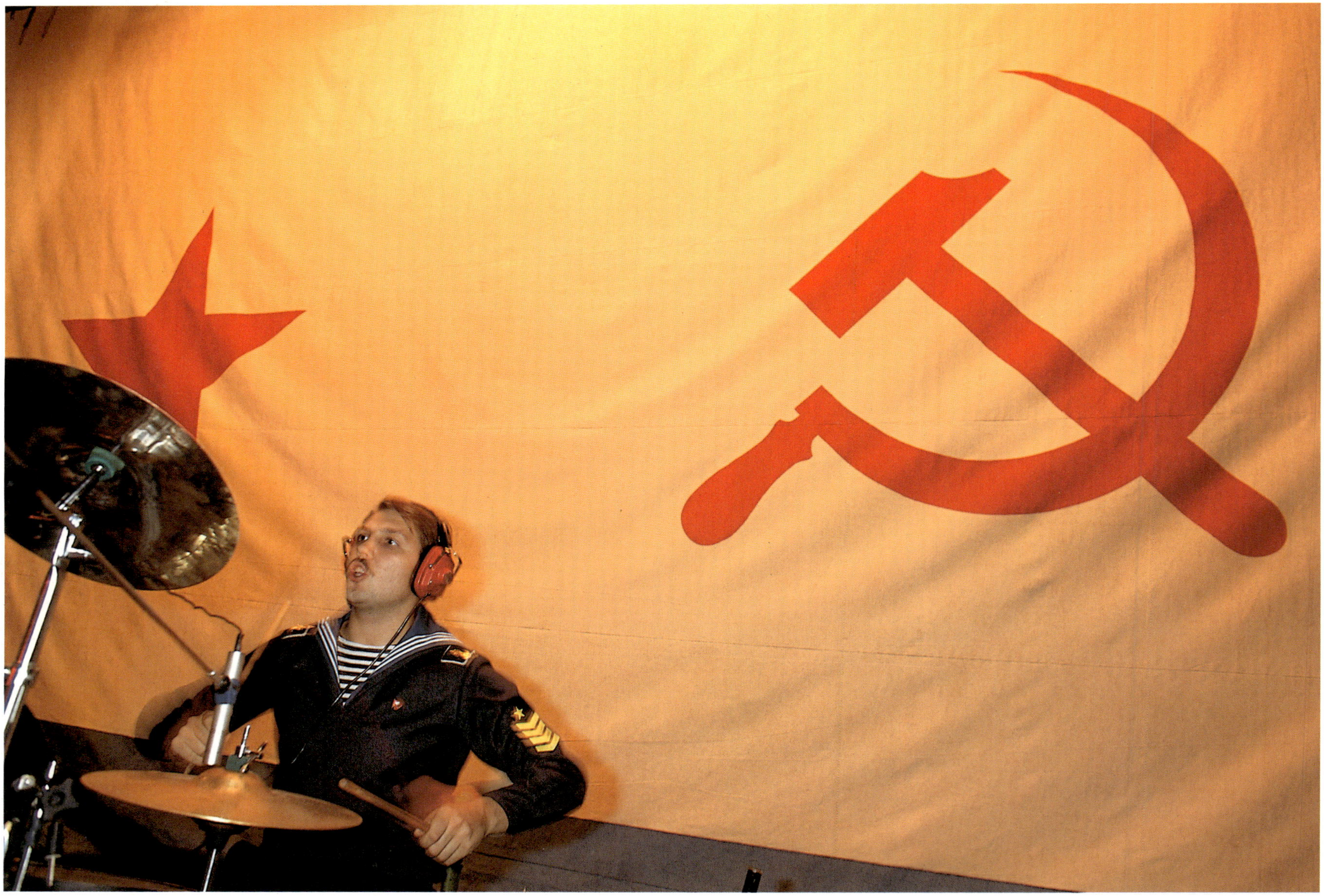

Above • Peaceful drumming by 'Captain Nemo', the band from the Red Navy. In the disco at the Frunze military academy in Leningrad (St Petersburg) the cadets with their pay of twenty roubles are no longer as popular amongst the unmarried girls. Demobilized officers have neither jobs nor apartments; many feel like lepers. (March 1990)

Facing page • Within the Soviet Union's recovery programme, the personal reward for effort is a suntan. With Lenin's blessing. In December 1920 he issued a decree 'on the use of the Crimea for the therapeutic treatment of workers'. In the Socialist battle for productivity at least, the front still stands: every year, seven and a half million Soviet citizens spend their holiday in the Crimea. To get Lenin off their chest? (July 1990)

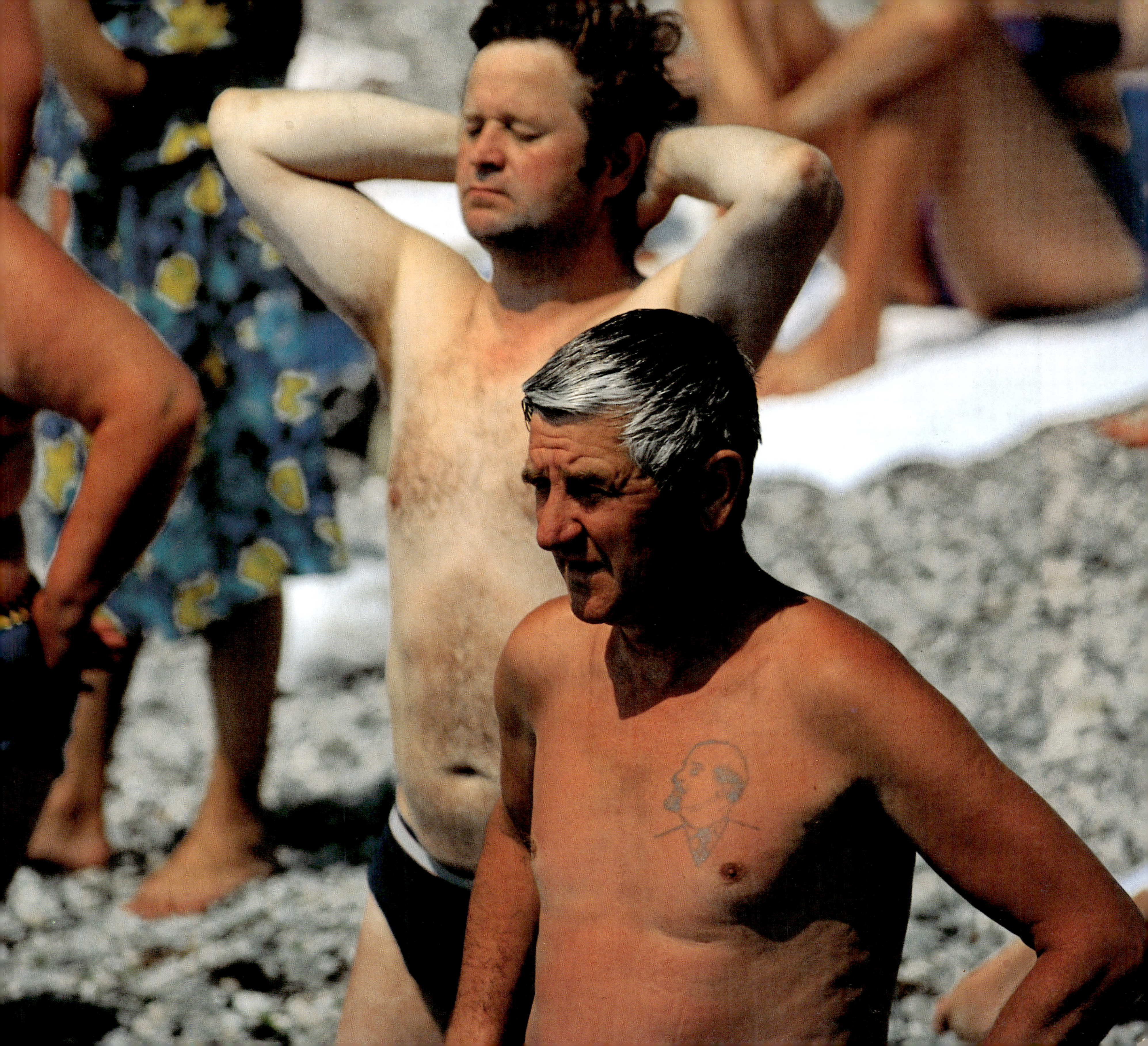

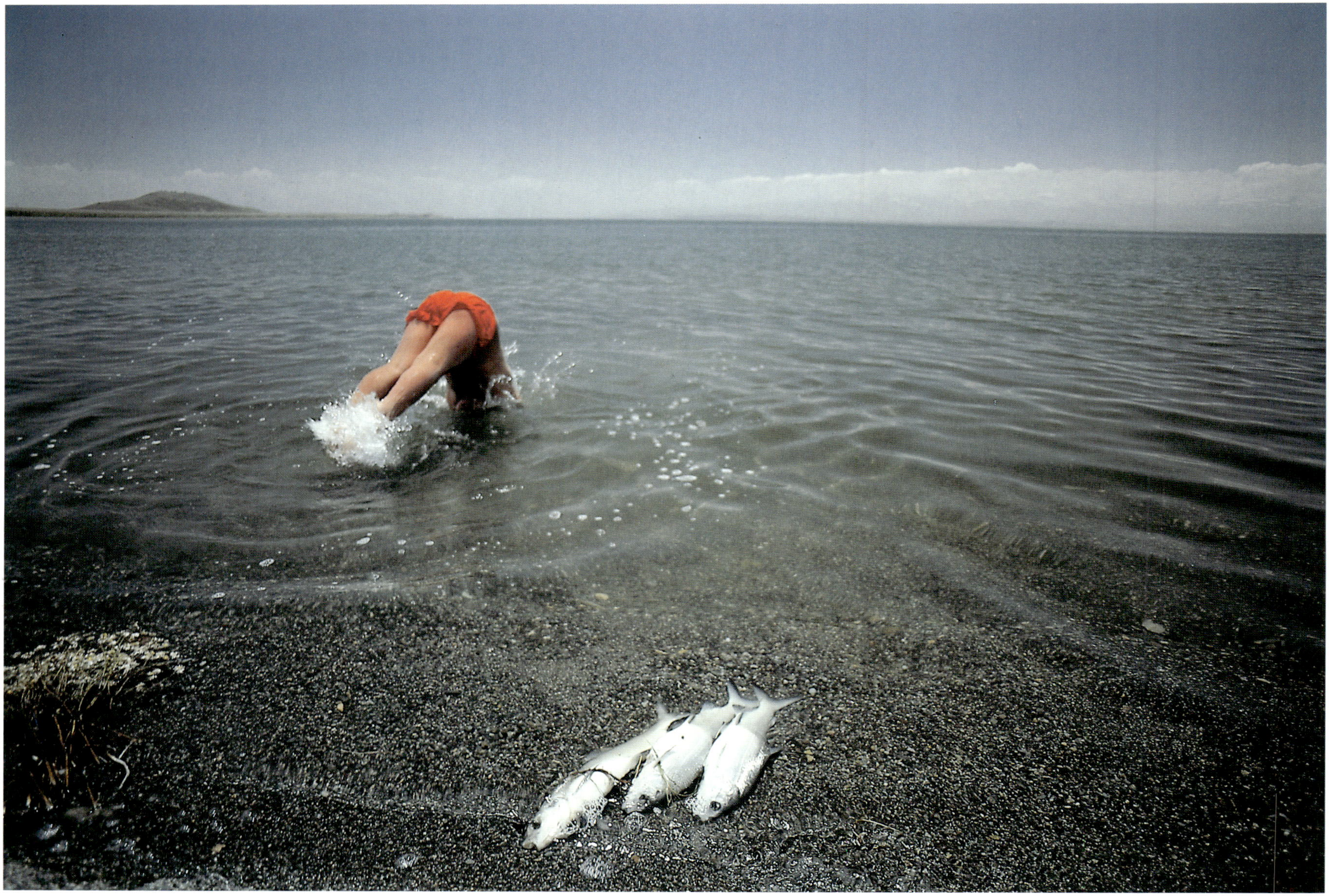

The glittering waters of Lake Sevan, known as the 'Pearl of Armenia', have now become a fishes' graveyard. Factories drain their waste directly into the lake and the ground water. For the local people, more important even than deliveries of basic foodstuffs from the West is information about the poisoning of the lake. But they lack even the most basic measuring instruments. And perhaps it is better not to know anyway. (August 1986)

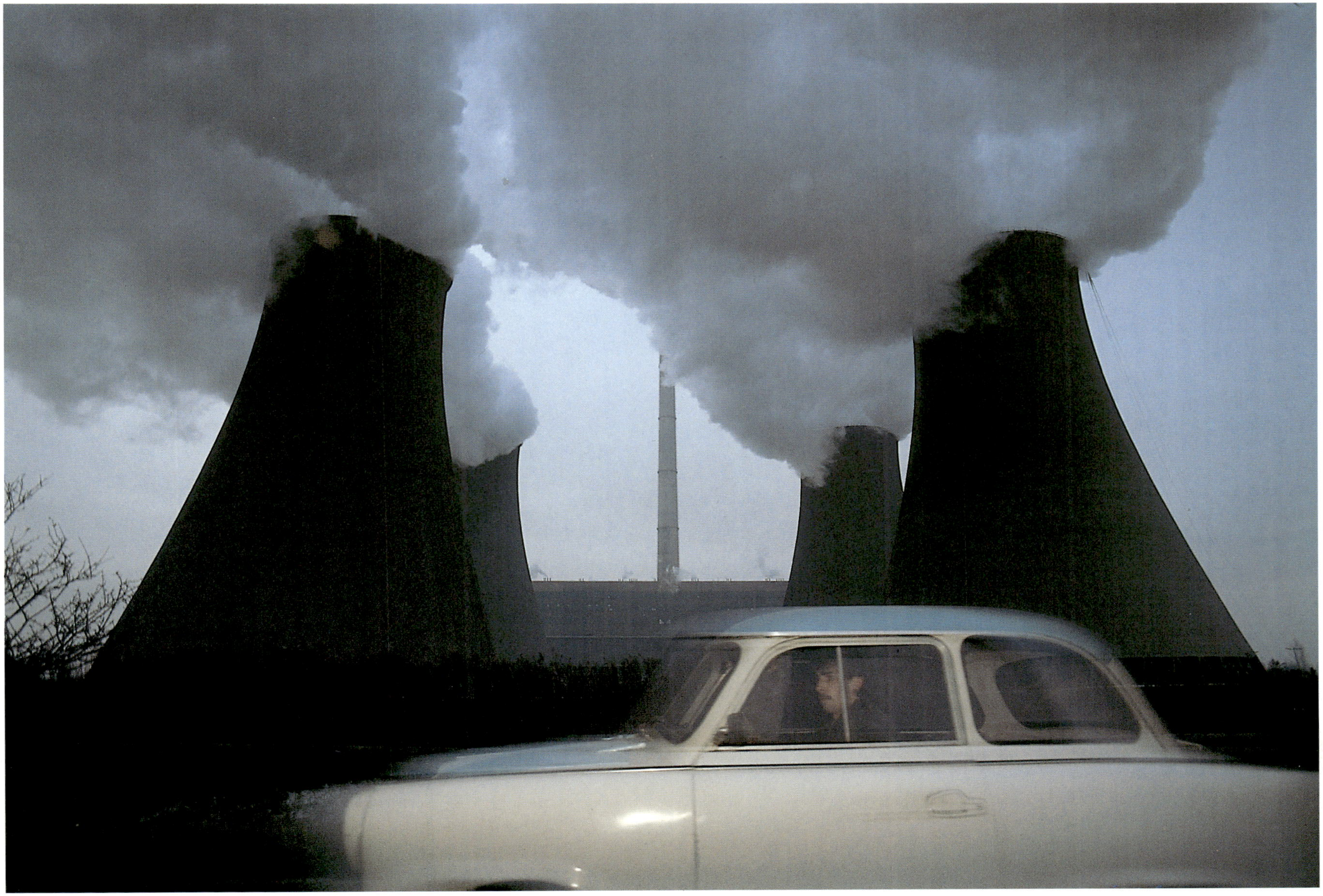

The poetic name of Espenhain, 'aspen grove', only makes the ecological catastrophe in the former German Democratic Republic even more surreal. Nature has no place in Saxony's industrial zone. Clouds of steam from the power station darken the sky, and smoke mushrooms from the chimneys of the briquette factory. In burning the brown coal, four-fifths of the energy produced escapes unused. East German citizens bear it – perforce – with equanimity. At least inside the Trabi the world is still in order. (February 1990)

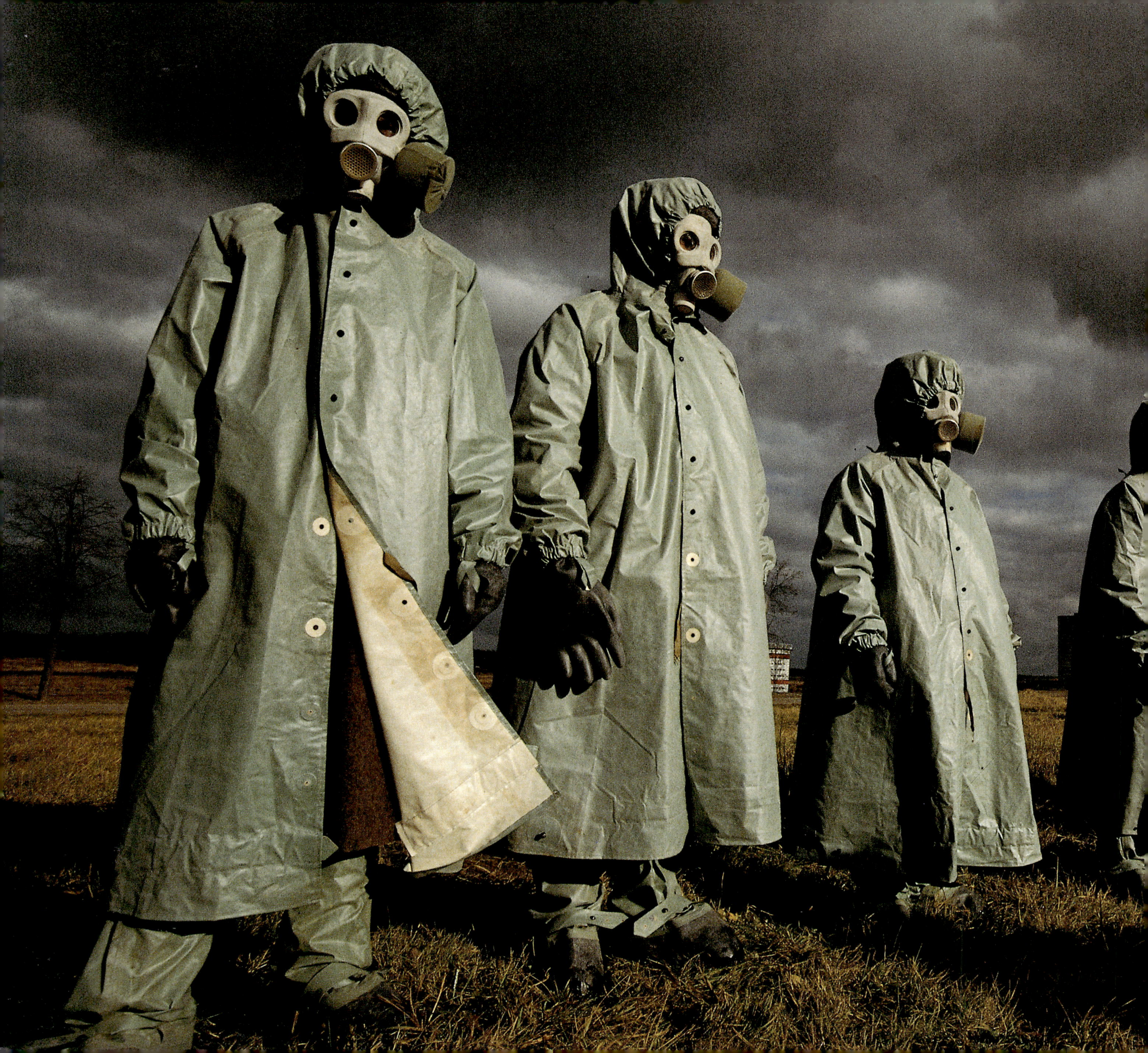

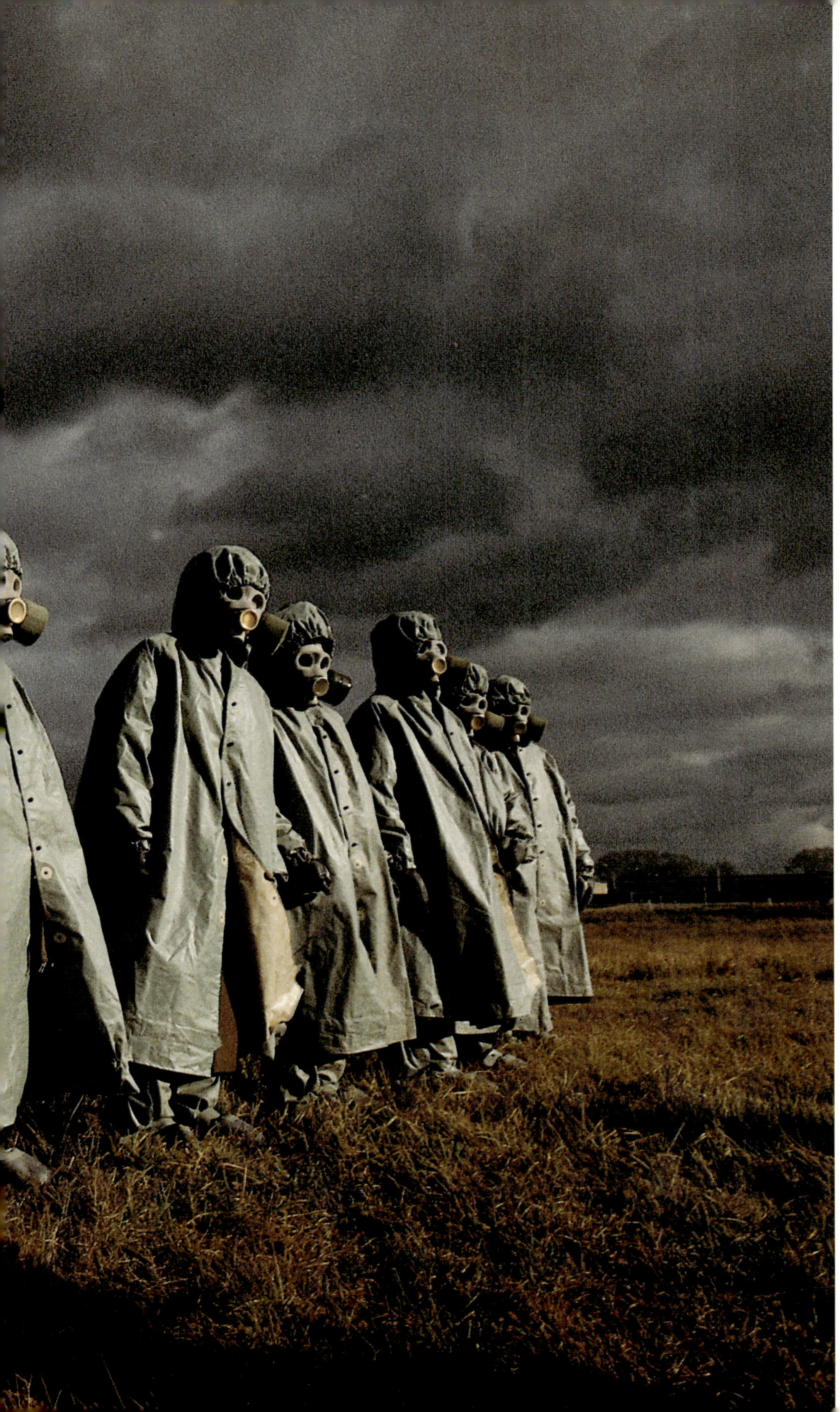

Greeting the dawn. . . . In an exercise in the Moscow area, soldiers from the Kantemirov Division prepare for ABC (atomic, biological and chemical) warfare. This élite unit of the Red Army is today taught in political classes that there can be no victors in such a conflict. Total war is neither just nor revolutionary. (January 1990)

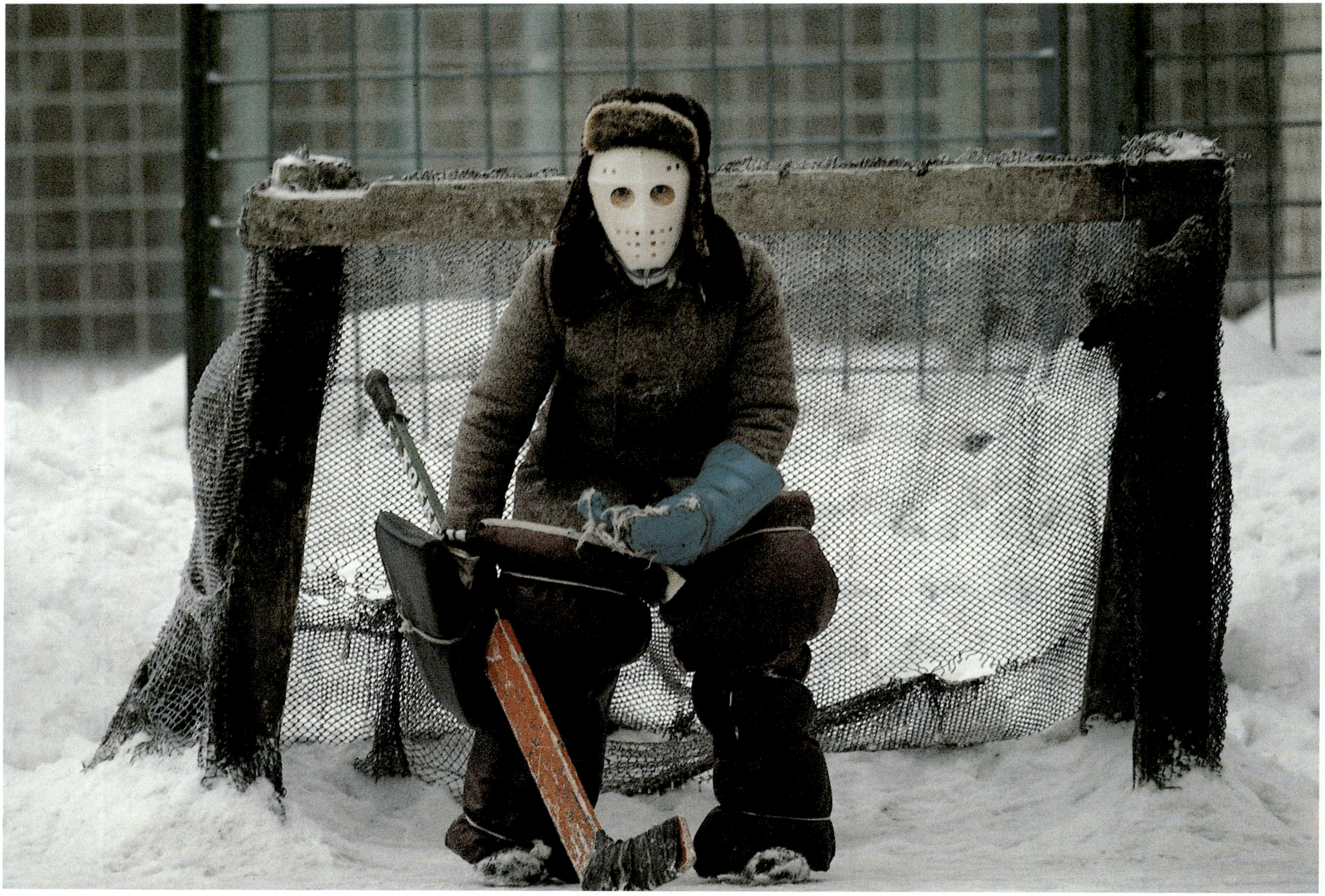

The Moscow winter transforms frozen playgrounds into ice-hockey stadiums, where street teams pitch heated battles between home-made goals at temperatures of −20°C (−4°F). (April 1988)

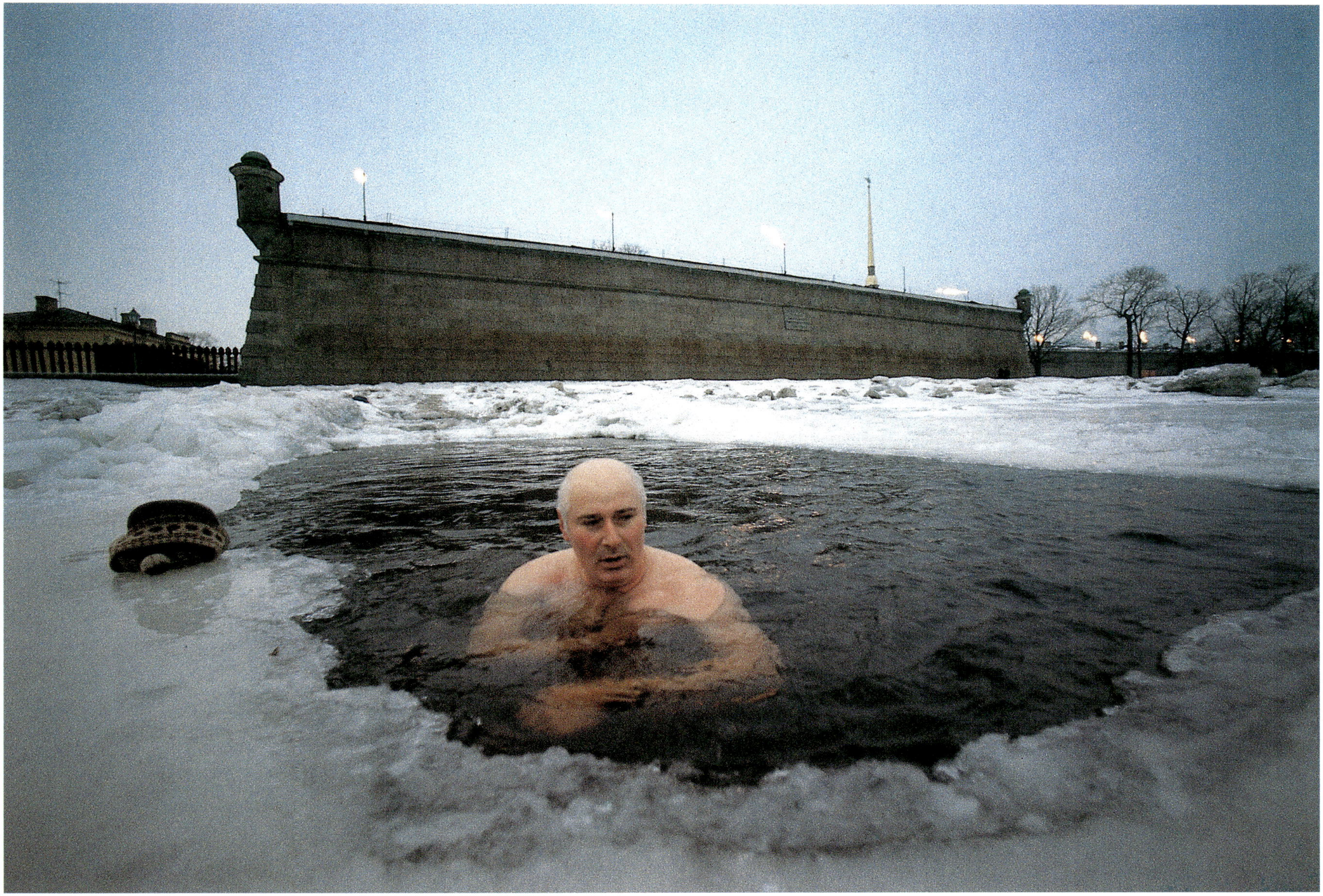

Everyone complains about the weather. Except a true *morzh*, or walrus. For that is what St Petersburg's residents call the cold-resistant heroes who clear a hole in the ice of the Neva even at −20°C (−4°F). The Peter-Paul Fortress in the background is used to such a chilling sight. (February 1989)

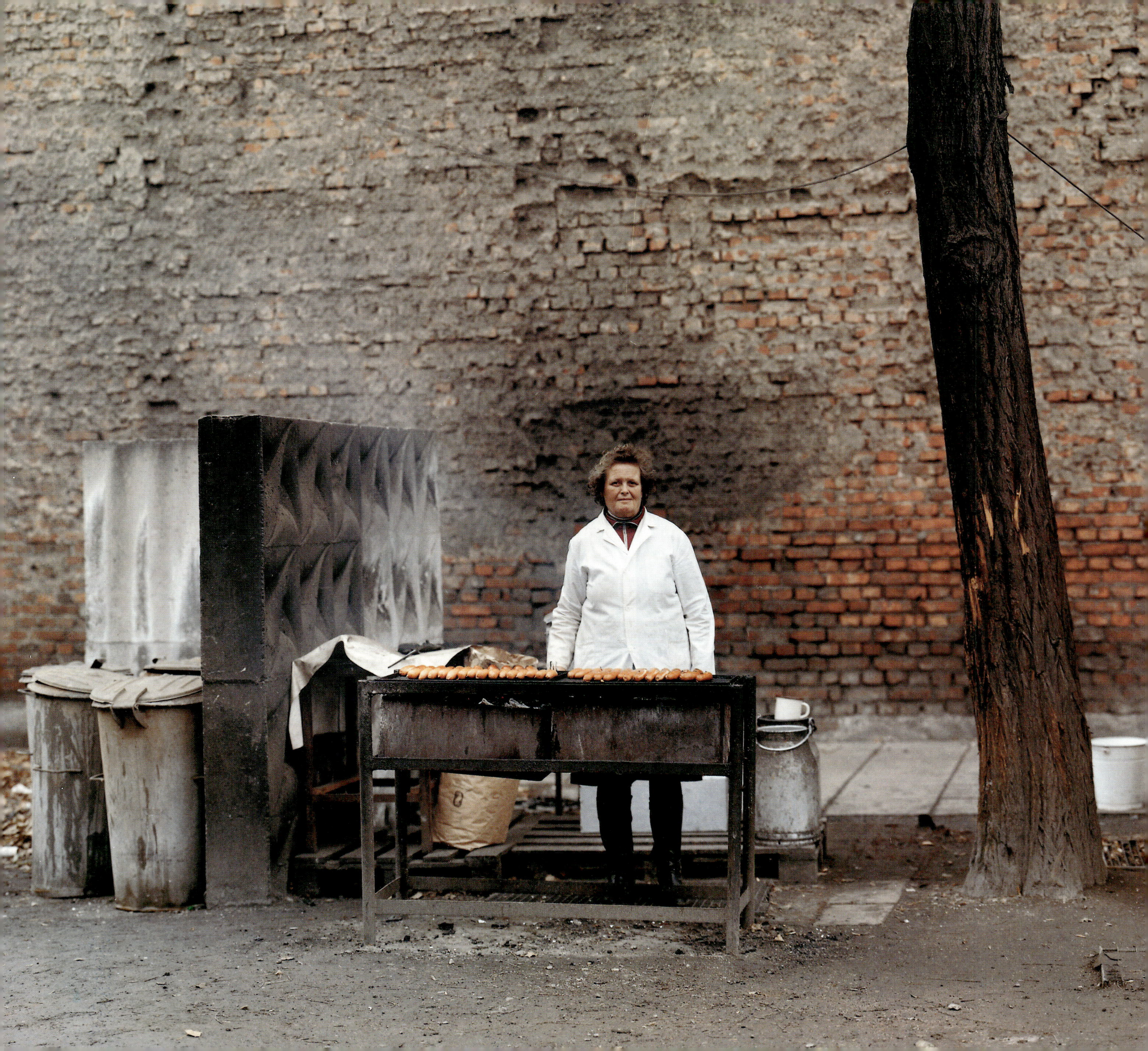

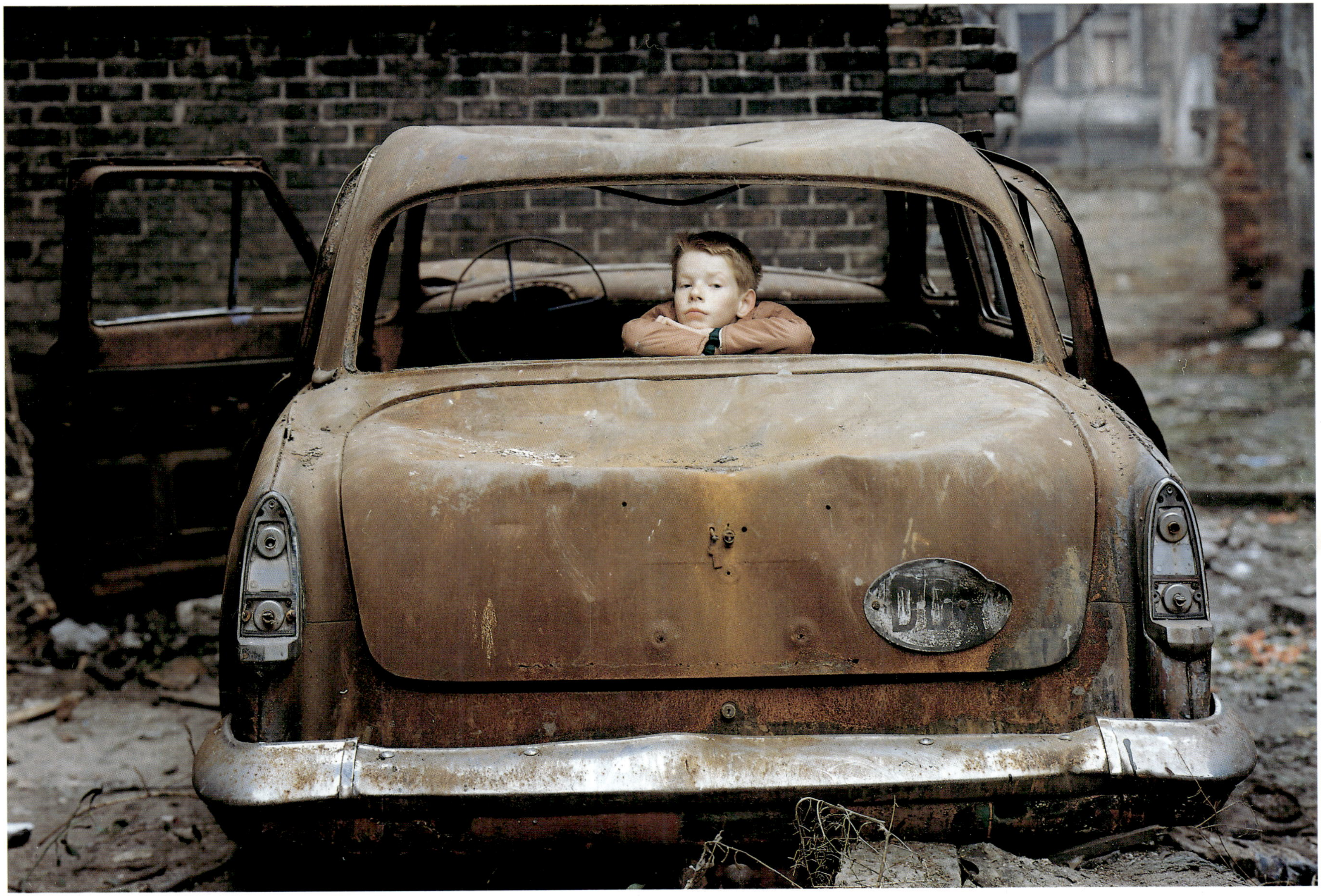

Facing page • *Bratrost* on a bomb site. Else Lohrke has been selling Thuringian sausages on an Erfurt bomb site for twenty years. She has got used to the dustbins and coalheaps in her 'restaurant'. What else can she do? In the universal drabness of its façades, the GDR seemed a country where the fifties would never end, the post-war period never pass. Every morning a fresh start, every evening a catastrophe. (April 1990)

Above • Looking forwards backwards. The burnt-out shell of a once much-loved Volga sits in a soulless corner of Dresden's Neustadt district. Hard to believe it ever went at all, let alone for forty years. (February 1990)

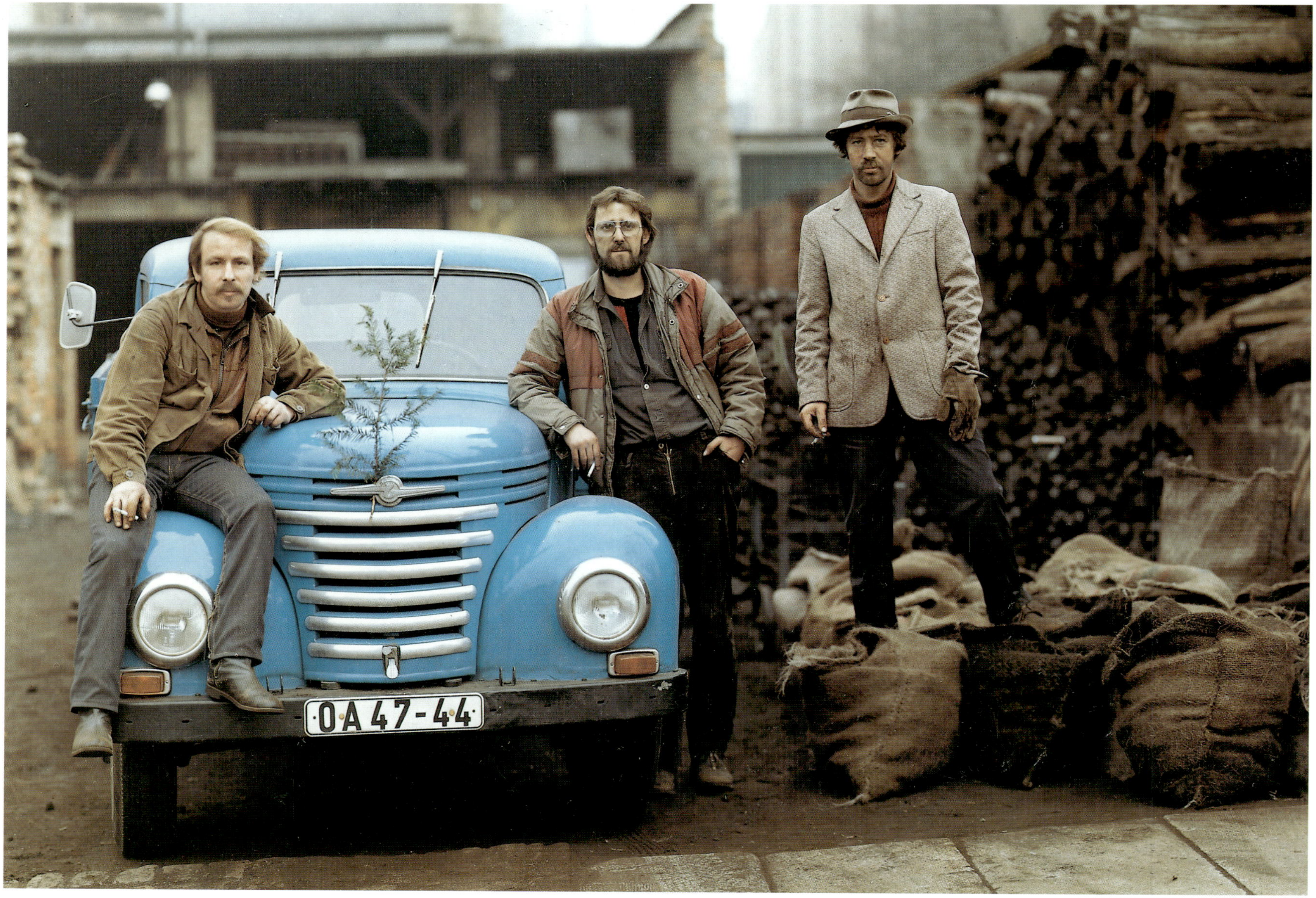

Above • Survival in the back yard. Coal merchant Kruschel's team and their prize possession: a 1953 Barkas truck, with Christmas decoration. Private firms in the GDR were effectively debarred from purchasing new equipment. So Kruschel's men made do with what the State no longer had a use for: a vintage vehicle and – as their business premises – a piece of land flattened by the Dresden firestorm of 1945. (January 1990)

Facing page • 'Find your niche!', the categorical imperative of Soviet citizens, meant seeking out privacy, as here in Moscow. Only off the prescribed path, only off the straight and narrow, only in a concealed courtyard was there a prospect of being a real person for once. It is not Lenin, but the Good Soldier Švejk, with his sense of the possibilities of a situation, who is the true patron saint of 'pragmatic' Socialism. (July 1989)

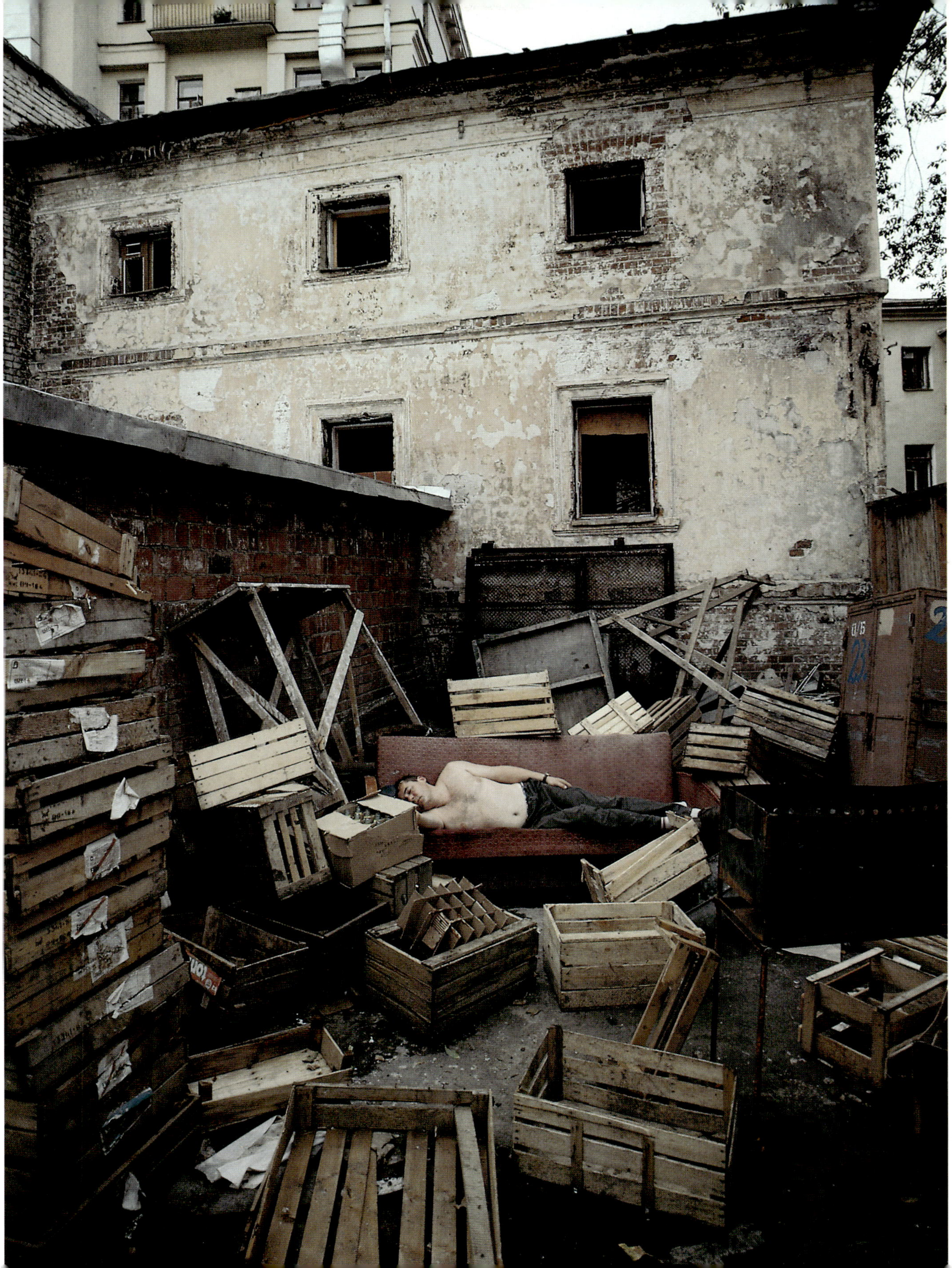

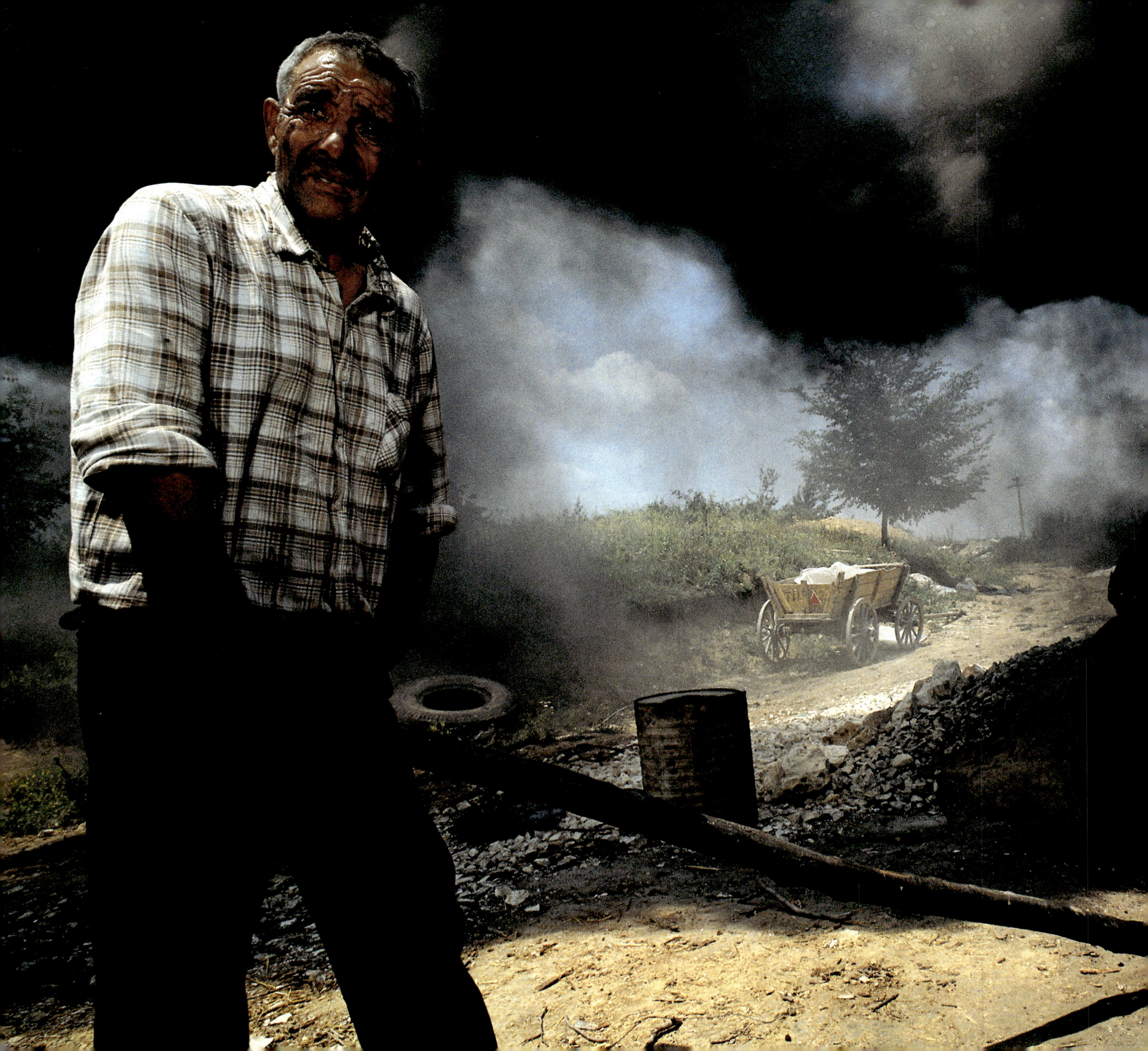

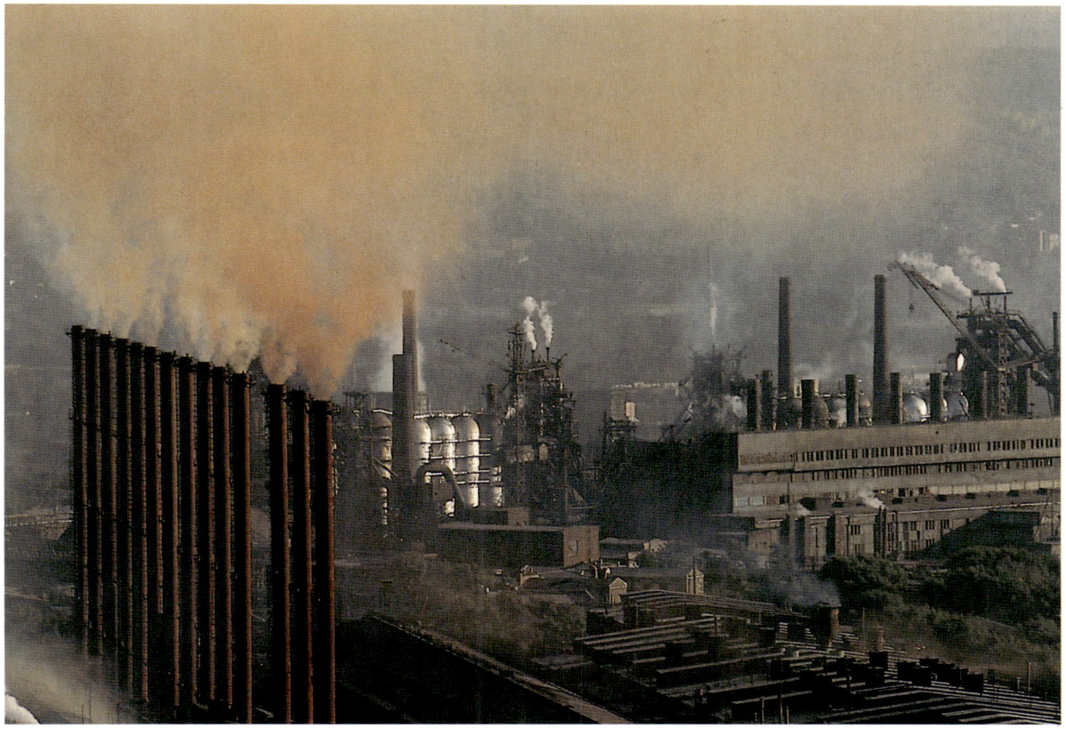

Above • The sky above the Kuzbas industrial region (USSR) is red. Every chimney belches joyful tidings of the 'steelinist' programme: expansion of heavy industry at any price. There has been no departure from this ideology up to the present. Ecological catastrophe has long since struck broad areas of the Soviet Union. (March 1990)

Facing page • A charcoal-burner in Bulgaria. The techniques used to burn the charcoal have been the same for as long as people can remember. The sky is black – but the soot has a human face. (August 1990)

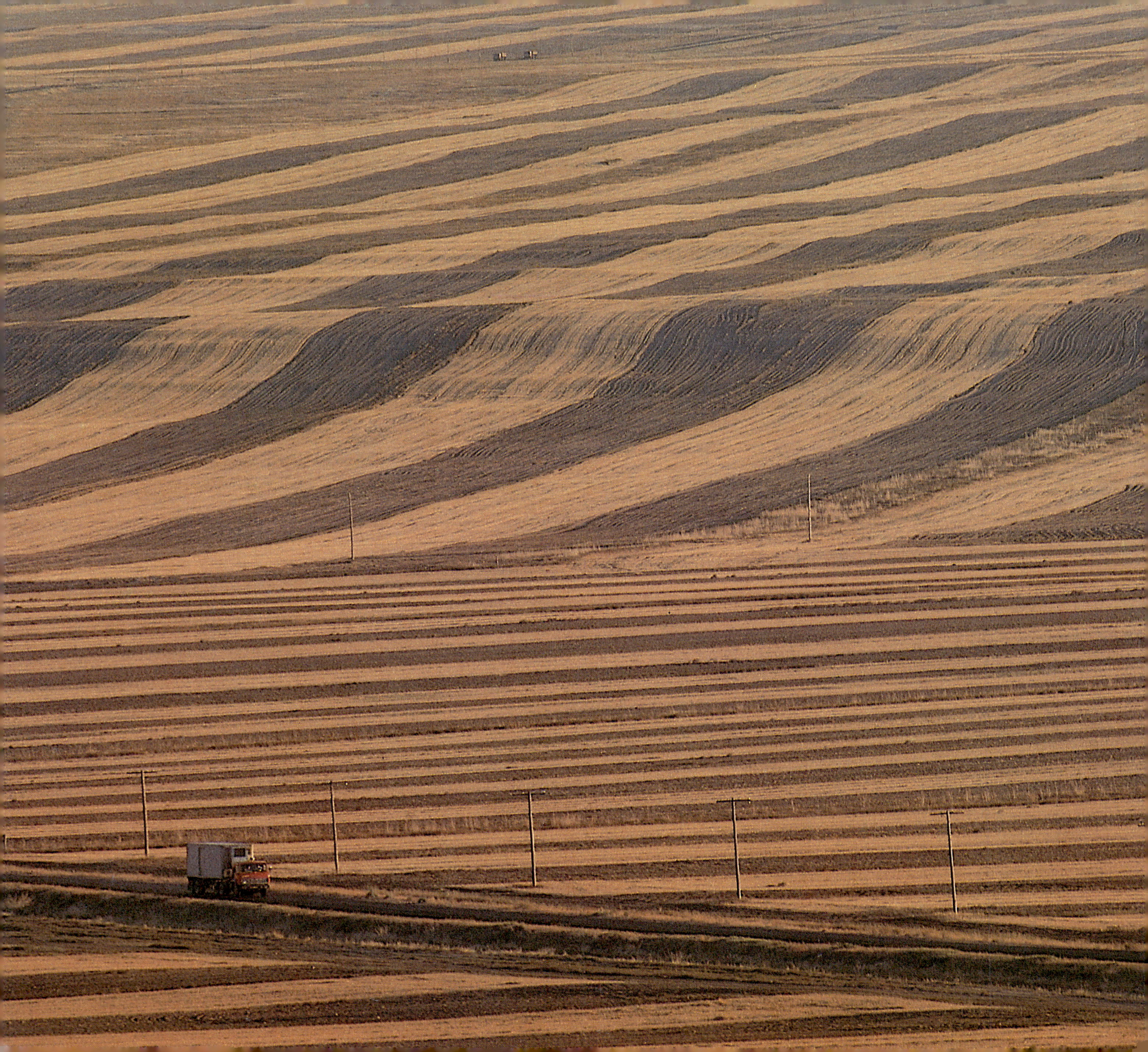

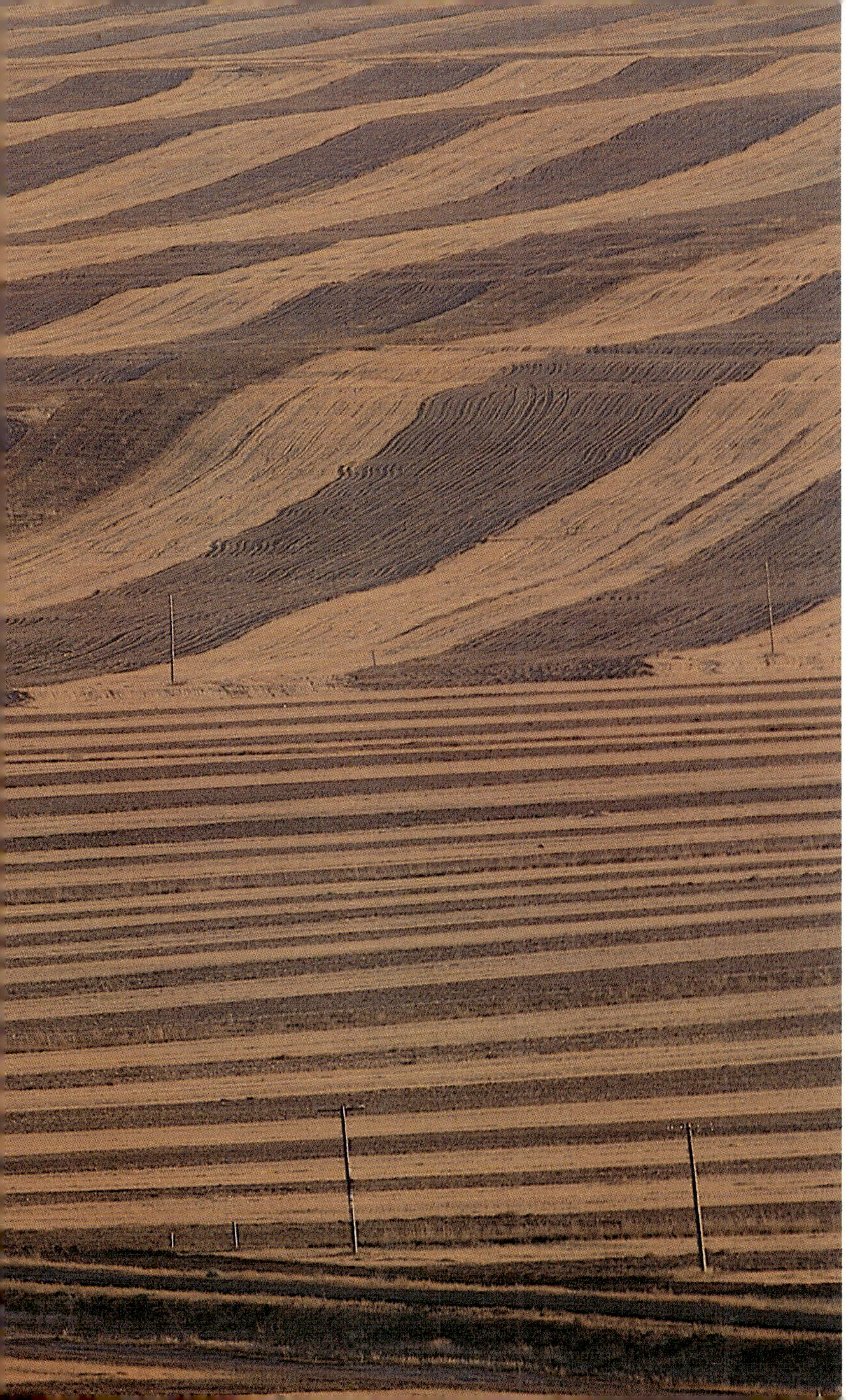

Zebra stripes against the steppe winds. As a means of preventing erosion, collective farmers near the Mongolian border plough their wheat fields in strips. At least it helps break the monotony of the single-crop system. (March 1990)

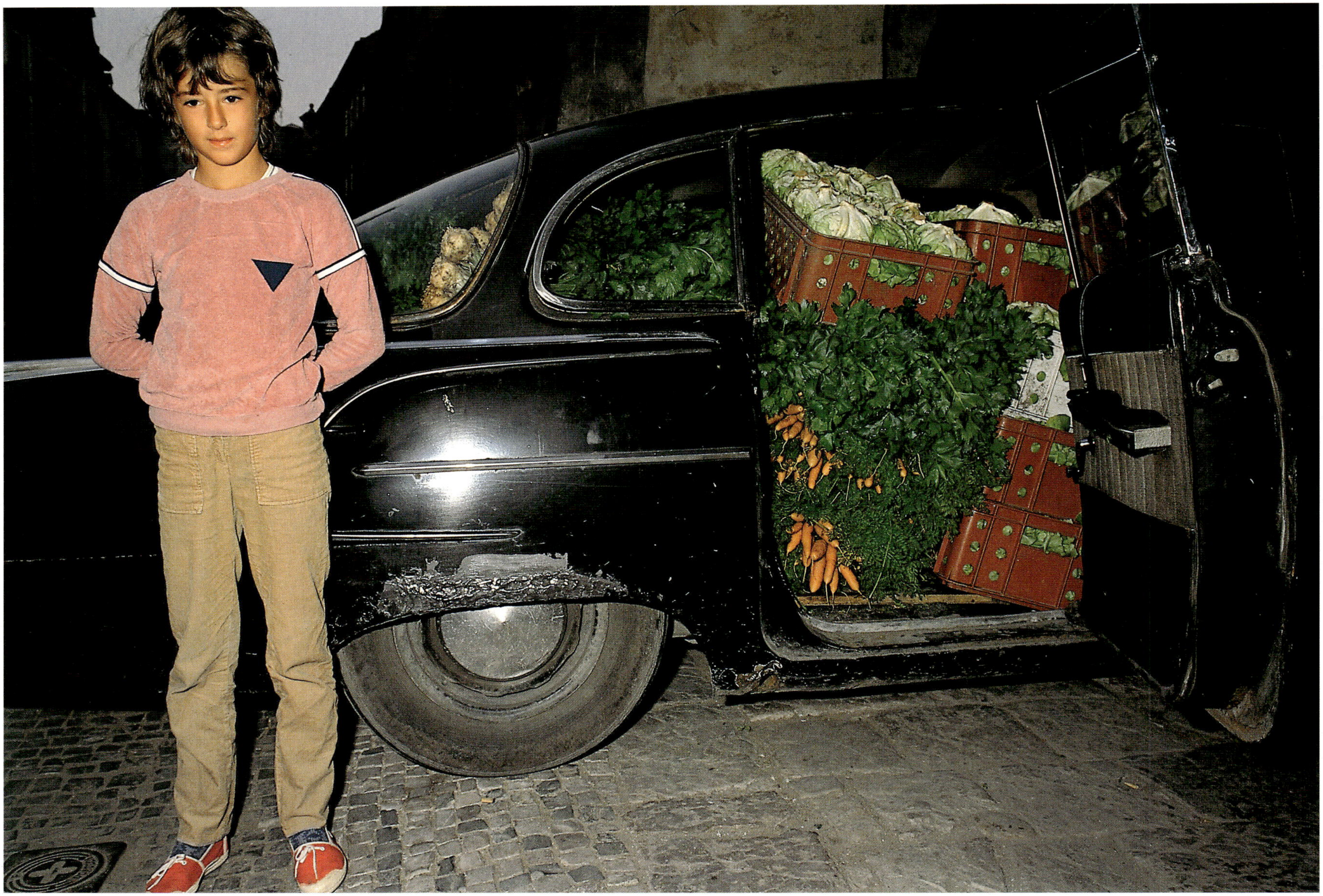

State limousine turned vegetable cart. This Tatra 603 once transported the flower of the Czechoslovakian *Nomenklatura*. With the reorganization of the car fleet, a Prague market trader replaced wilting power with fresh carrots. (May 1988)

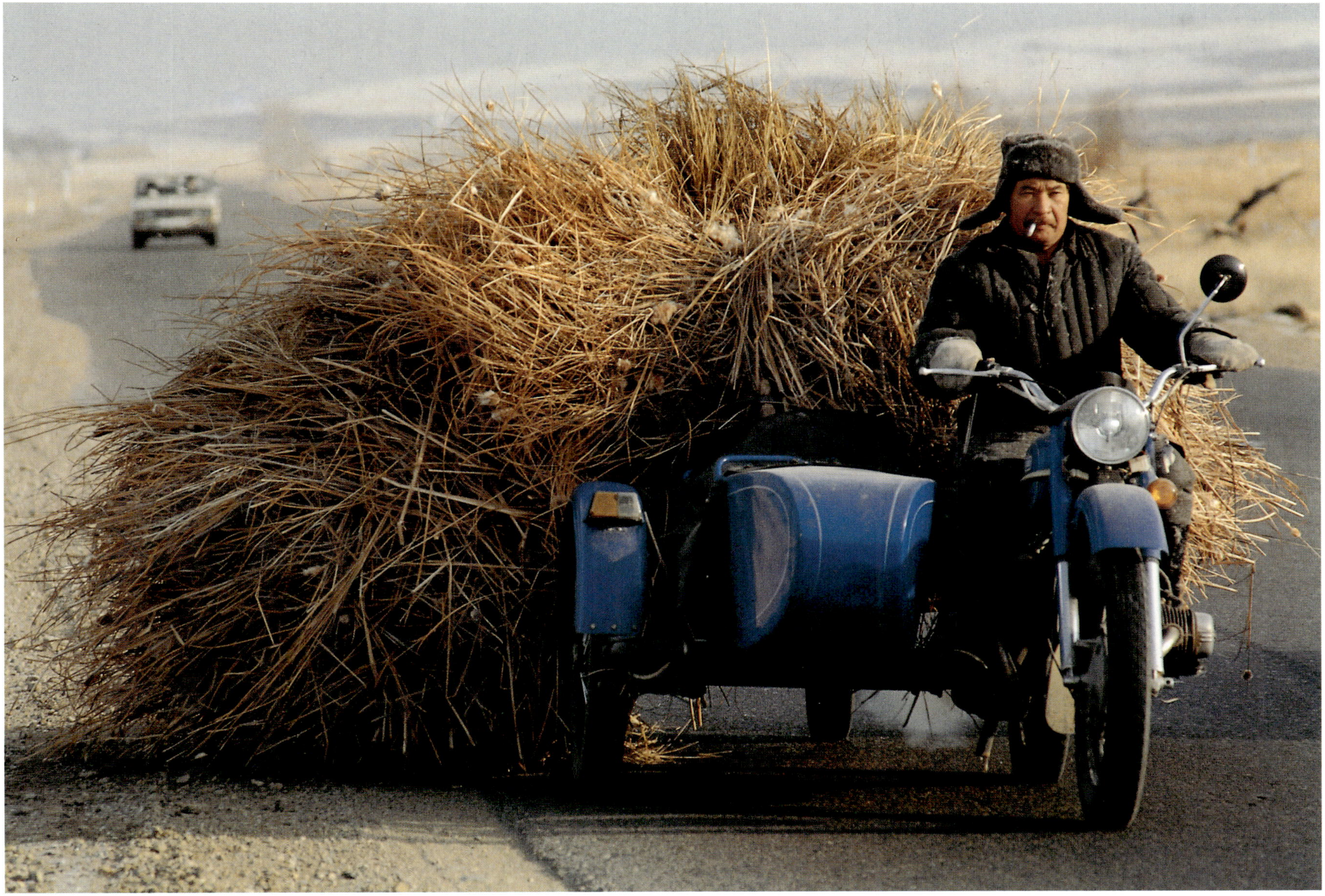

Improvisation is everything in a command economy. Where centralized Soviet planning deprives the local farmer of his tractor, the side-car of a motorbike must serve to bring in the hay. (March 1990)

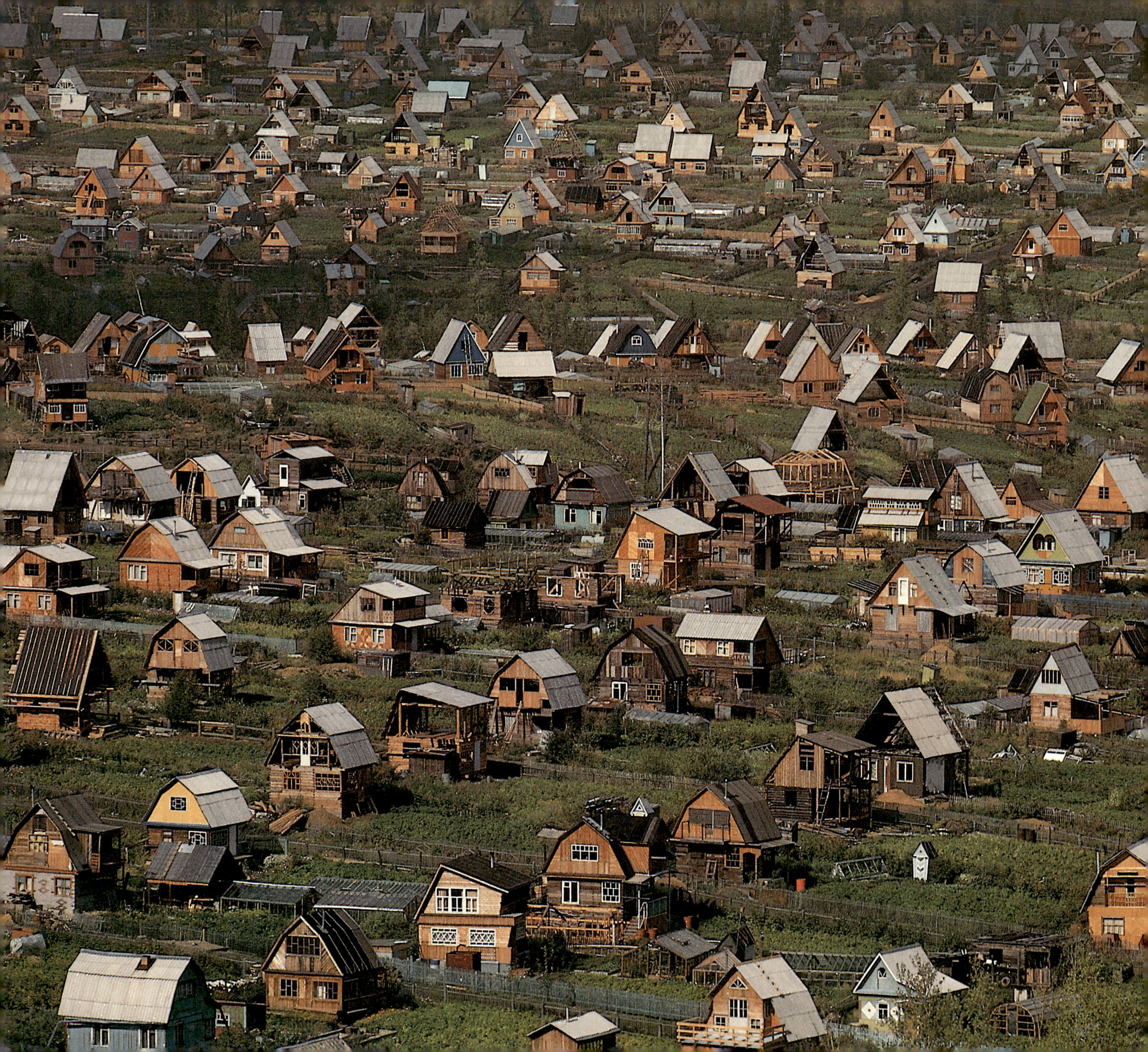

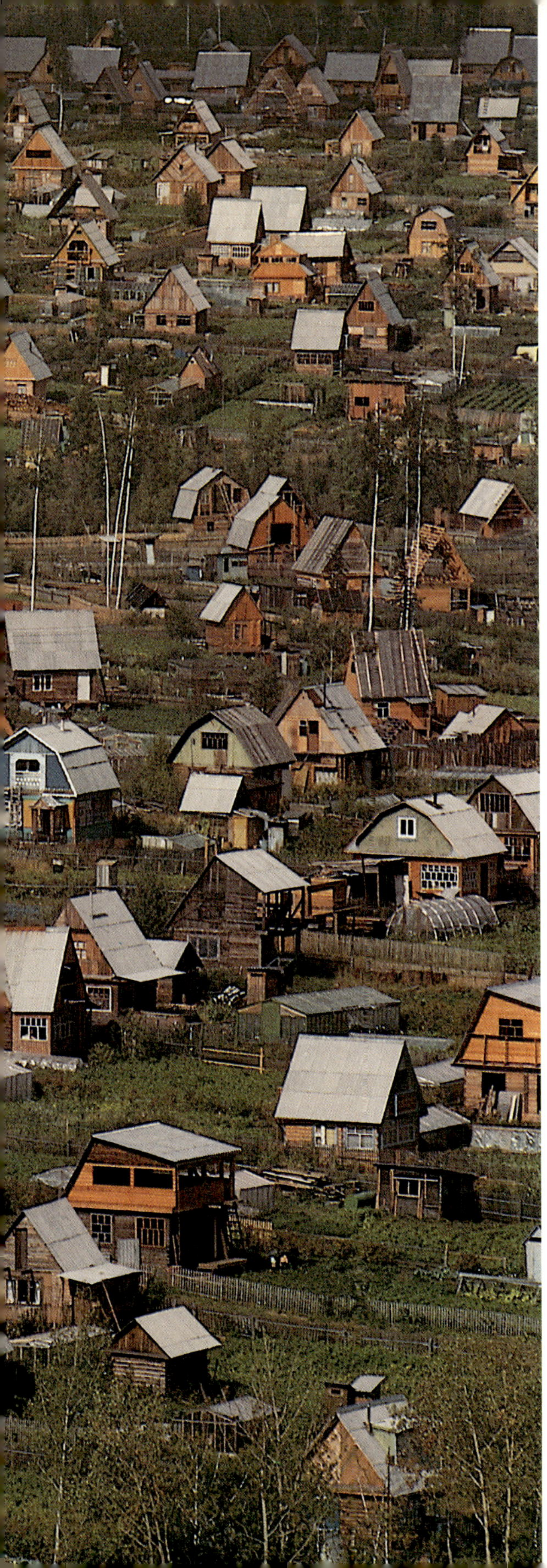

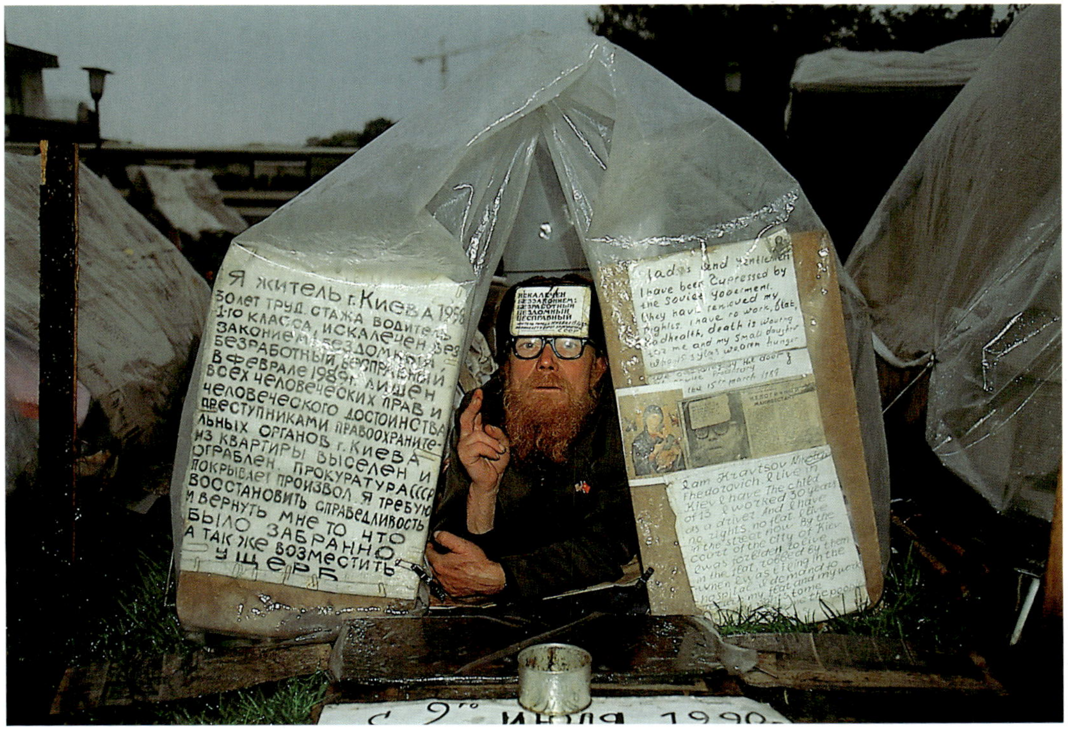

Above • Victims of the great 'reorganization' have neither thatch nor dacha over their heads. In the winter of 1990, the Soviet empire's new poor erected a city of tents in Red Square – in full view of the Kremlin. The bulldozers moved in shortly before Christmas. (November 1990)

Facing page • Where the collective disperses into individuals. The dacha is just as much a part of Communism as the hammer and sickle. It serves as oasis and refuge. A society-free zone where the Soviet citizen can simply be human. (April 1990)

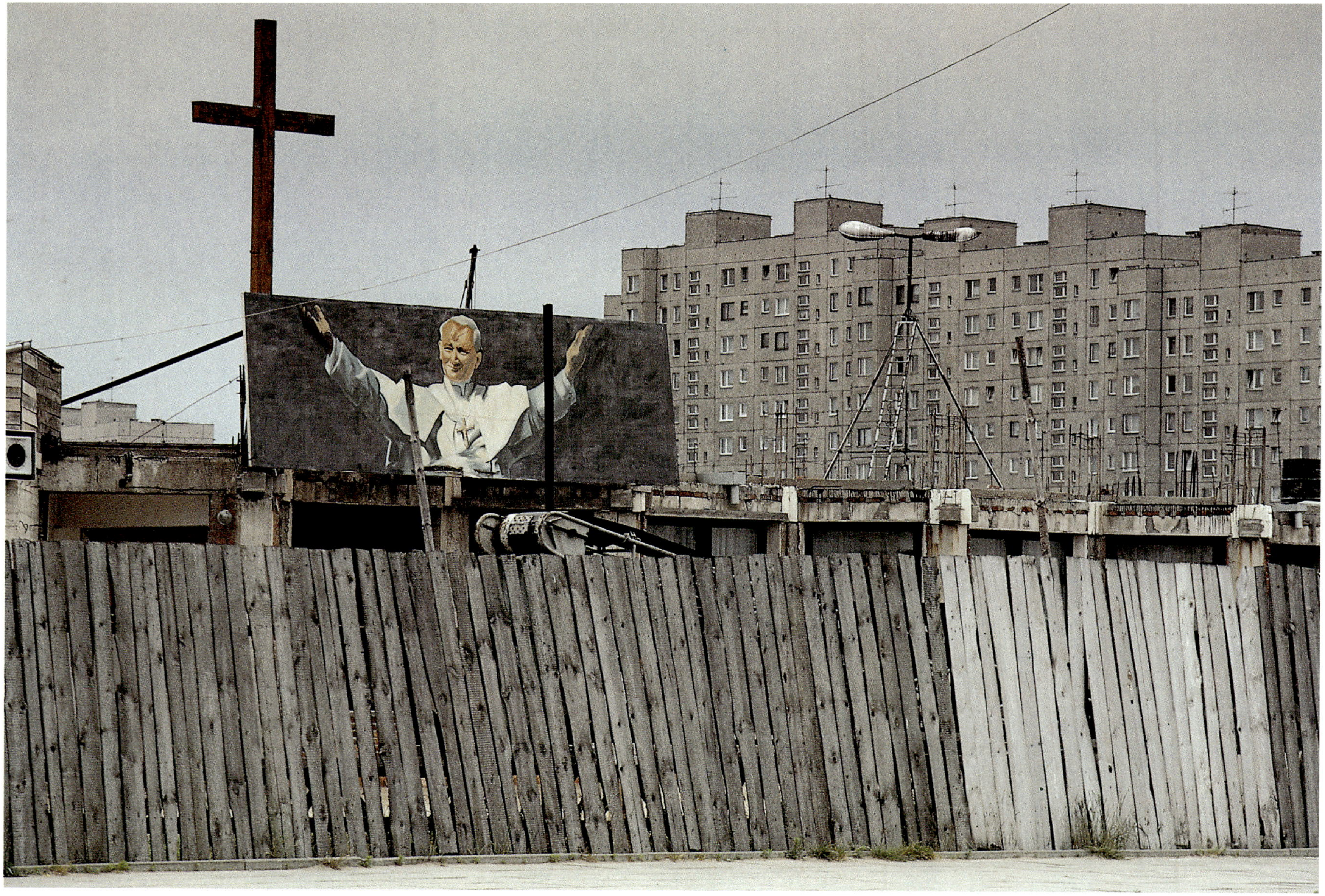

Above • In Poland, faith still moves mountains and walls. While Gdansk's town planners complained about the lack of construction materials for urgently needed housing, a new cathedral with a 60-metre (200-foot) spire arose in the suburb of Wrzeszcz. Labourers will work for their Pope often for no pay, and material shortages are unknown. The Lord moves in mysterious ways. (June 1989)

Facing page • The orthodox Communists' crusade against religion is over, and the cross can now be remounted on top of the dome. As here at the monastery of the Saint of Kronshtadt in St Petersburg, almost all such crosses were removed from the roofs of Orthodox churches after the Russian Revolution. Buildings were destroyed or used as storehouses for coal and potatoes. The Russian State lacks the money to maintain its historical monuments. Another reason to give them back to the Church. (June 1990)

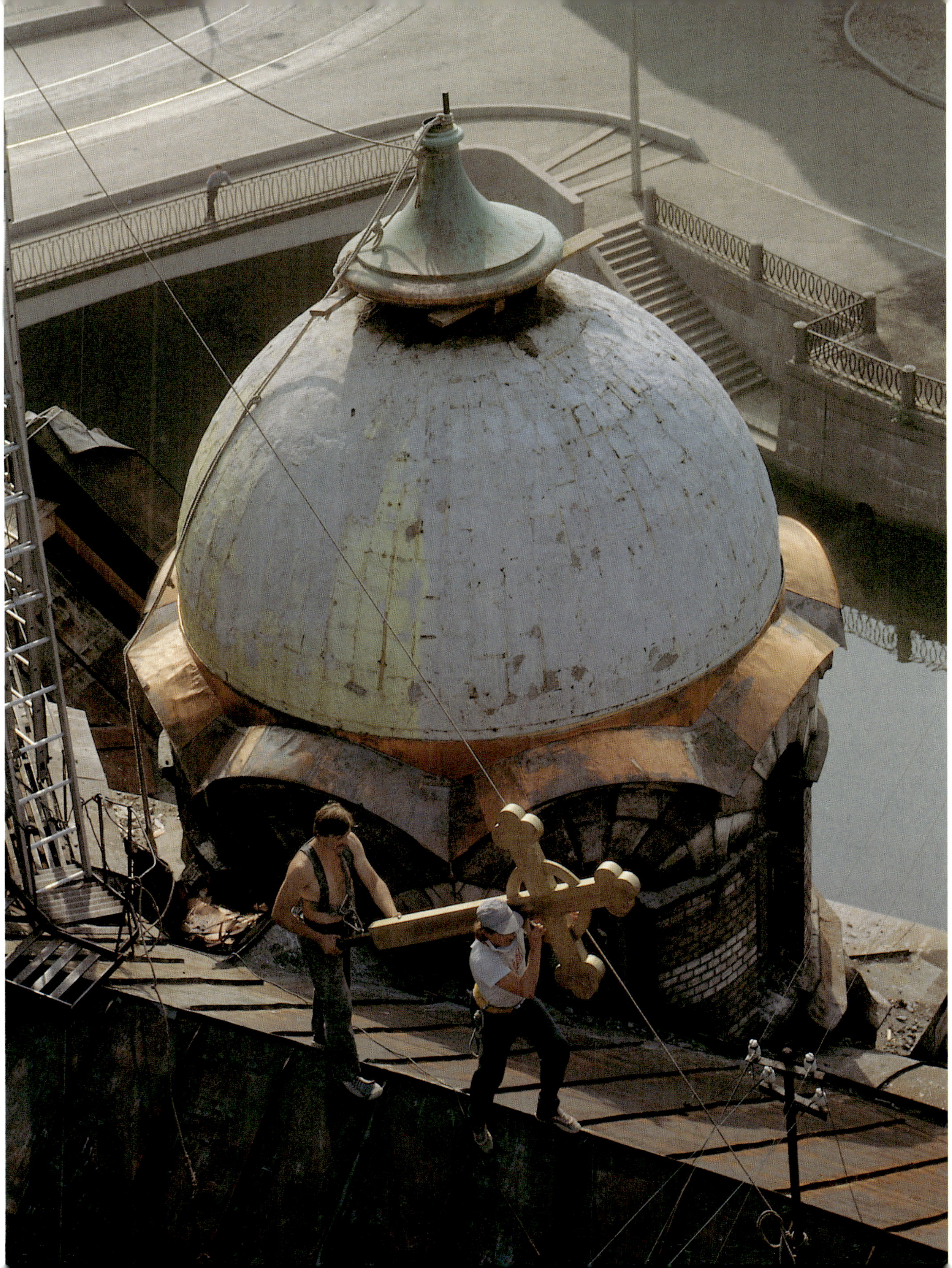

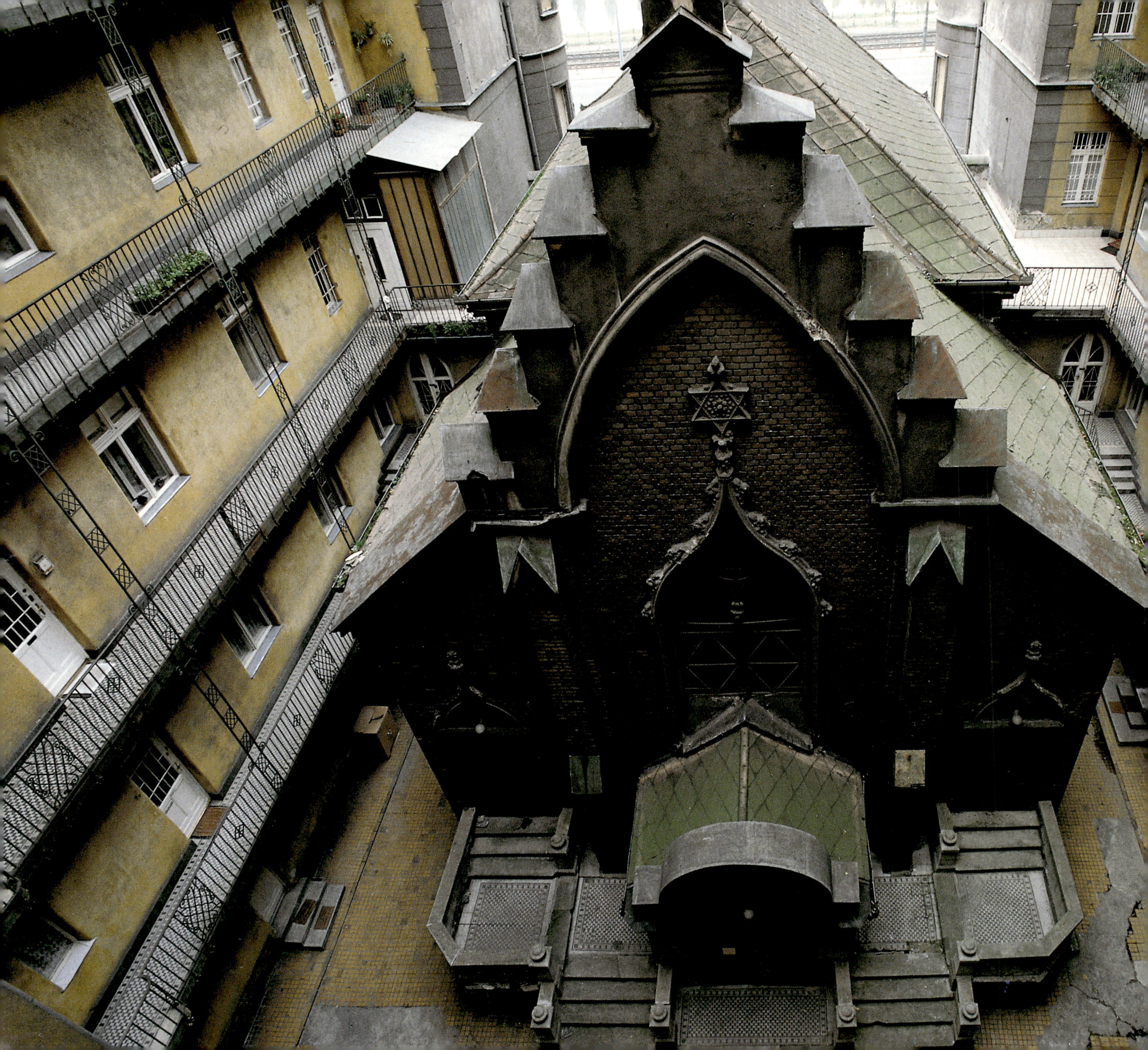

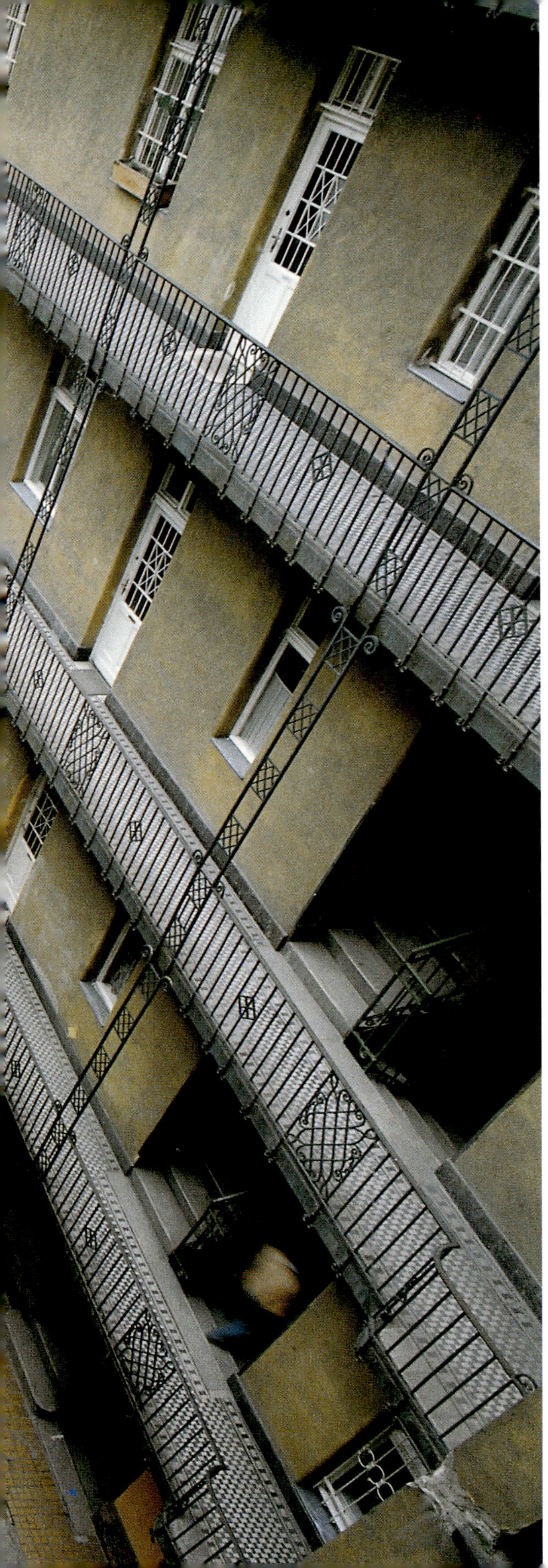

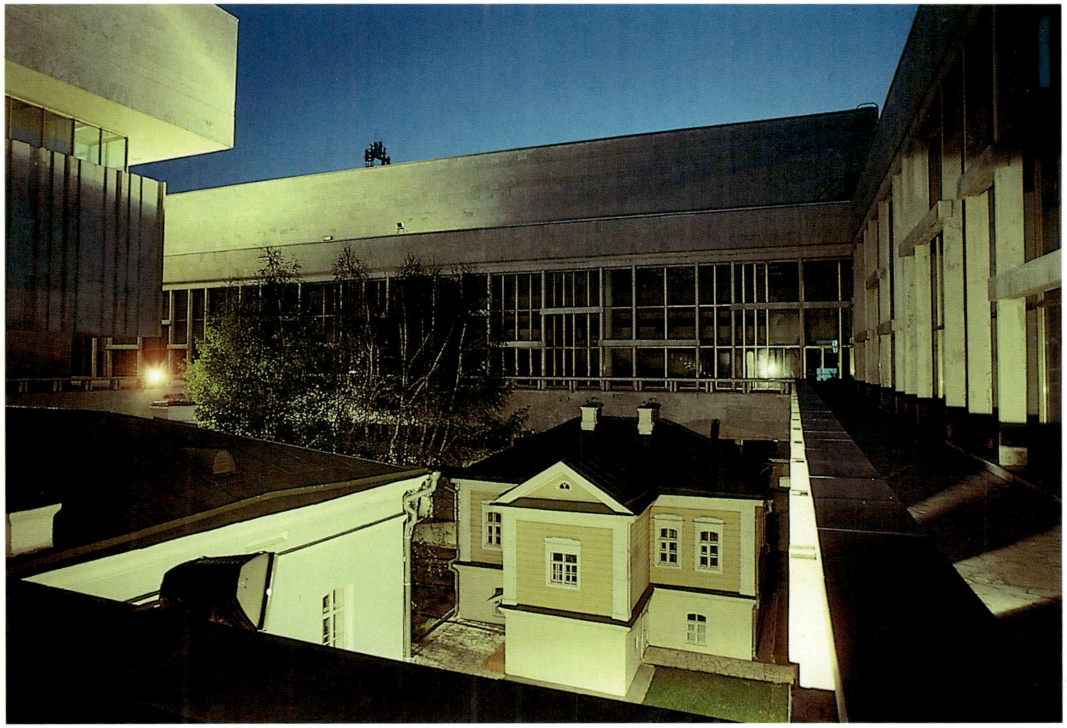

Above • A Bethlehem of Bolshevism: the home of the Ulyanov family in the Russian town of Ulyanovsk, which is unlikely to bear the name of its most famous son for very much longer. The monuments to Vladimir Ilyich Ulyanov, otherwise known as Lenin, are standing on unsteady foundations. In most East European cities they have already been melted down or toppled over. Surrounding the Ulyanov home, however, is the Museum of the Great October Revolution, a protective wall of marble to keep out the changing times. (May 1988)

Facing page • Protected by the houses around it, the synagogue in Lajos Street in Budapest has survived both war and holocaust. It was built, for lack of space, in the courtyard of a newly finished residential block in the Jewish Third District in 1910. In 1944 the Jewish community was forcibly relocated to the opposite bank of the Danube, and Gentile families moved into the apartments overlooking the synagogue. Today there are 100,000 Jewish Hungarians living in Budapest, the only city in Eastern Europe with a fully developed religious infrastructure: rabbinical schools, ritual baths, kosher shops – and a synagogue in the back yard. (July 1987)

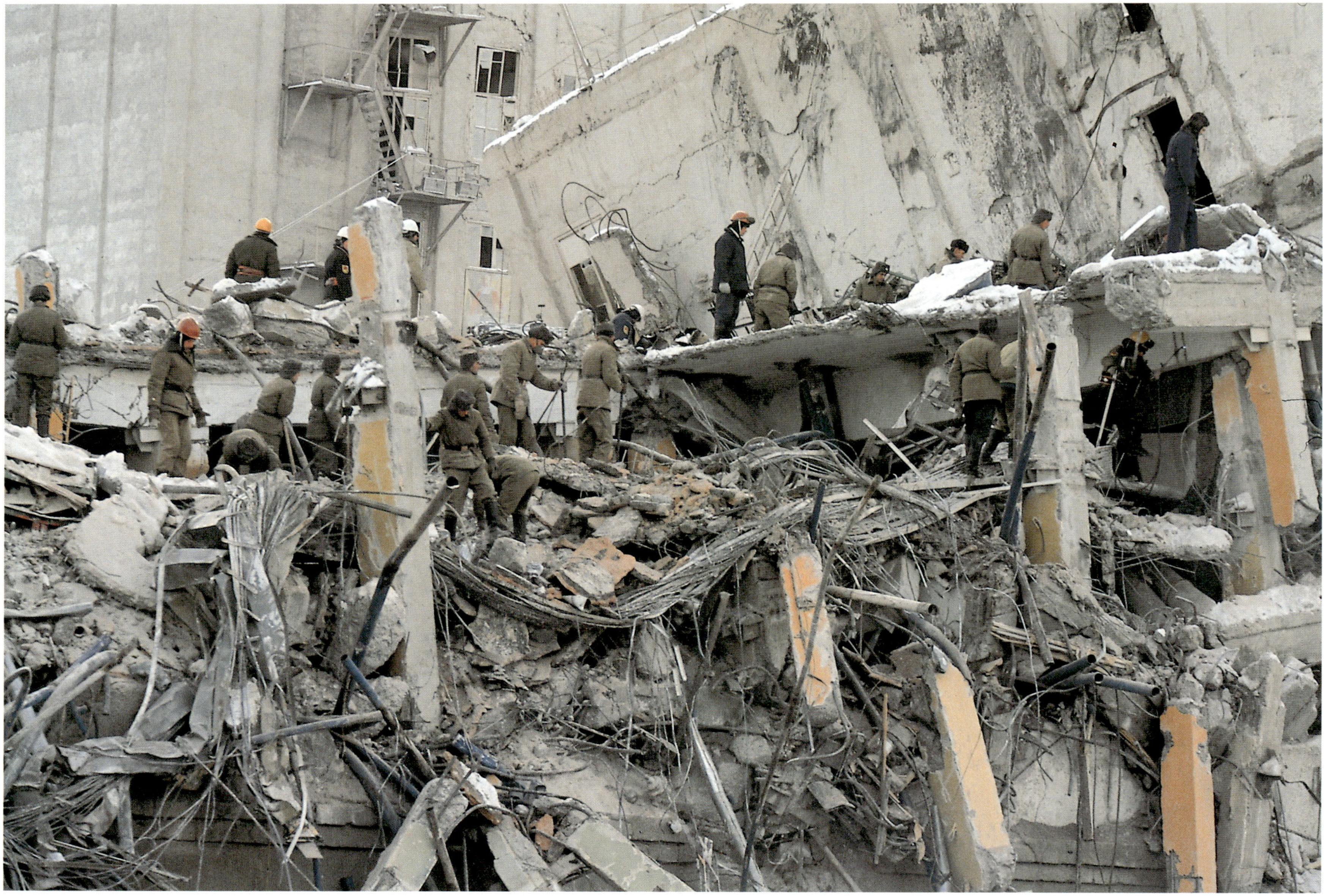

The last Judgment lasted thirty-eight seconds. On 7 December 1988 the earth quaked in Armenia, a land which has borne more than its fair share of pain and suffering this century. Many buildings – thrown up in the Brezhnev era with nothing but quotas and speed in mind – were reduced to rubble. Like this bread factory in Spitak. 365 towns and villages were partially destroyed, 58 totally. More than 24,000 people lost their lives. Political tremors followed not far behind: hostile Azerbaijanis blocked traffic routes into Armenia, deliberately obstructing reconstruction work. (December 1988)

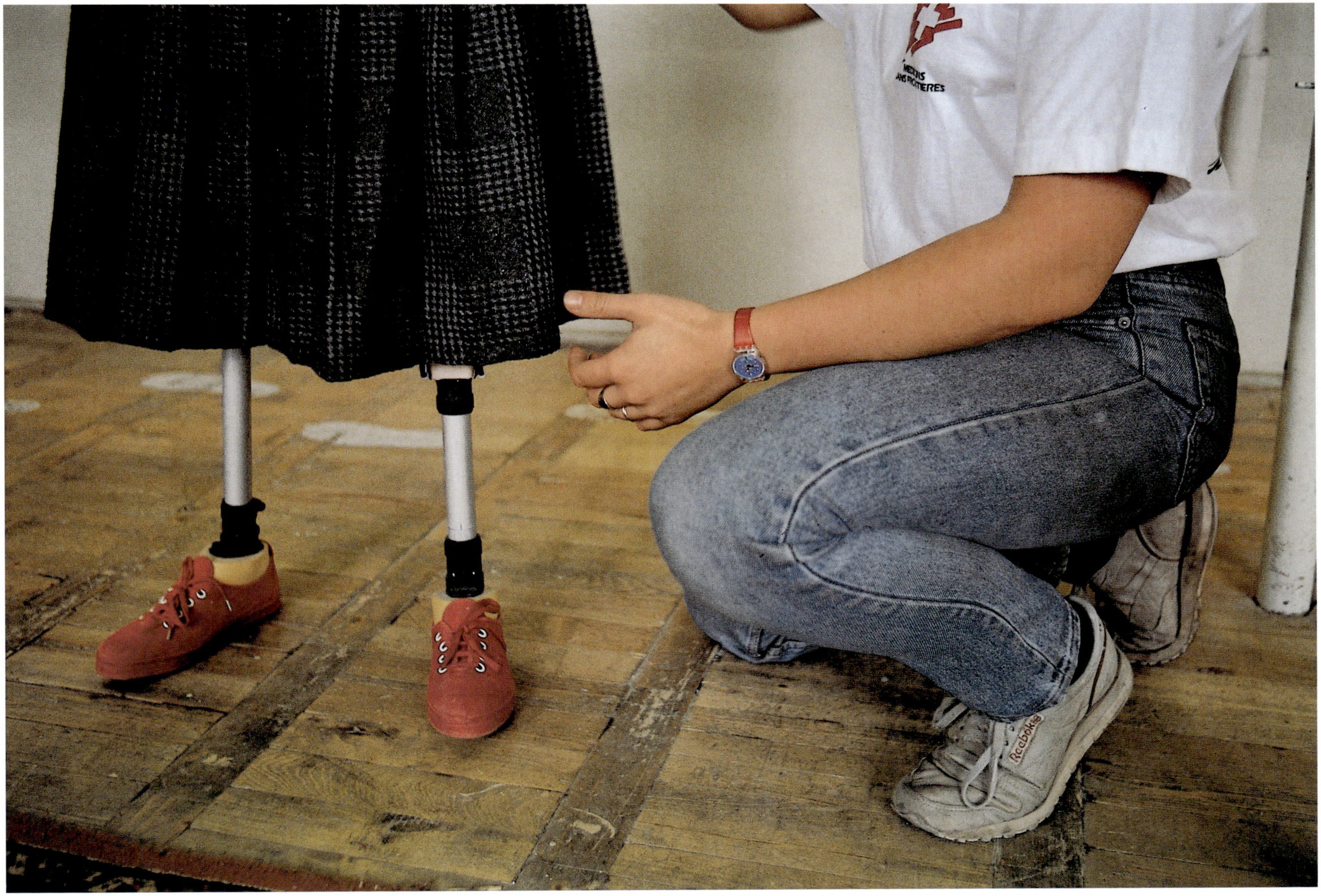

The political tremors are still being felt. The ruins which were there for everyone to see in Armenia were also those of an era. The Soviet State had made no provision for effective disaster-relief measures. For the first time in its history, the German Red Cross set up a prosthesis workshop, teaching people to walk all over again. (July 1989)

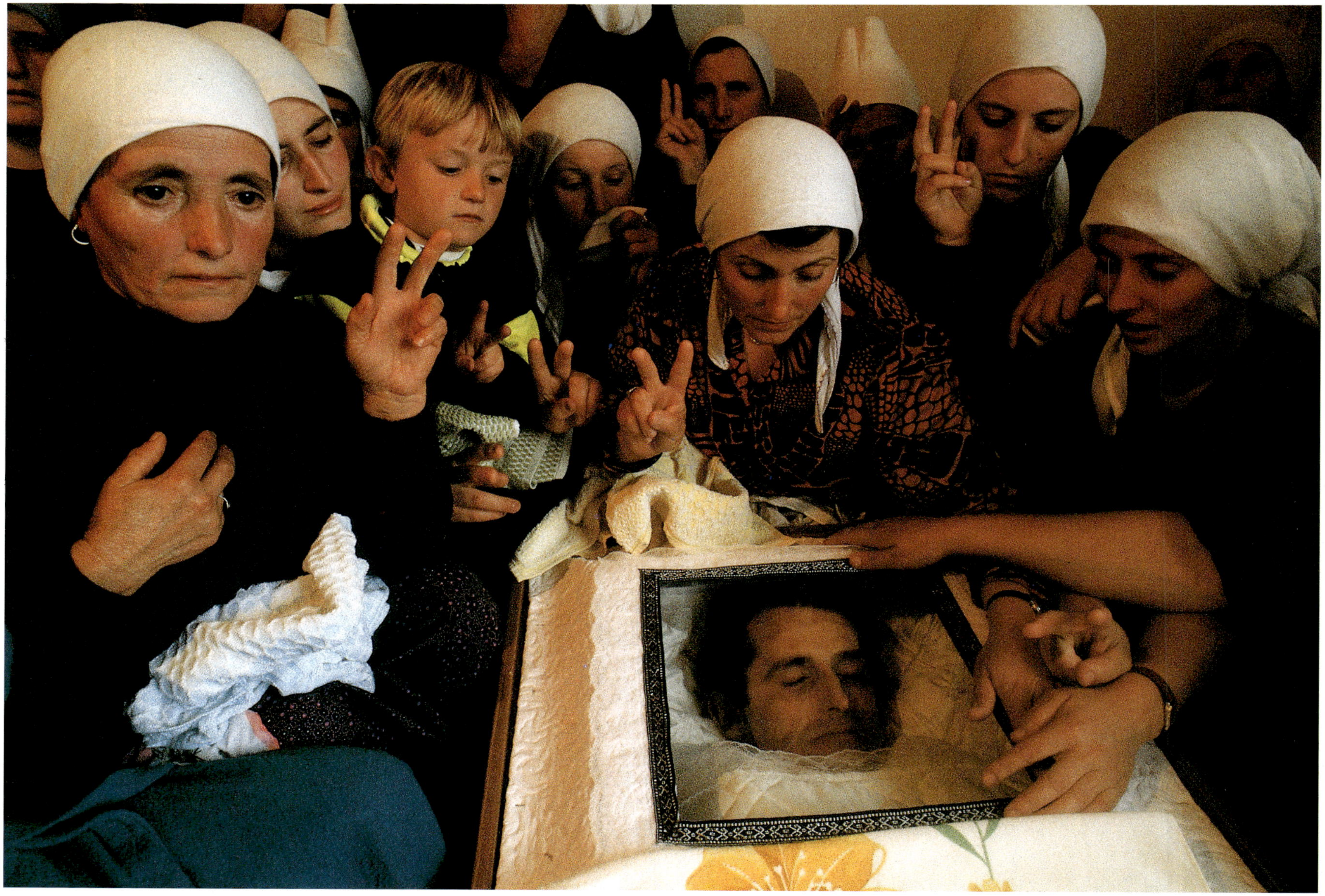

Haxhi Osmanaj, aged twenty-eight. Emigrated to Offenbach in Germany, shot one evening and brought home dead to Kosovo. 'It was Serbs', insists the family, although the police have no proof. For hours Haxhi Osmanaj is celebrated and mourned by the womenfolk of the clan. The burial, according to Islamic rite, is then performed by the men. Thus it has always been, and thus it will remain, in the Albanian southern province of Yugoslavia. (April 1990)

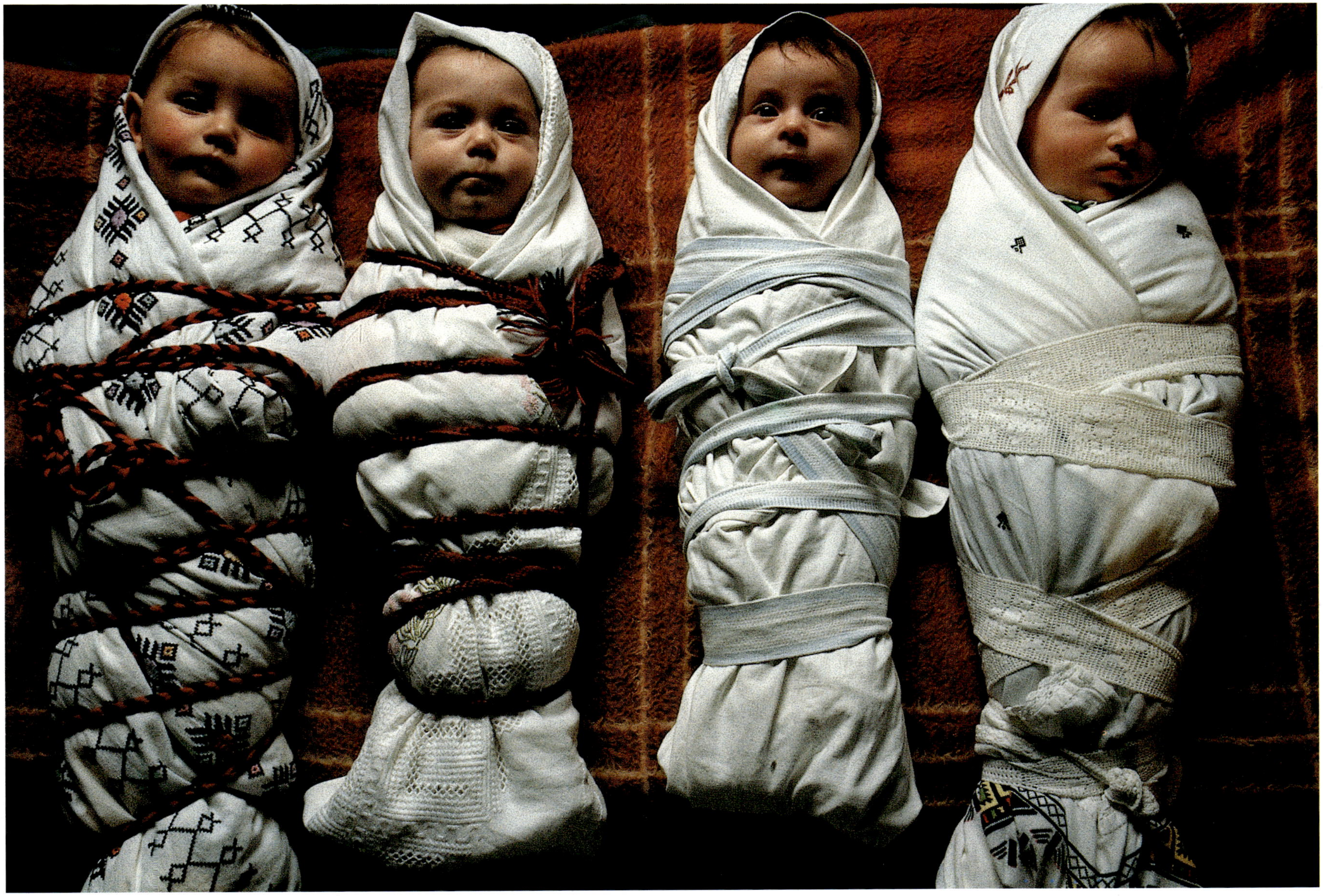

Four young Albanians wait for liberation. In Kosovo, babies are still wrapped up like mummies according to old custom. The large size of Albanian families is a thorn in the flesh of the Serbs, who fear for their own hegemony. The average age in Kosovo today is twenty-one. 'Each of their families has more children than tiles on the roof', mock the Serbs. (April 1990)

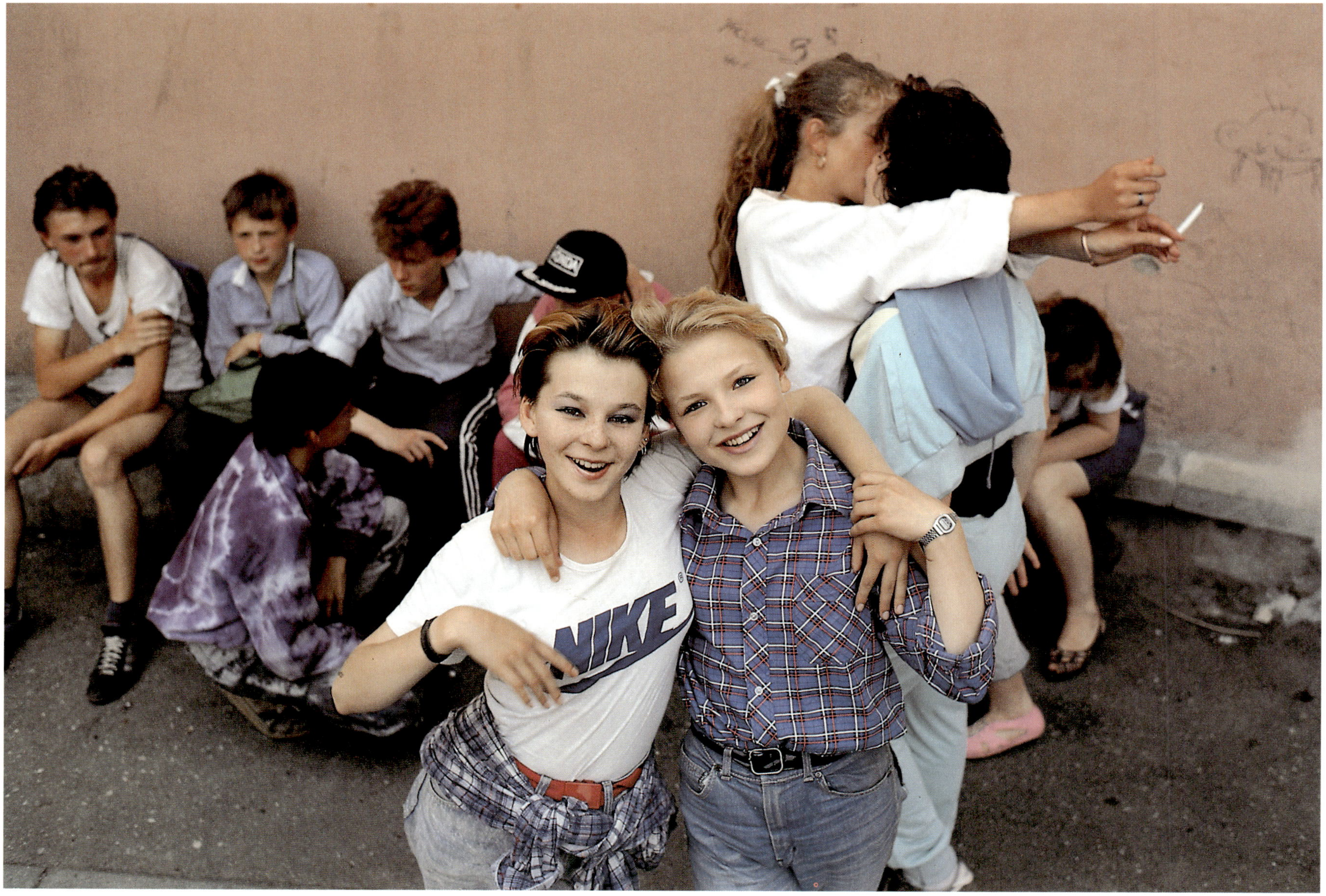

The *Children of the Arbat* have turned into Western-style kids. Anatoly Rybakov's famous novel described life in Moscow's Arbat district in the fifties, the years of harsh Stalinist rule. For the young people in Gorbachev's Arbat, that's all in the murky past. Post-Socialism has long since begun. (July 1989)

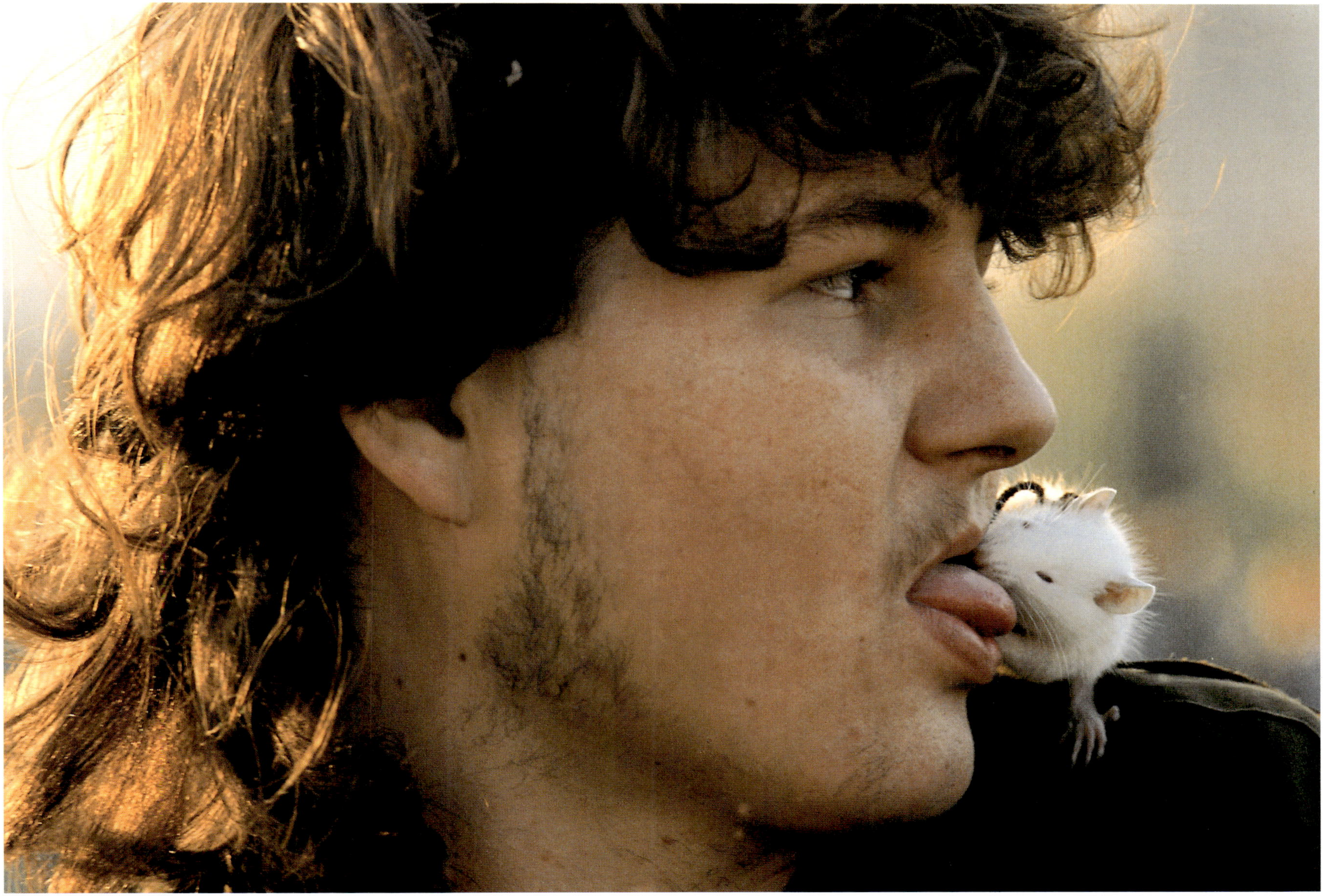

A kiss from a rat in a beastly encounter on Prague's Charles Bridge. Young Czechs have picked up the customs and rituals of their Western cousins in no time at all. Fur collars are back in fashion. (September 1990)

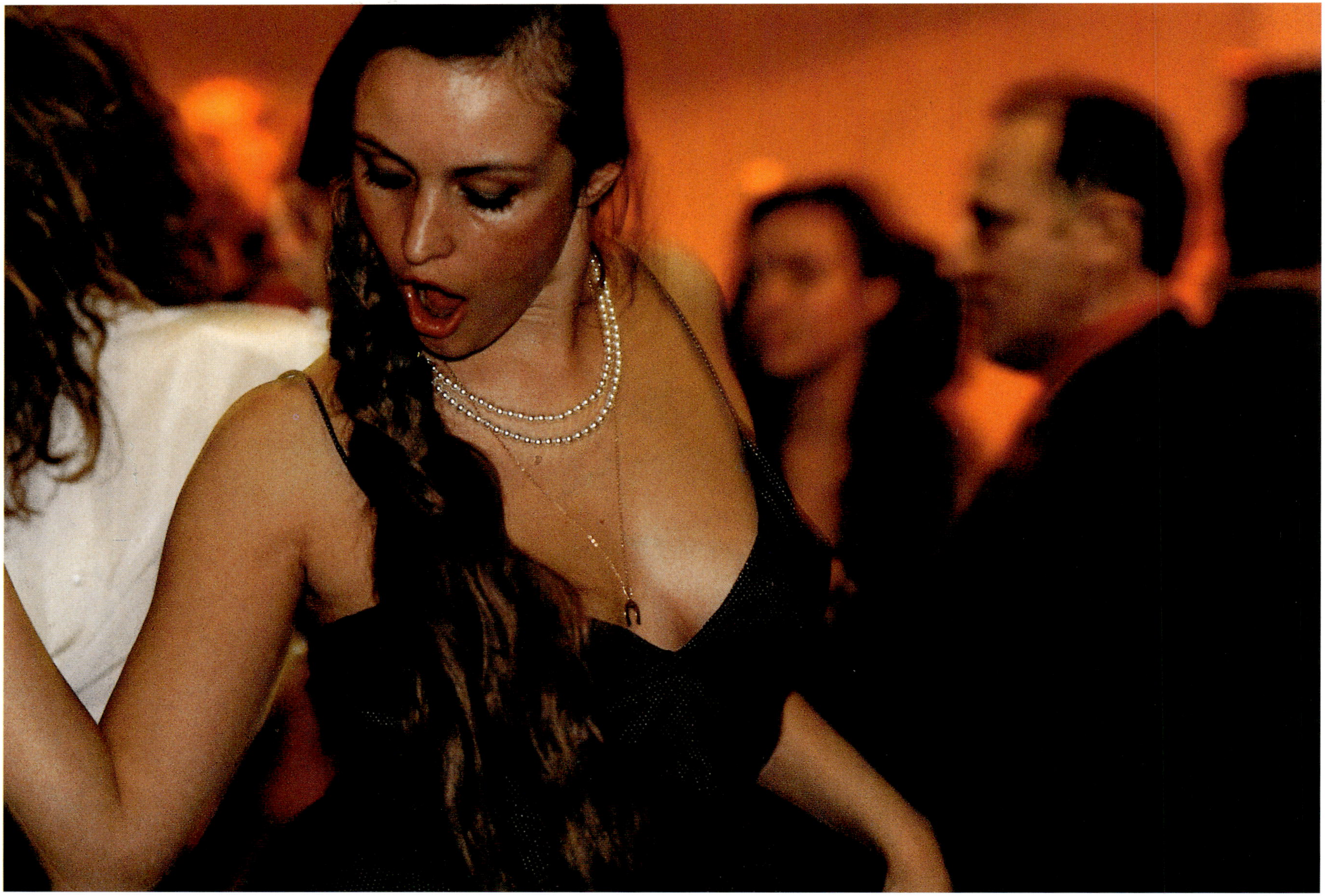

The body as liberated zone: Western body language being practised in Moscow's Olympus nightclub. For one night the collective disintegrates into partying individuals, and Narcissus can show off on the dance floor. (May 1989)

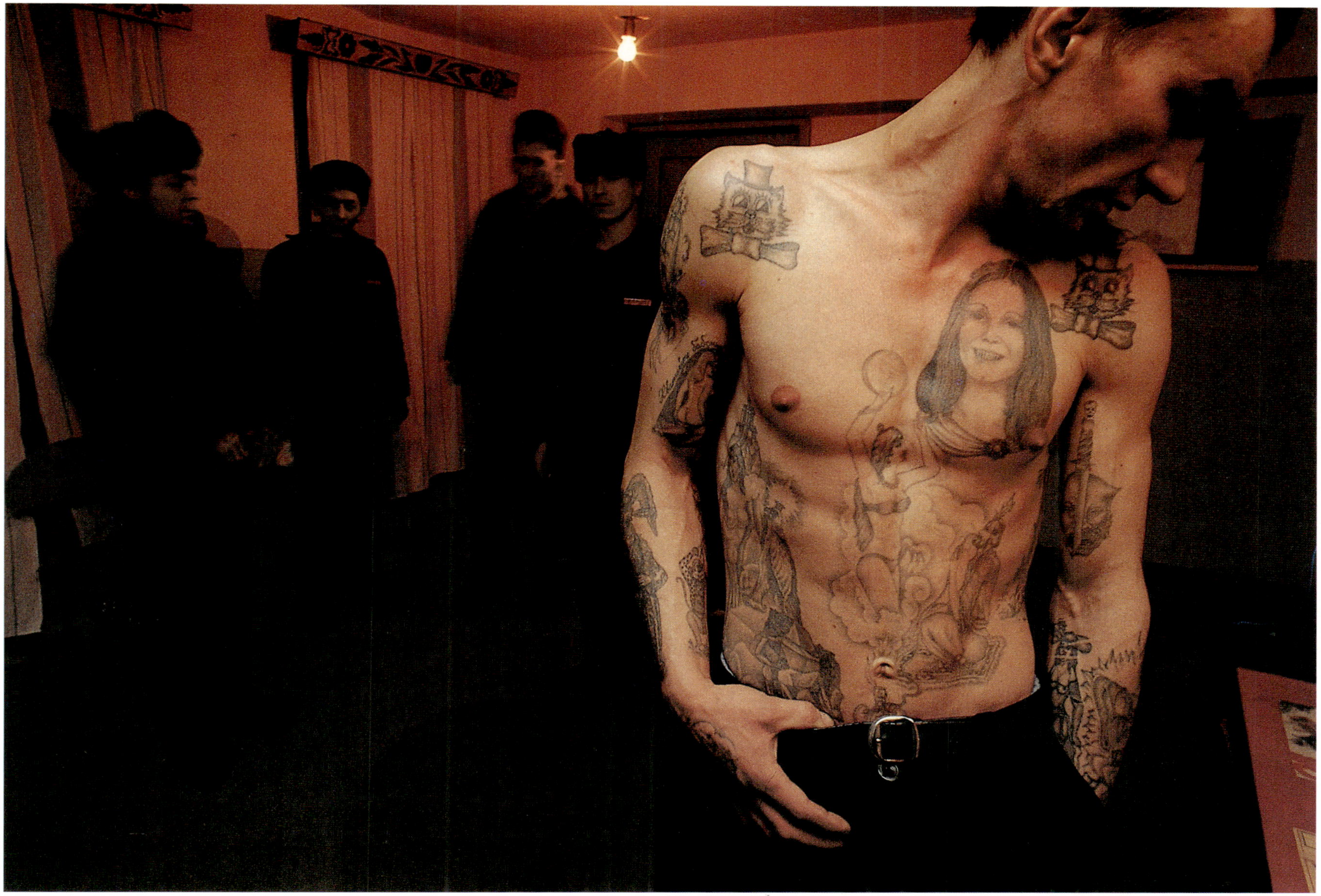

The body as private refuge, as skin-deep Utopia. The prisoner of a Siberian gulag has had the delights of *A Thousand and One Nights* tattooed into his skin. The face on his breast will never grow old. And will always be smiling. (March 1990)

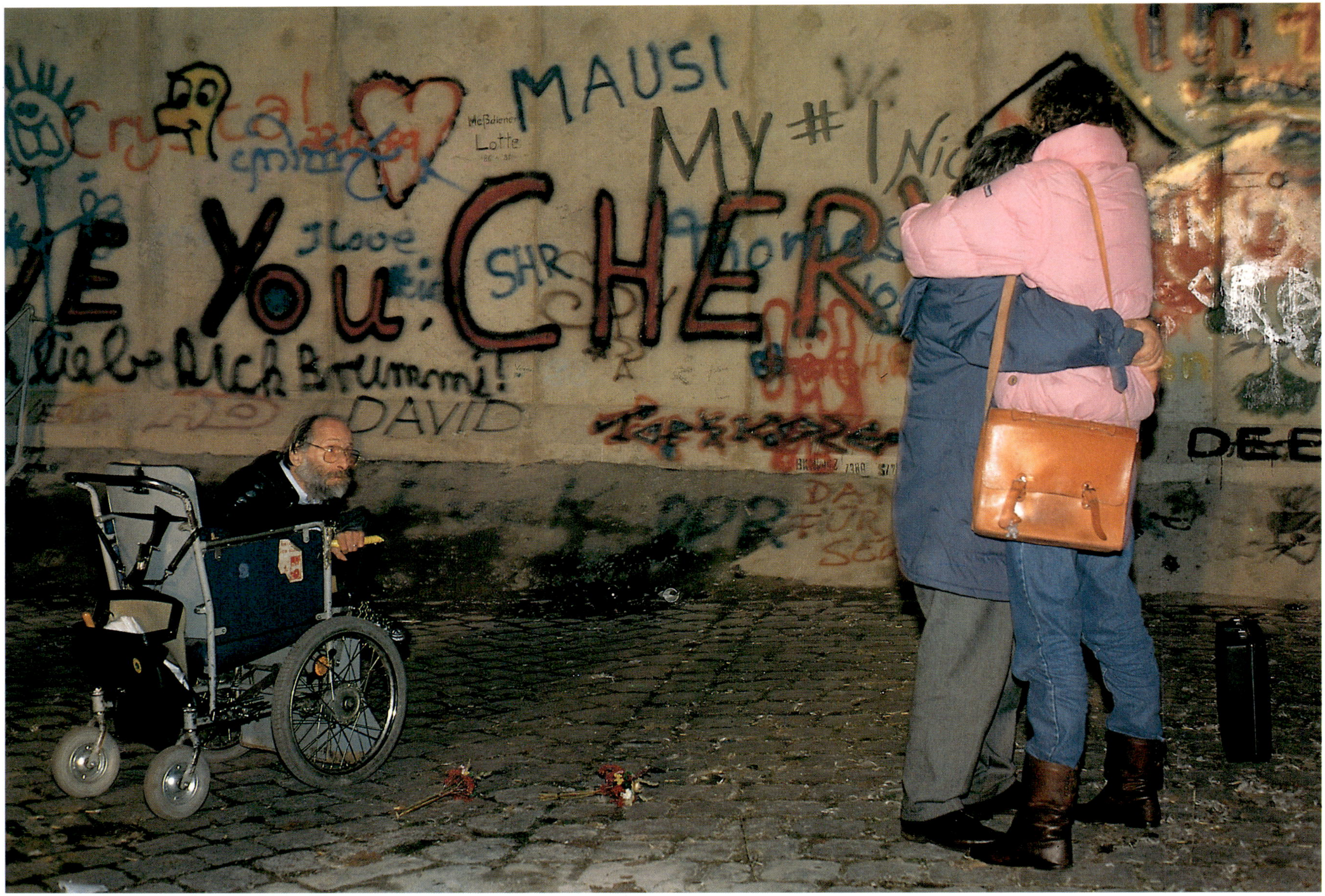

Amaaaazing. . . . The Berlin wall has suddenly started to crumble. You knock a hole in it and simply step through! This couple was one of the first to open a gateway to the West with a hammer and chisel. Incredulous, they hug themselves simply 'because it's so wonderful'. (November 1989)

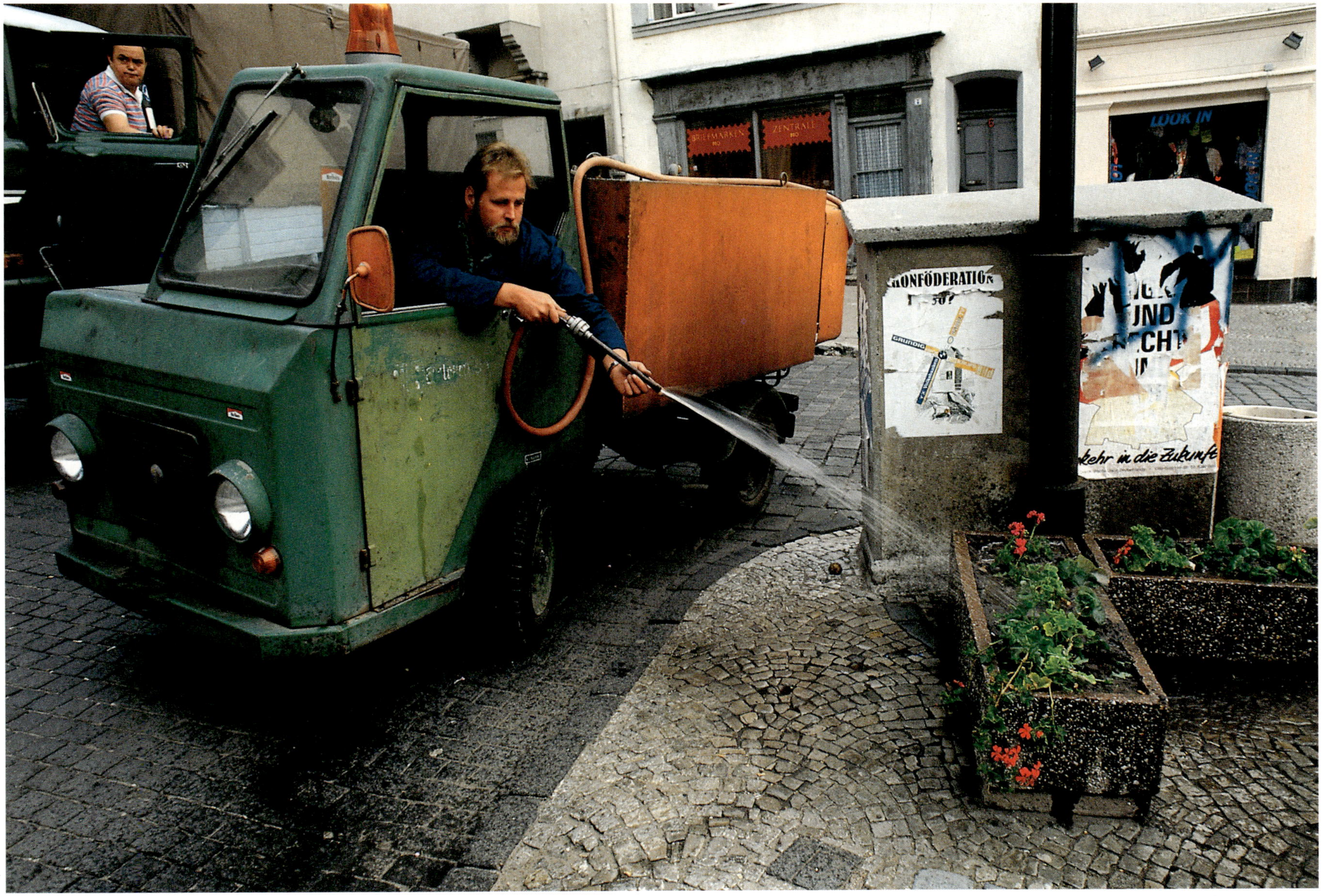

Caring for the environment in Thuringia. Centrally planned flower troughs are tended from a safe distance with a powerful jet. The double-think of East German society encouraged little secluded havens of peace to flourish like geraniums. In the face of the countless demands imposed by the State, the new, Socialist, man retreated behind his mask and his front door and became a petty bourgeois. Alongside the juxtaposition of loud-mouthed Party optimism and obvious narrow-mindedness, there emerged a personal, very German, aesthetic of 'small is beautiful'. (May 1990)

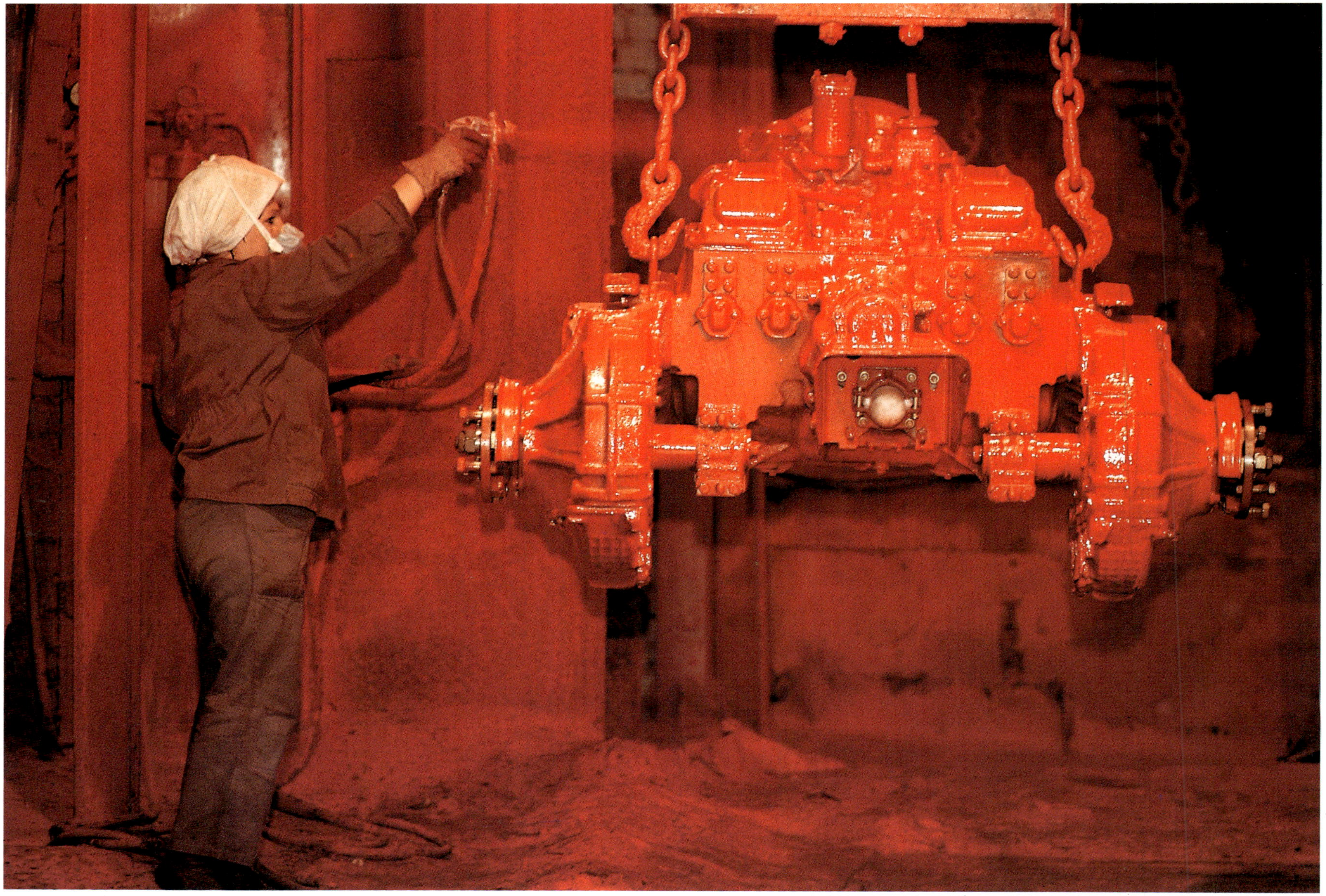

Above • The end of a red legend: the 'Felix Dzerzhinsky' tractor factory in Volgograd was one of the first set up after the Revolution by the proletarian State. Shortage of parts means the assembly lines often stand idle for hours at a time, while the workers have to put in illegal Saturday shifts just to meet their target quotas. The proportion of rejects is twenty-seven per cent. The women working in the paint shop have to make do with a flimsy face mask. Those who fail to meet their quotas get no place in the holiday home. (May 1989)

Facing page • Pop Art is dead. Long live Poop Art! Moscow artist Mikhail Rozhal-Fyodorov finds new inspiration in a caviar snack during a creative break from work. (May 1989)

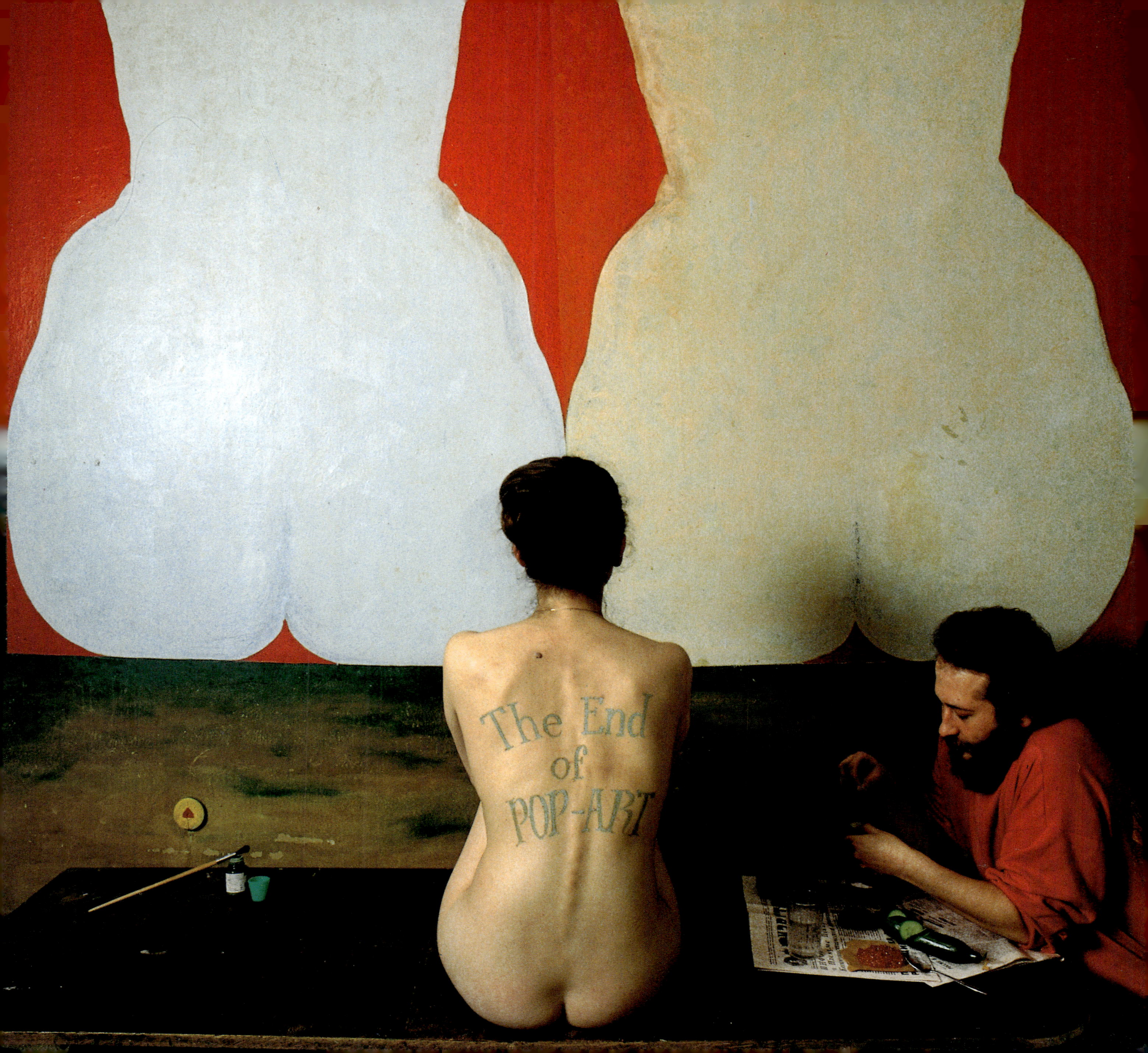
The End
of
POP-ART

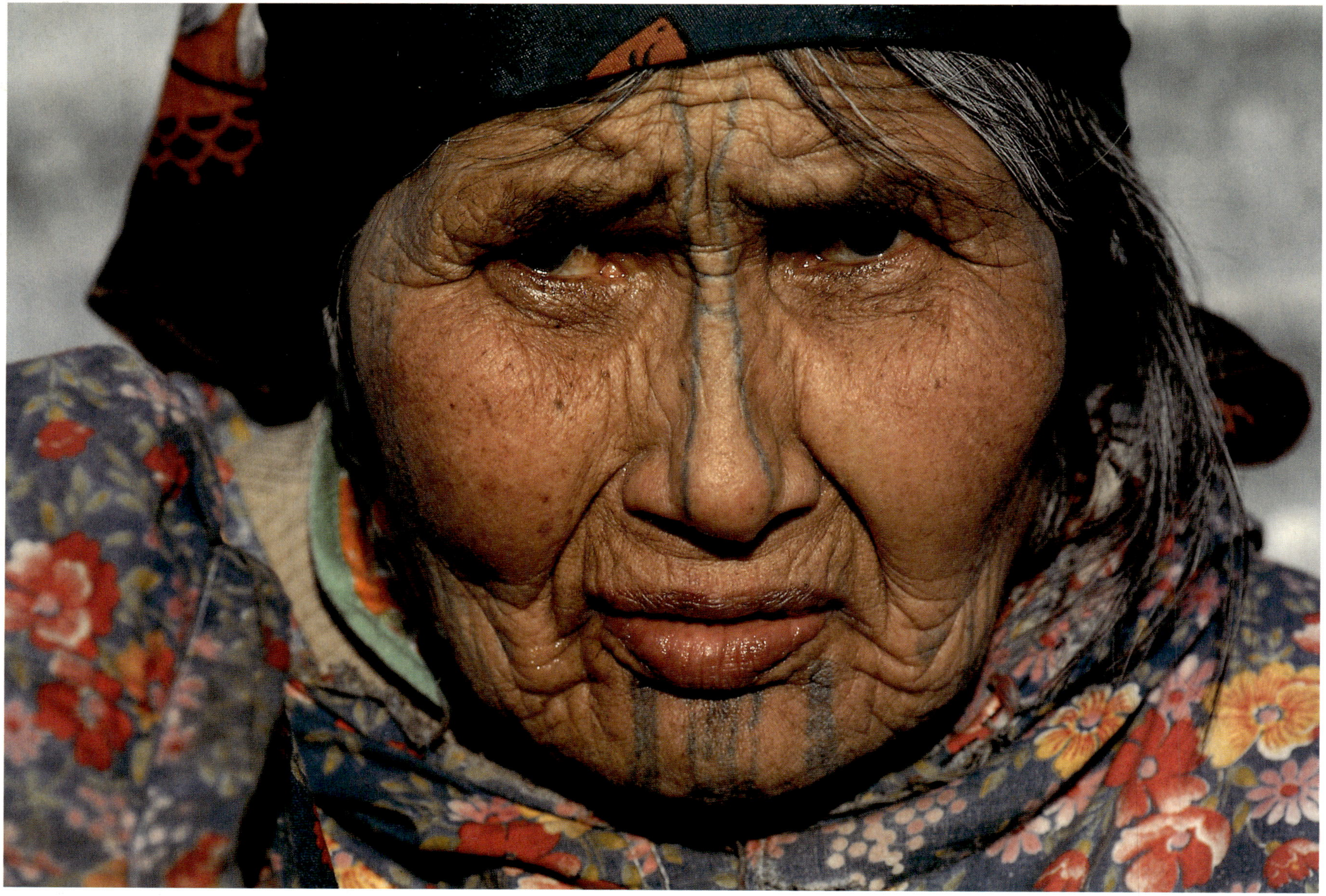

Above • The easternmost East. This Eskimo woman has spent her long life in Uelen, an Eskimo settlement on the headland facing Alaska. Traditional tattooing and the Arctic climate have etched her face into a veritable map, but without any sense of direction. (March 1990)

Facing page • Off to become a man, decorated with leva bills and silver tinsel. For many years Bulgaria's Islamic minority was forbidden to practise its religion. Muslim names had to be dropped. Now, after Zhivkov's fall, they are making up for lost time. In villages in the Rhodope mountains, such as here in Valkosel, people gather to celebrate circumcision ceremonies. And call themselves by their old names. (February 1990)

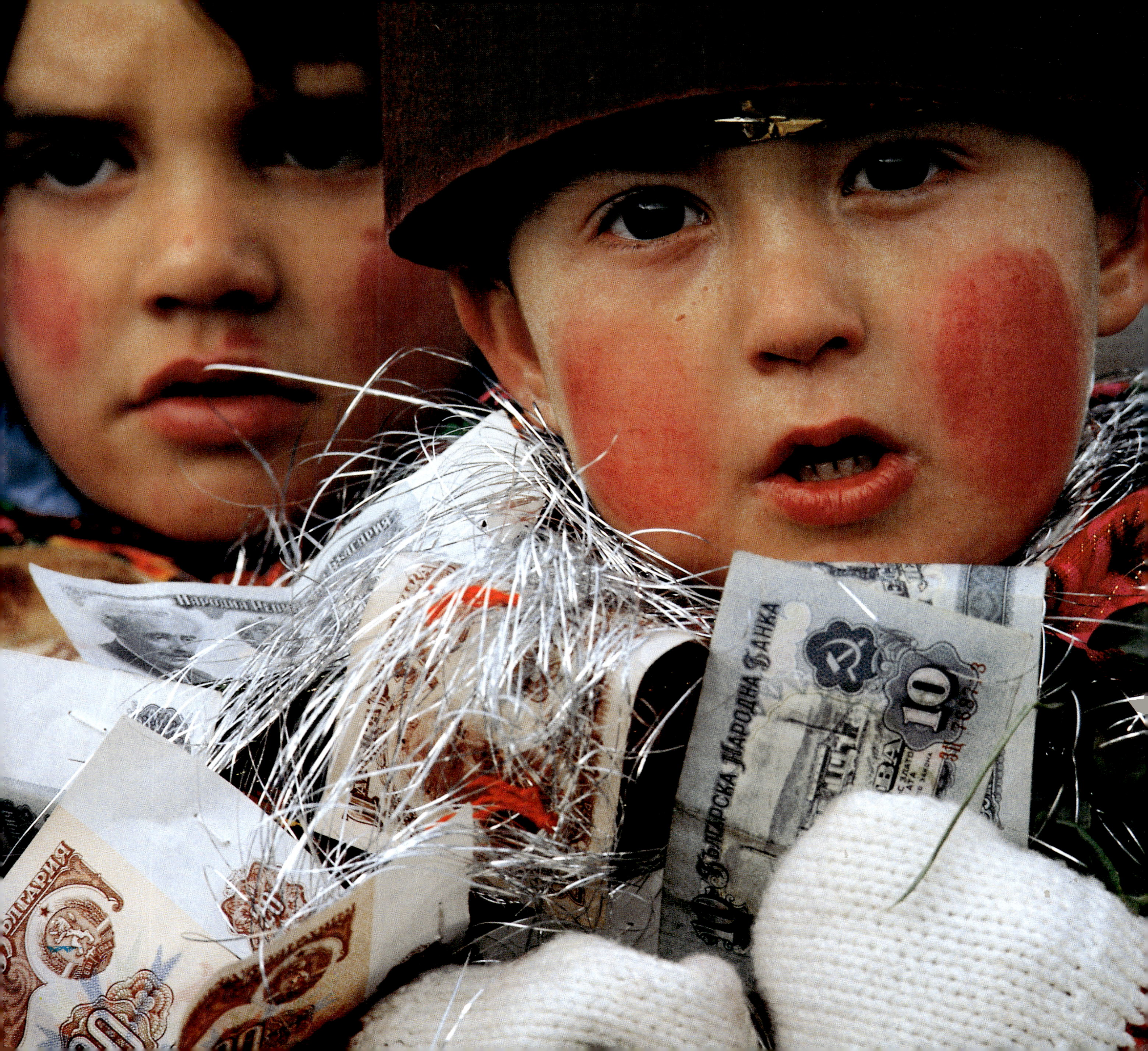
БЪЛГАРСКА НАРОДНА БАНКА
10
БЪЛГАРИЯ

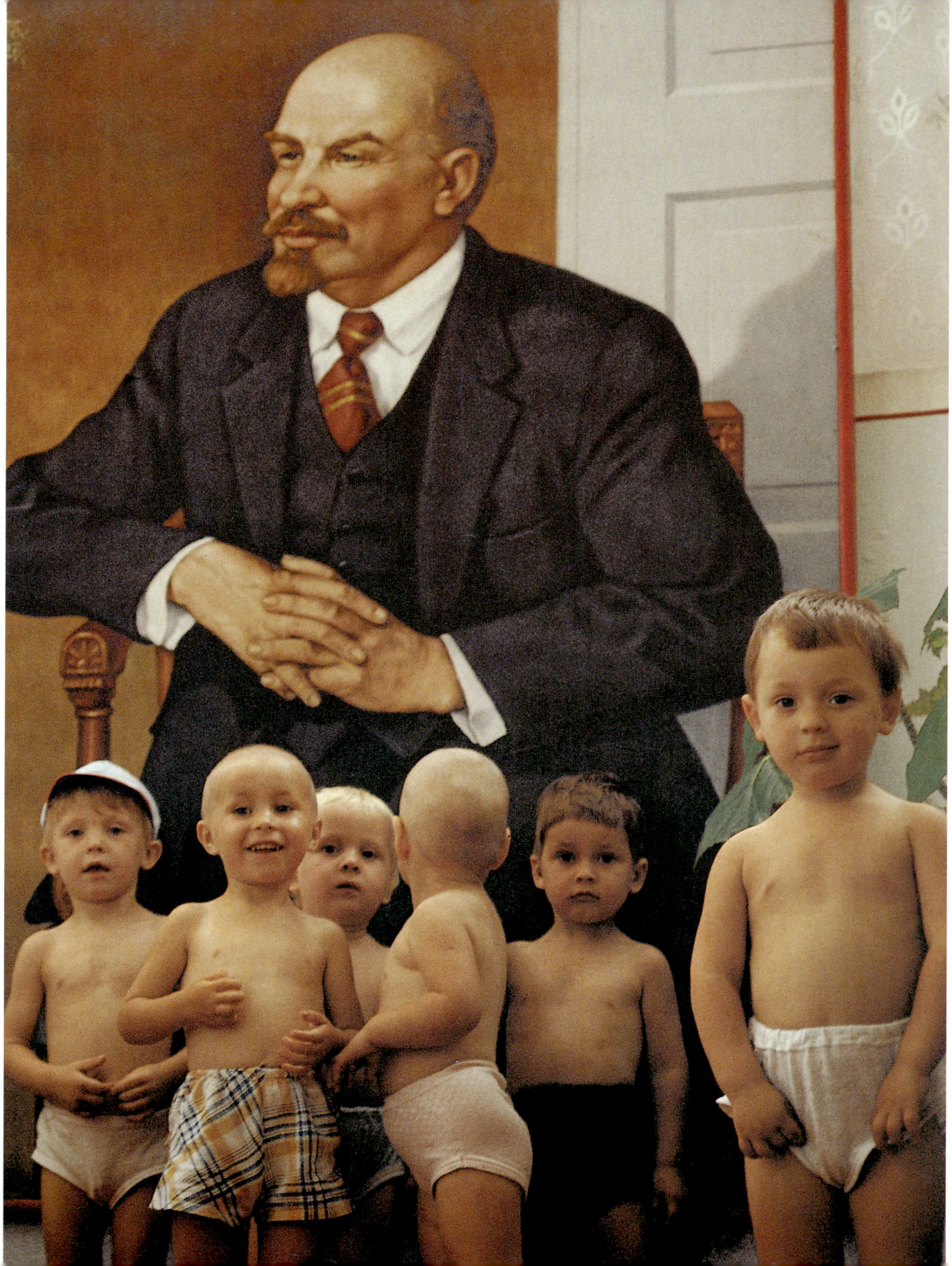

Suffer the little children to come unto me. In an atheist Soviet Union, Lenin had to stand in as ersatz God. He himself was opposed to personality cults, but his successors knew that Russians need icons. Here the kindergarten of the Ukrainian 'Victory of Communism' collective farm. (September 1988)

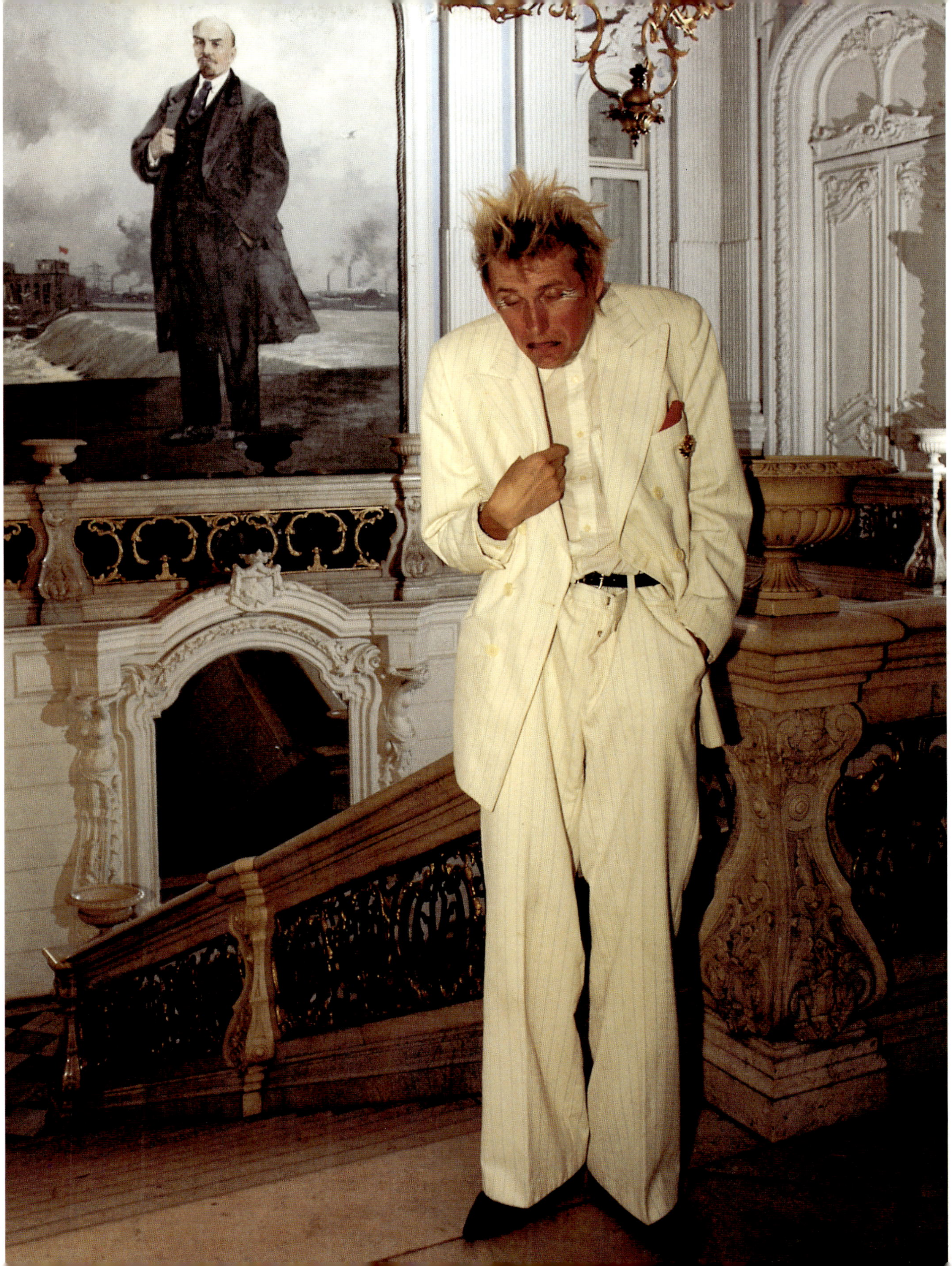

God is dead – even if He was only an ersatz God. Moscow rock singer Oleg Garkusha, from the group 'Auction', is allergic to the Lenin whose confident smile has accompanied him ever since childhood. Once everyone sees through it, the face will soon become a farce.
(August 1990)

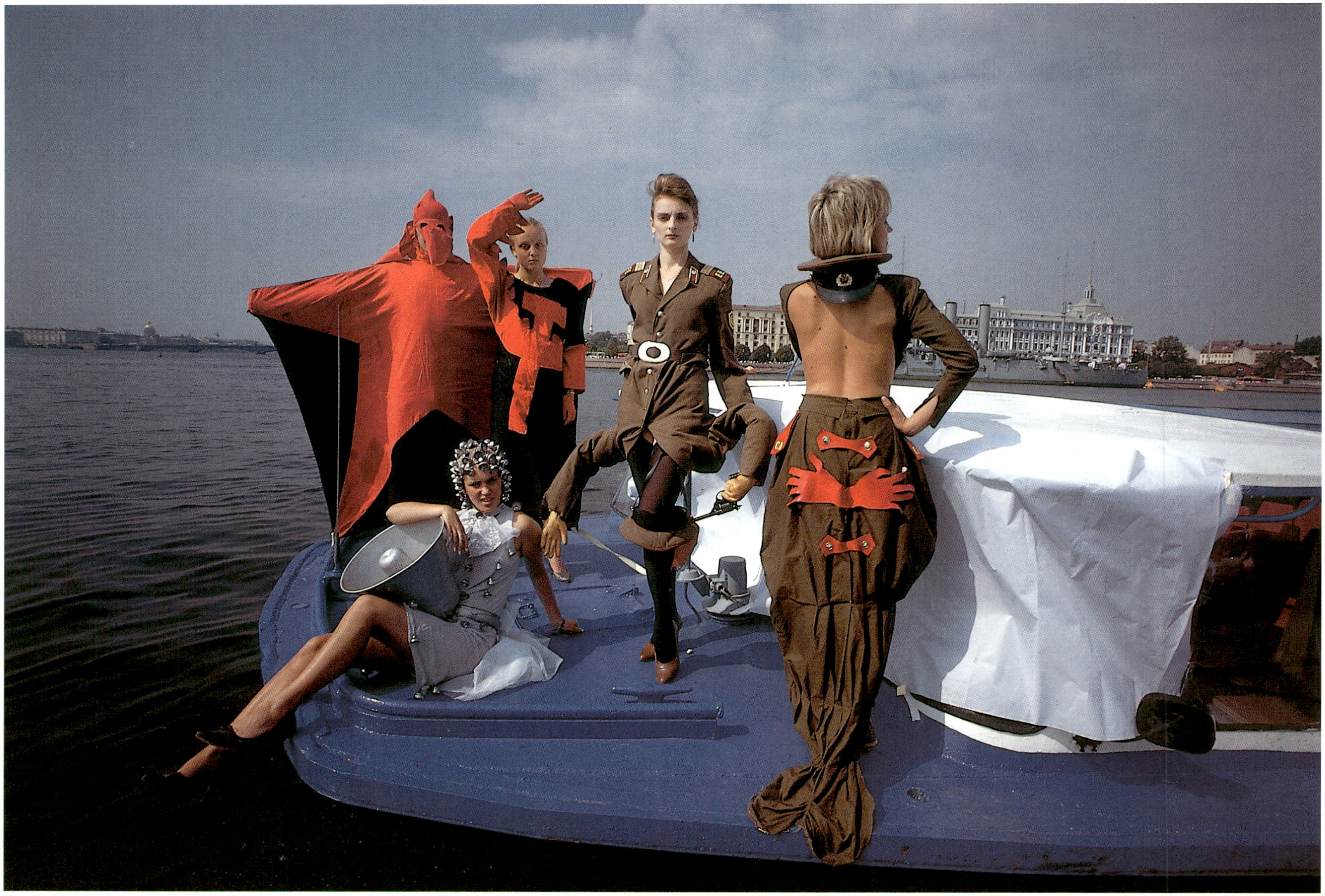

Above • Hammer and sickle as fashion gimmick. Afloat on the Neva, Leningrad (St Petersburg) fashion designer Sveta Petrova presents her spring collection. The *Aurora*, whose guns once signalled the start of the October Revolution, floats quietly in the background – a revered symbol turned incongruous backdrop. (August 1990)

Facing page • The decorations tinkle in waltz time when the band strikes up in Prague's Culture Park. Then even the senior ranks reveal the Švejk within, as they surrender to the miracle weapon of womanhood. Take note: even beneath a uniform there is only a (little) man to be found. (May 1988)

Overleaf • *Mother Russia* commemorates the battle of Stalingrad, the turning-point of the Second World War in the winter of 1942/43. 82 metres (270 feet) high, it is the tallest statue in the world. The veterans are not the only ones to return to the city, now called Volgograd, every 9 May. They climb Mamayev Kurgan hill, grave to countless thousands, where 1,200 pieces of shrapnel landed in a single square metre (ten square feet) of earth. At the foot of the monument, which weighs 8,000 tons, is the inscription '*Stoyat na smert*' – 'They stand until death'. The size of the memorial expresses the scale of the suffering which Hitler's war inflicted upon the Soviet Union. Twenty million dead. The people at the feet of the statue feel first and foremost their own impotence in the face of a tragedy wreaked by one (little) man. (May 1988)

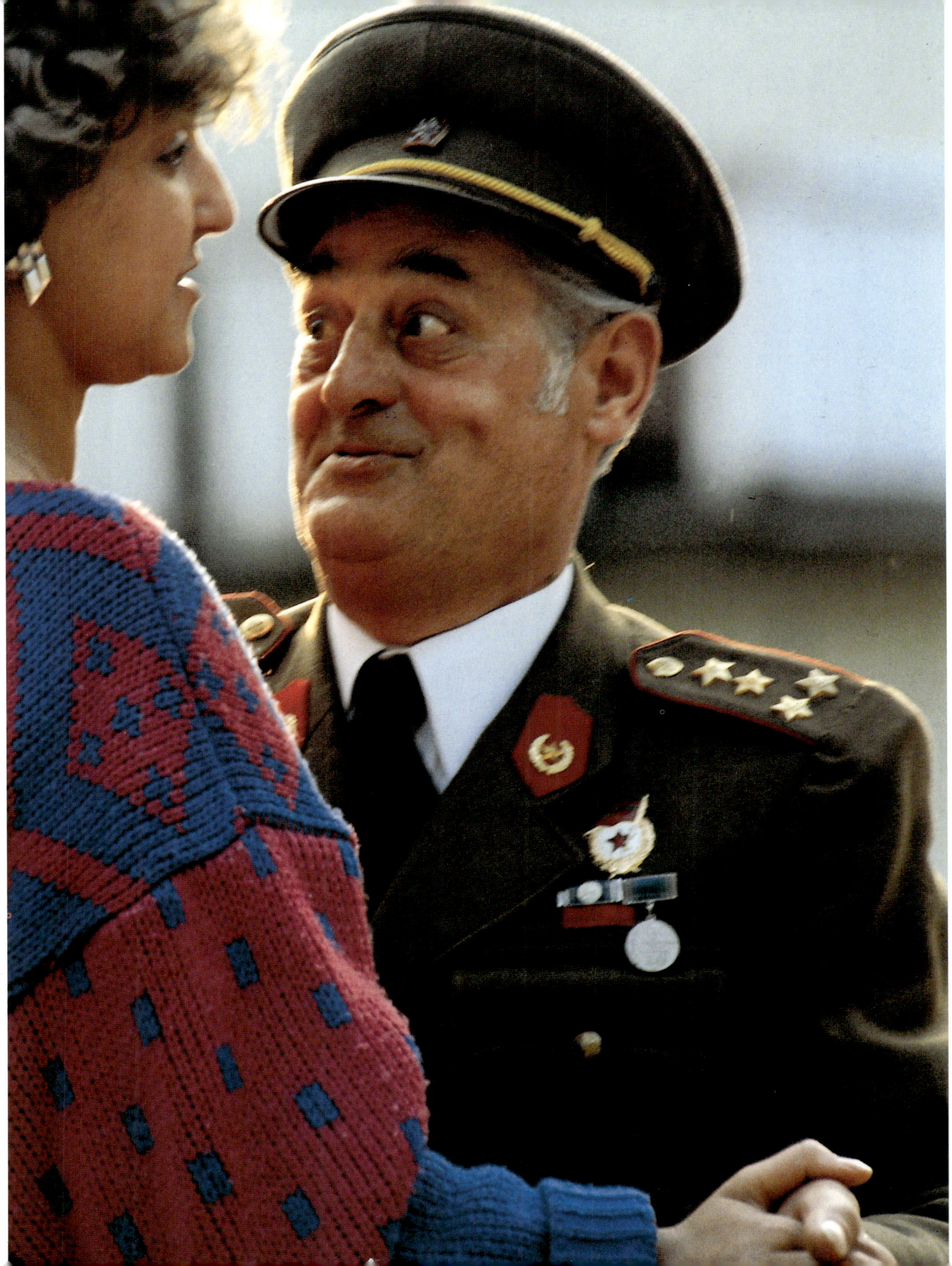

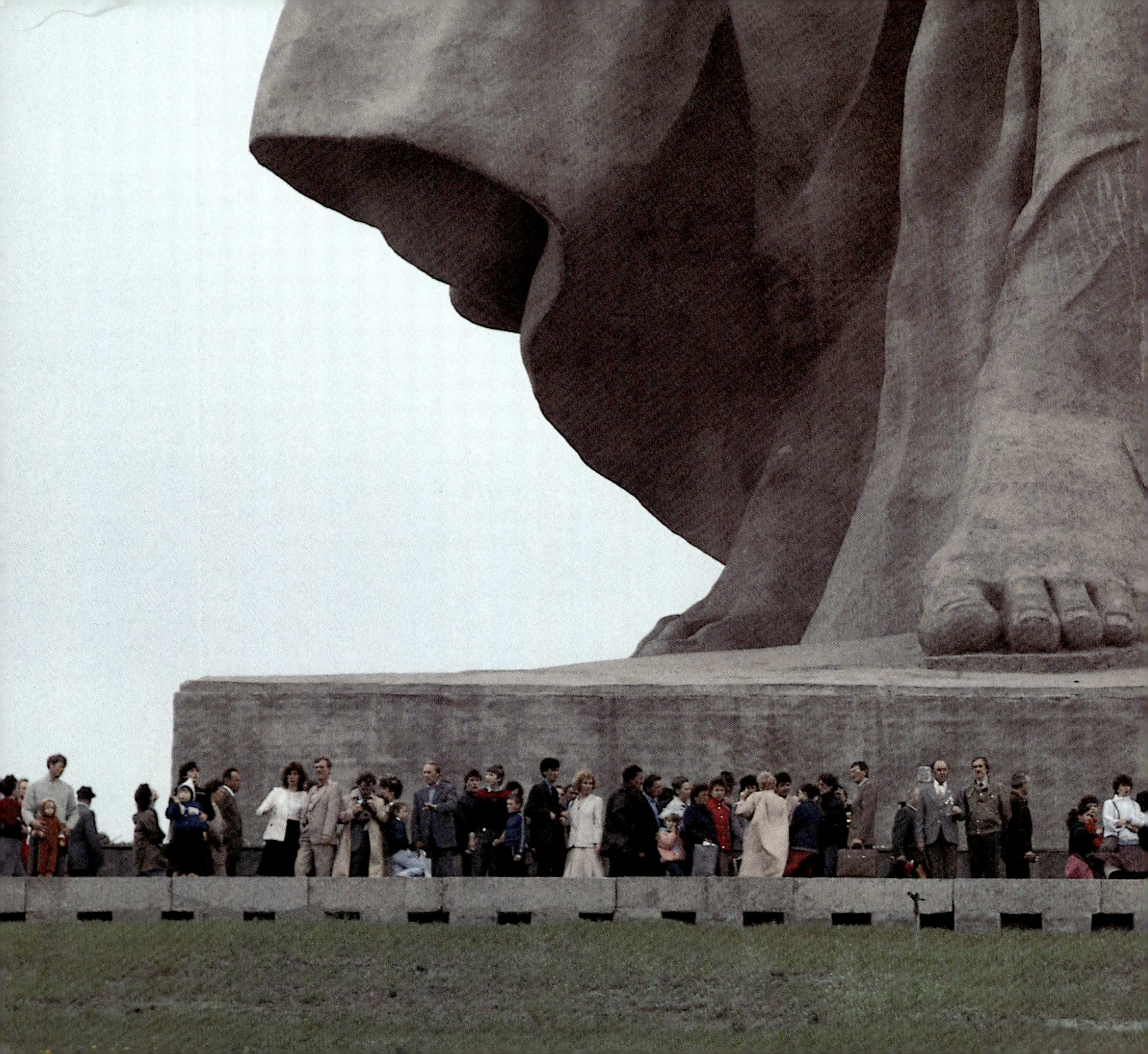

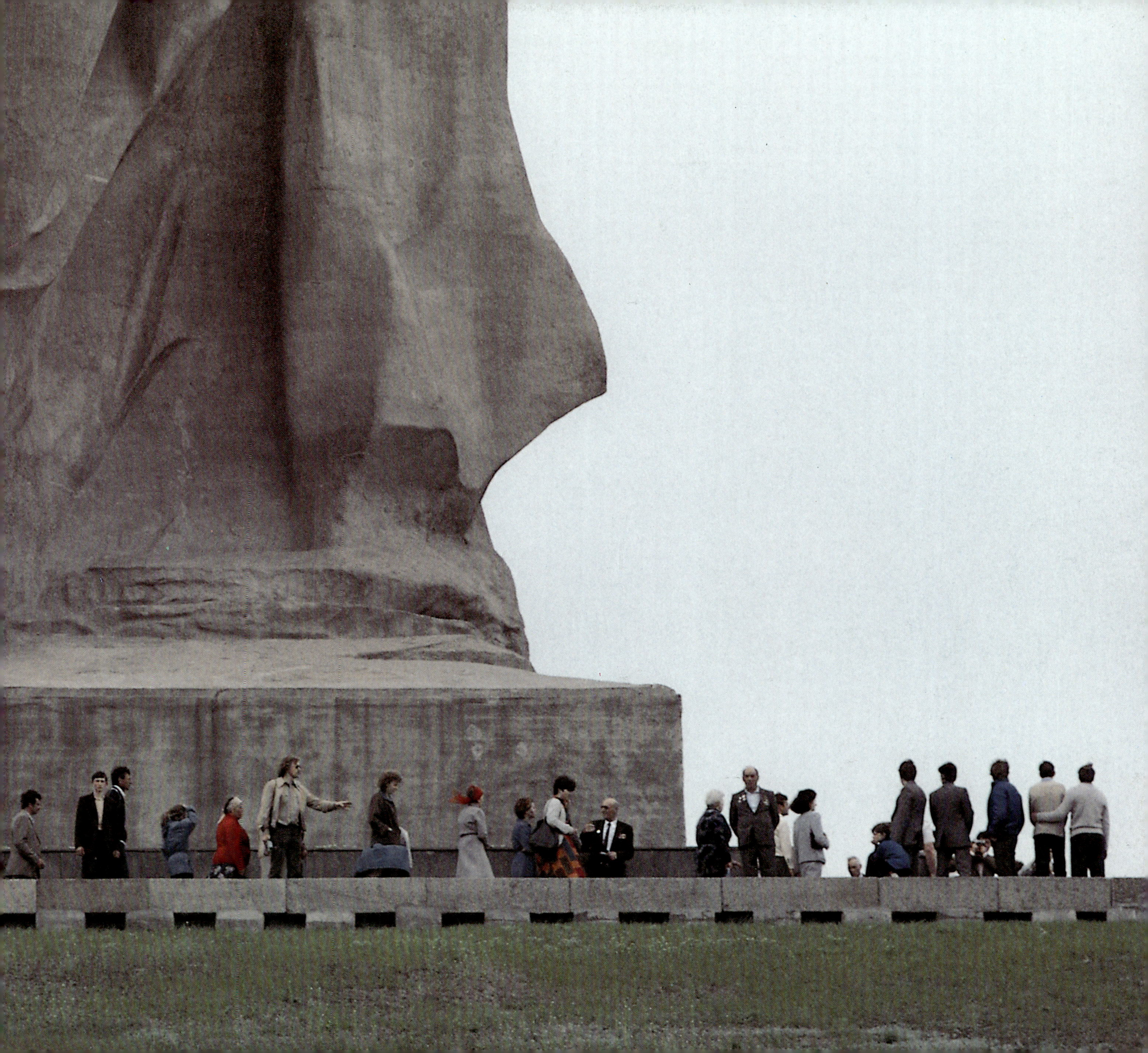

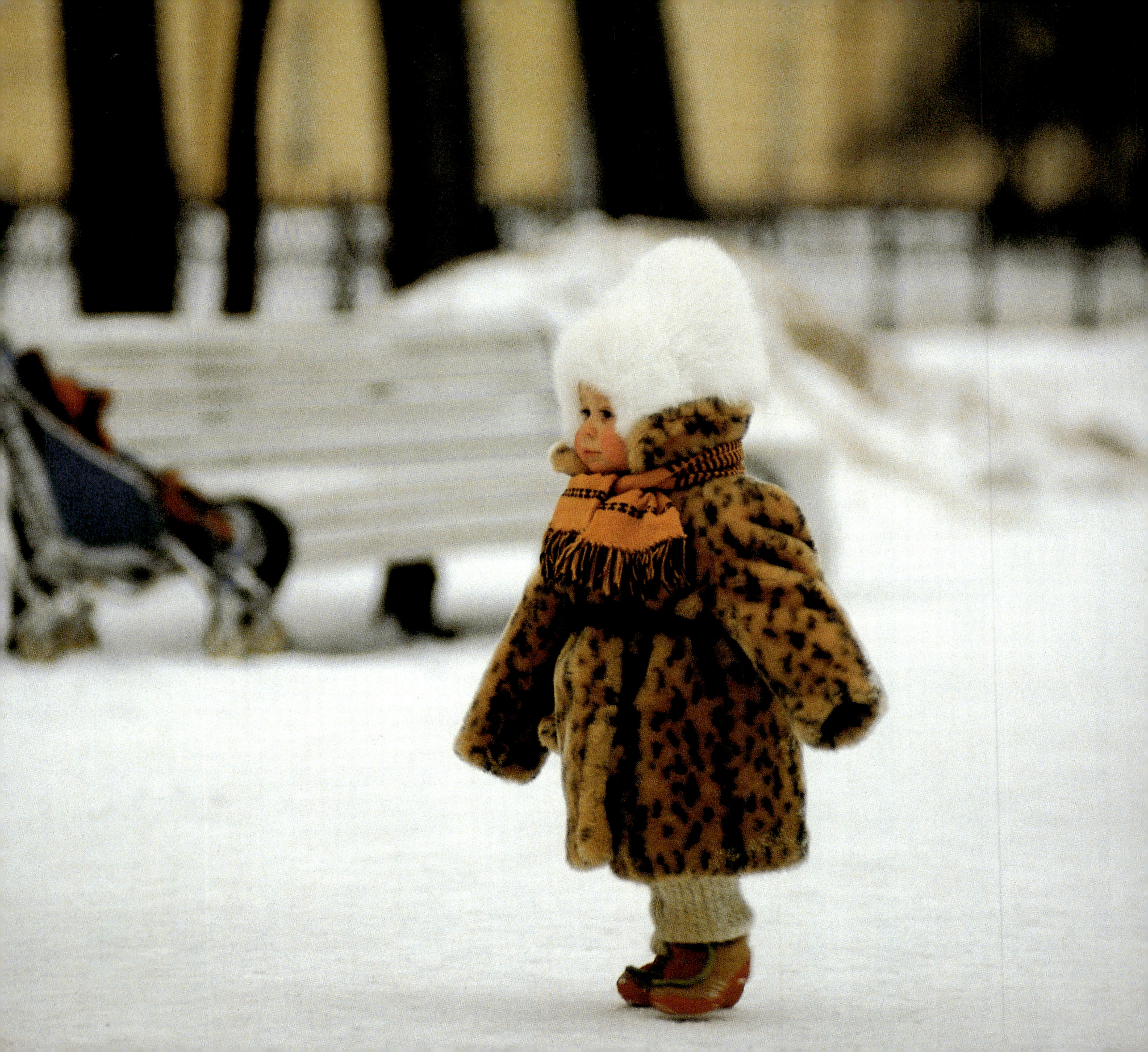

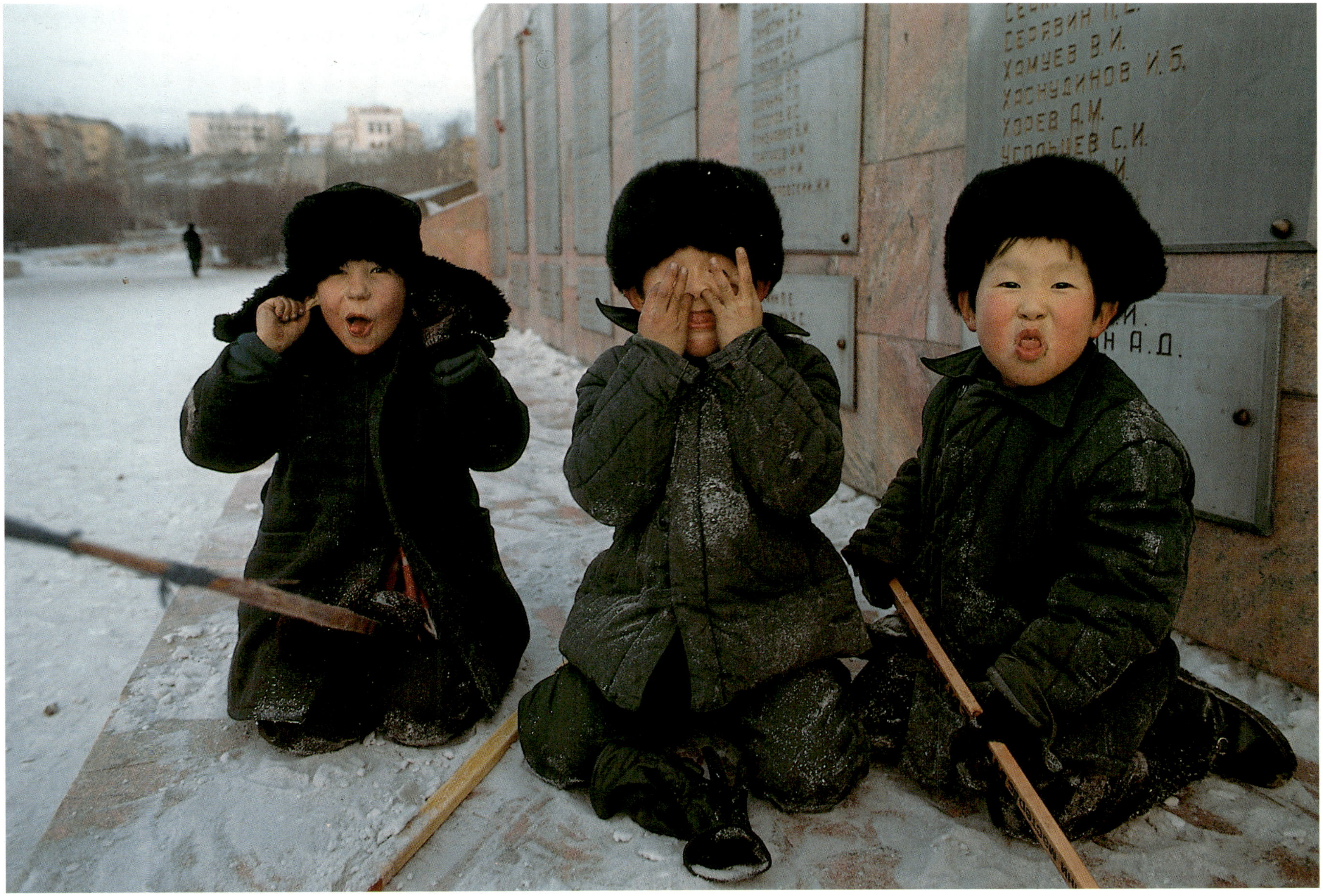

Facing page • Dolls may not feel the cold, but little girls do. Especially when they live in Vyborg, a seaboard city some 130 kilometres (80 miles) northwest of St Petersburg which has belonged to the Soviet Union since the Russo–Finnish winter war of 1939/40. It is horribly cold on both sides of the border, and you need to wrap up warmly – even if the only furs on sale are synthetic. For the world's largest fur producer exports its pelts to the West in exchange for hard currency. (February 1986)

Above • If Buddha could see them now! Buryat children pose cheekily and cheerfully in front of plaques commemorating the heroes of the Second World War in Ulan Ude, near the border with Mongolia. The Buddhist minority was suppressed under Stalin; perestroika is today arousing hopes of self-determination. (March 1990)

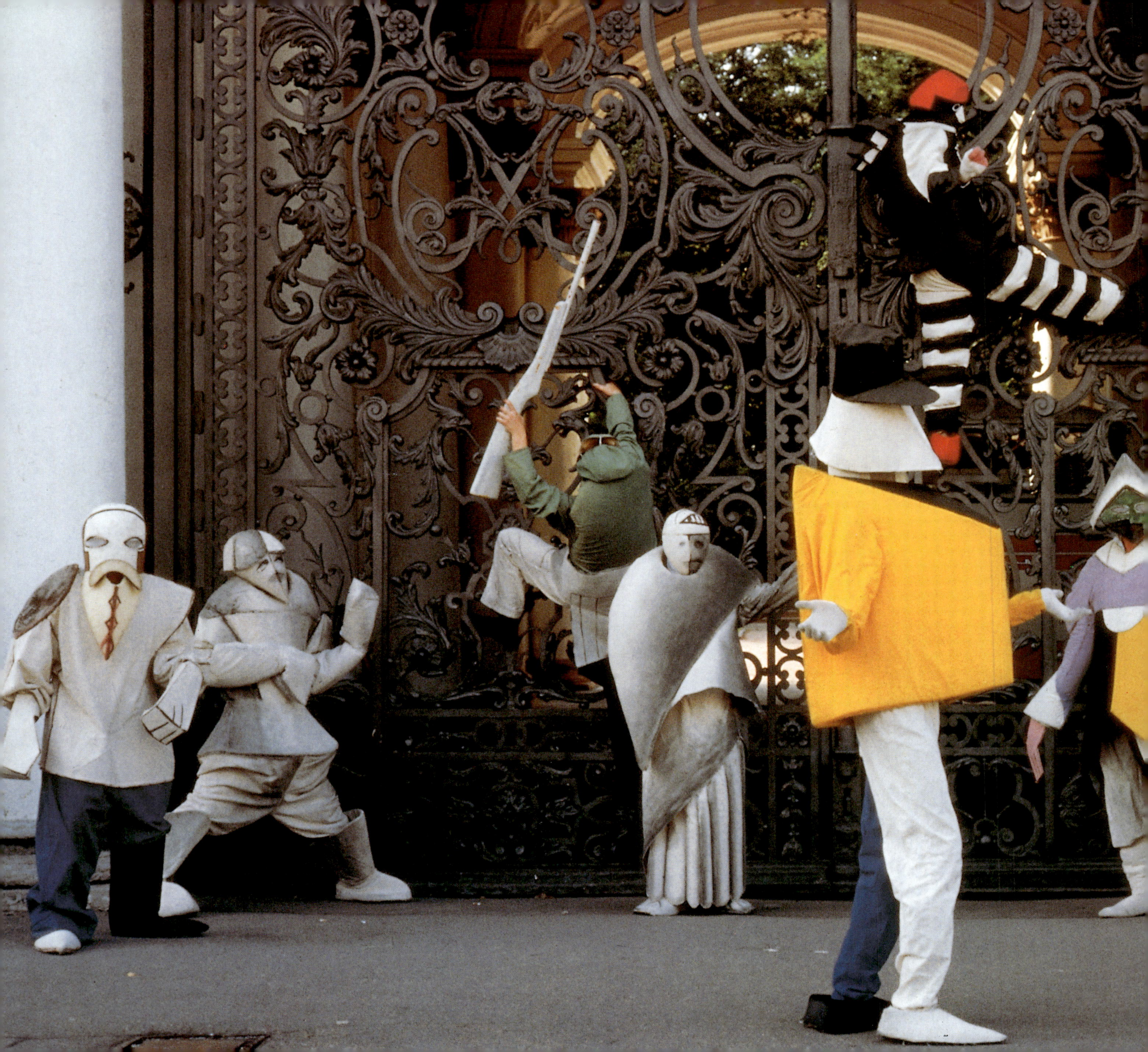

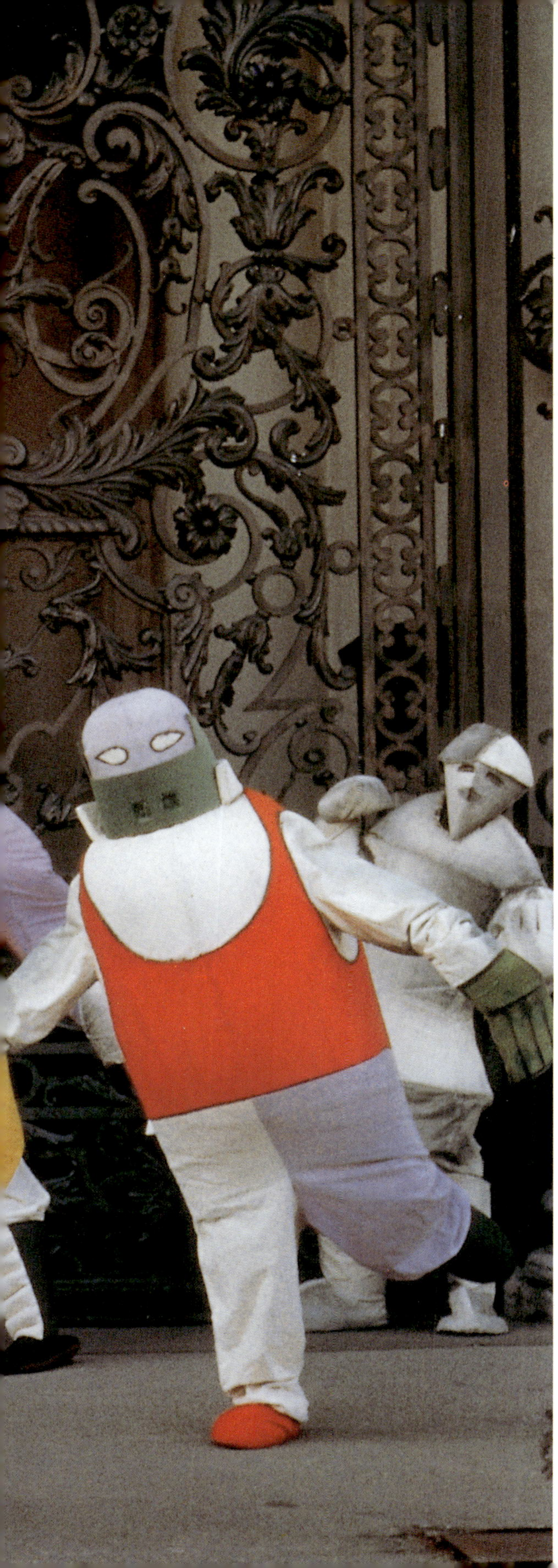

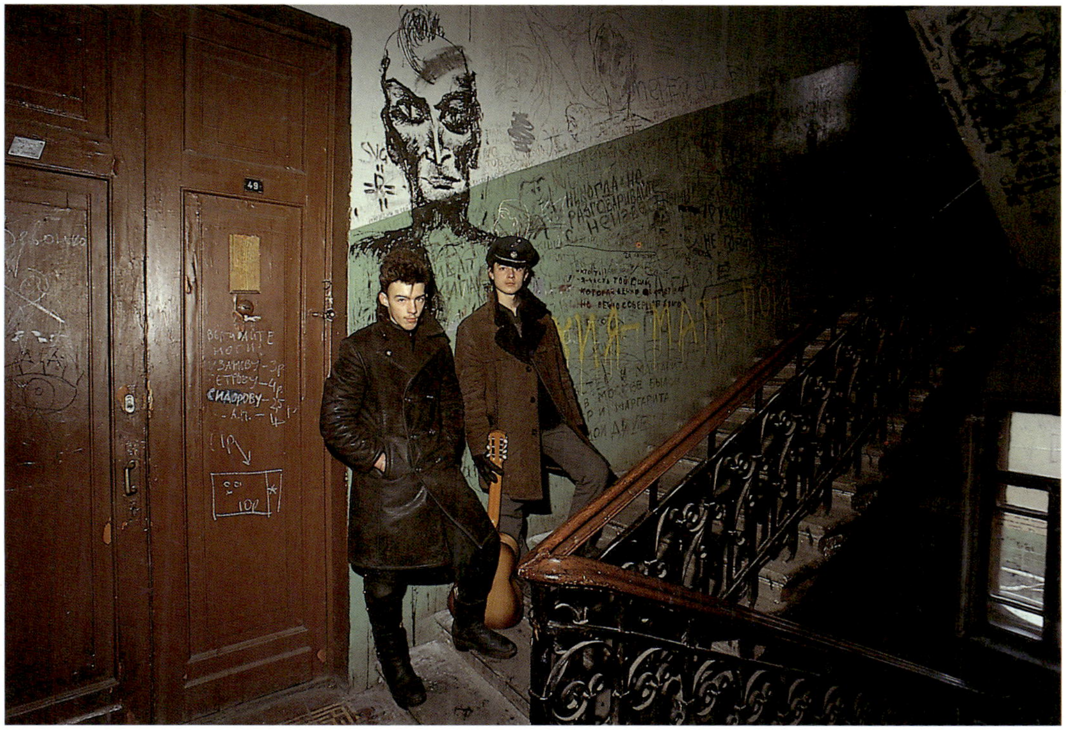

Above • The new symbols are under attack – and by no means purely symbolically. House No. 10 on Moscow's ring boulevard was the setting for Mikhail Bulgakov's *The Master and Margarita*. During the years of silence, the stairwell became a place of pilgrimage for underground artists and activists, for hippies and counter-cultures of all kinds. The walls are decorated with the icons of the Moscow 'Scene'. People meet, smoke, sing Wysotskii's ballads and dream of the reincarnation of the infernal Margarita. (February 1989)

Facing page • The old symbols are under attack. Even if purely symbolically. Seventy years after the storming of the Winter Palace in Petrograd (St Petersburg), the event which launched the October Revolution is being restaged by the Gala Gubanova theatre company. It was through these gates that the last Tsar was carried off by the Bolsheviks. The costumes were designed by the Suprematist painter Kazimir Malevich for Mikhail Matyushin's opera *Victory over the Sun*. (August 1990)

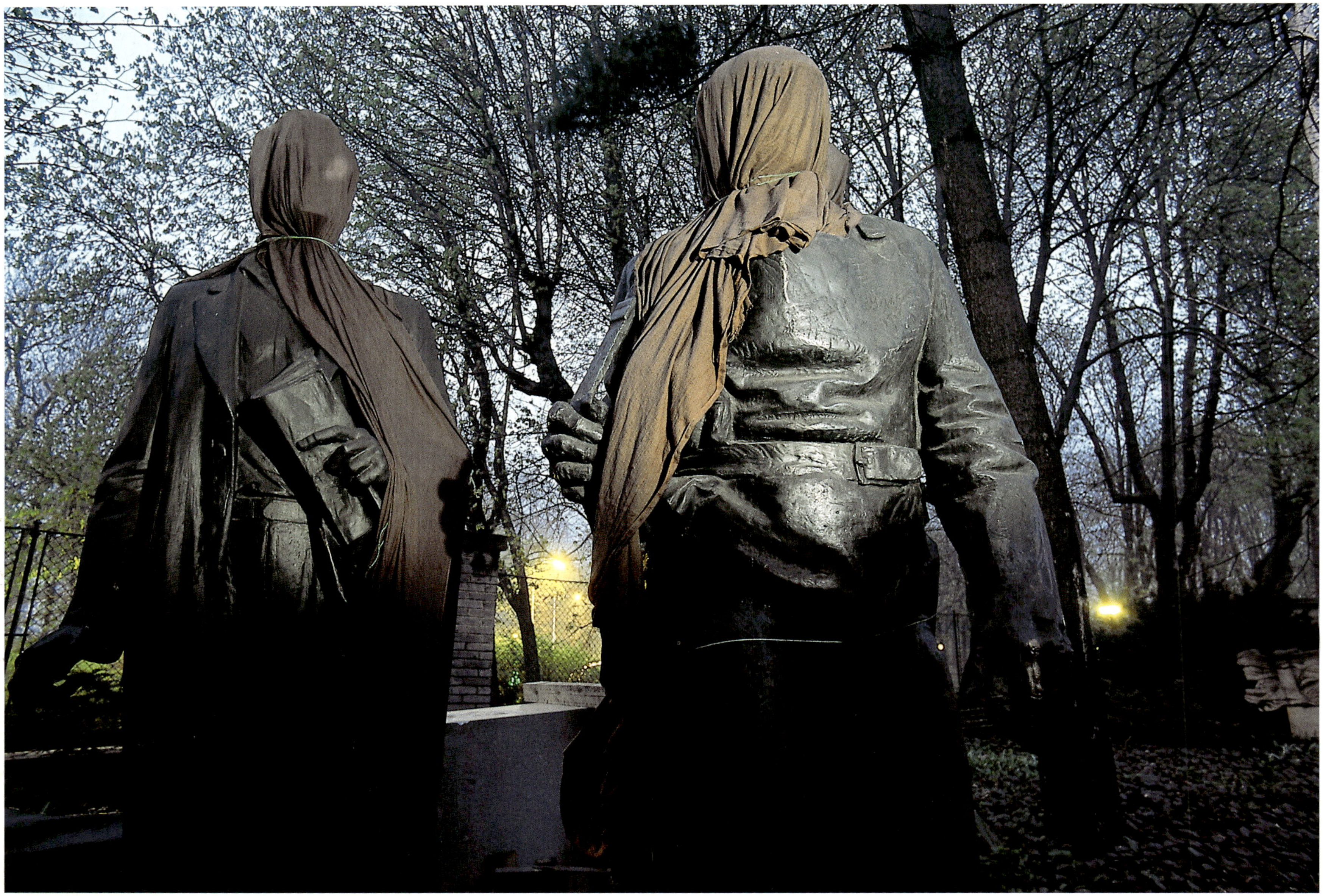

Above • Lenin keeps his composure. When things are going badly, disguise becomes a revolutionary's first duty. So as not to provoke the anger of its citizens any further, Prague's authorities sent Vladimir Ilyich into internal exile. They bagged up the soldier beside him, too – just to be safe. (September 1990)

Facing page • The winter which followed the Prague Spring lasted twenty-two years. In the early autumn of 1990, one of the Soviet tanks which had clattered in across the cobbles in 1968 rode quietly out of Wenceslas Square on the back of a transporter. It had stood there for two weeks, deliberately exposed to the scorn of the citizens of Prague. A panzer in the pillory. (September 1990)

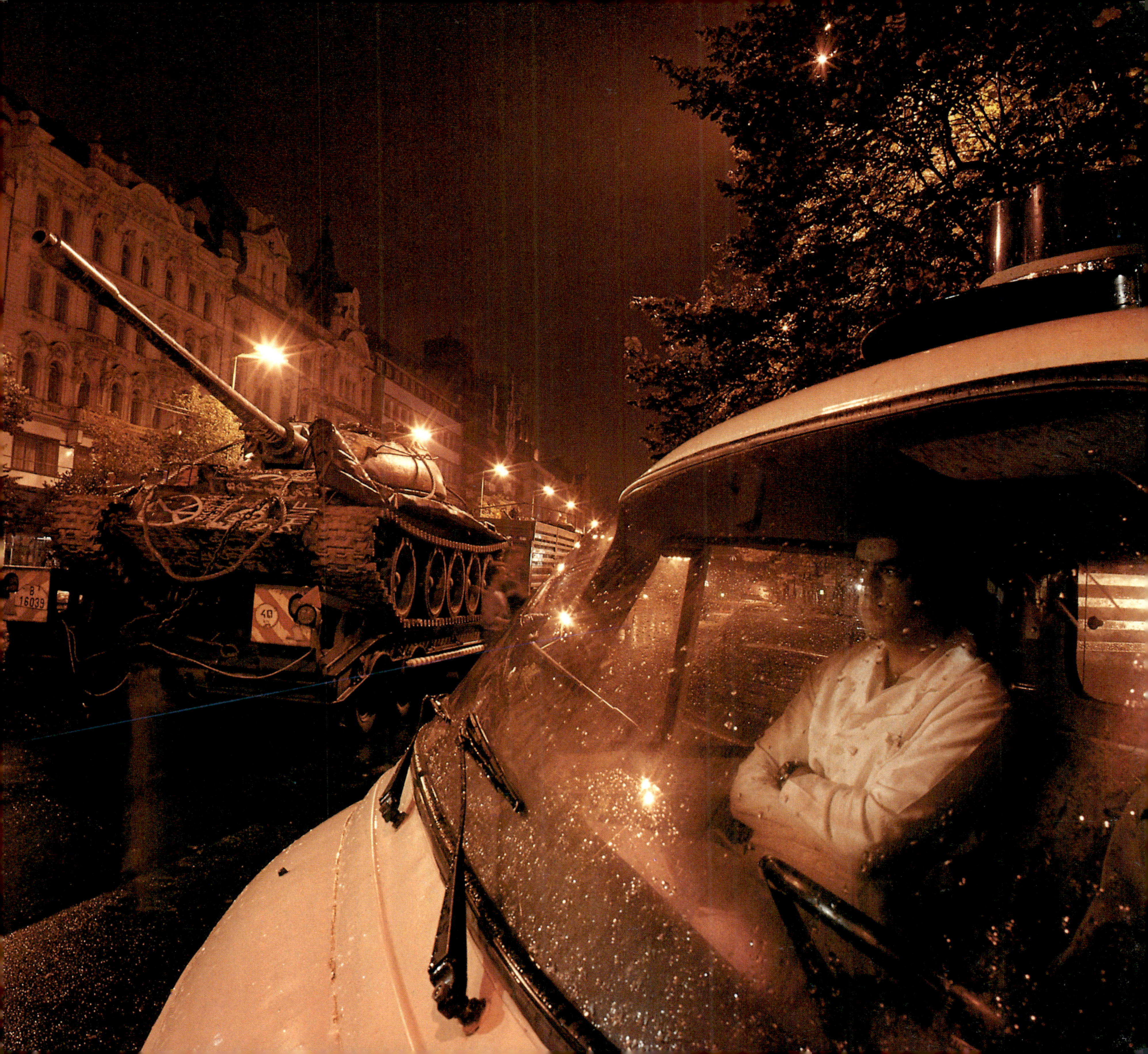
B 16039
40

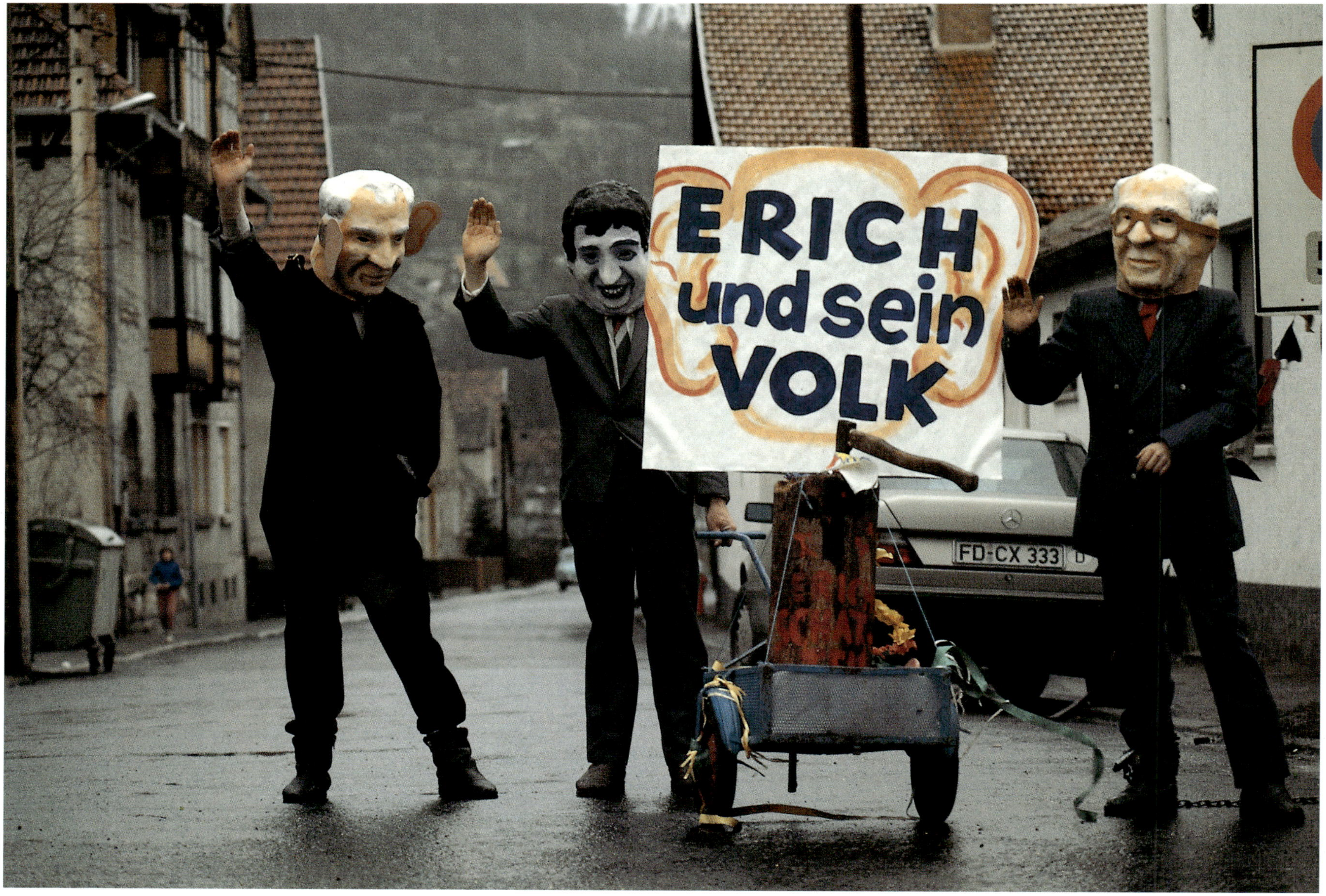

In Thuringia's 1990 carnival, fools unmask the follies of the old regime: 'Erich [Honecker] and his people', namely Nosy Parker and Eavesdropper with the big ears. Old comrades found it hard to laugh. (February 1990)

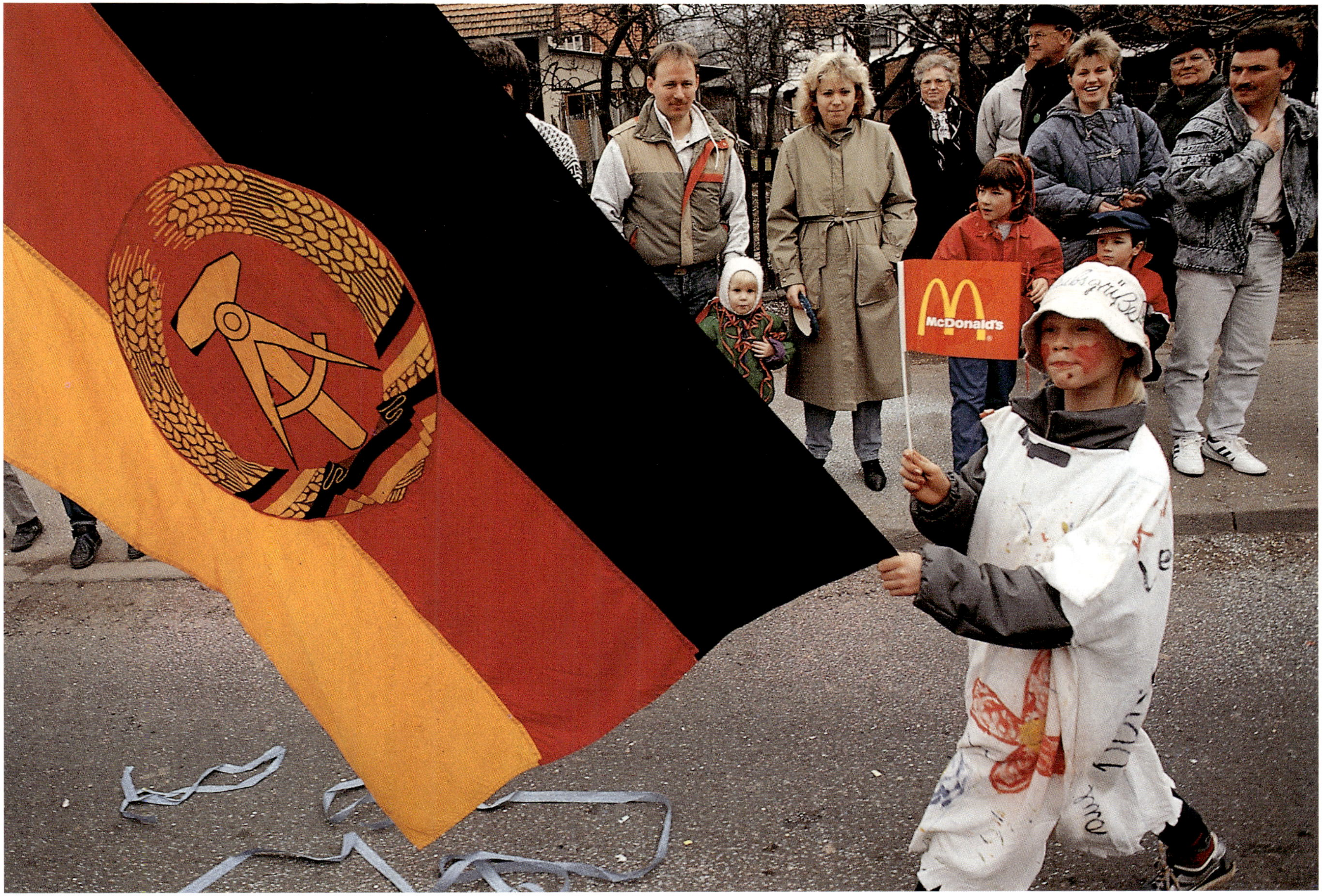

Forwards, and soon forgotten. . . . An alien flag from the Western world of wishes is carried in Thuringia's carnival parade just a few weeks after East Germany's collapse. So smoothly does Communism flow into Consumerism. (February 1990)

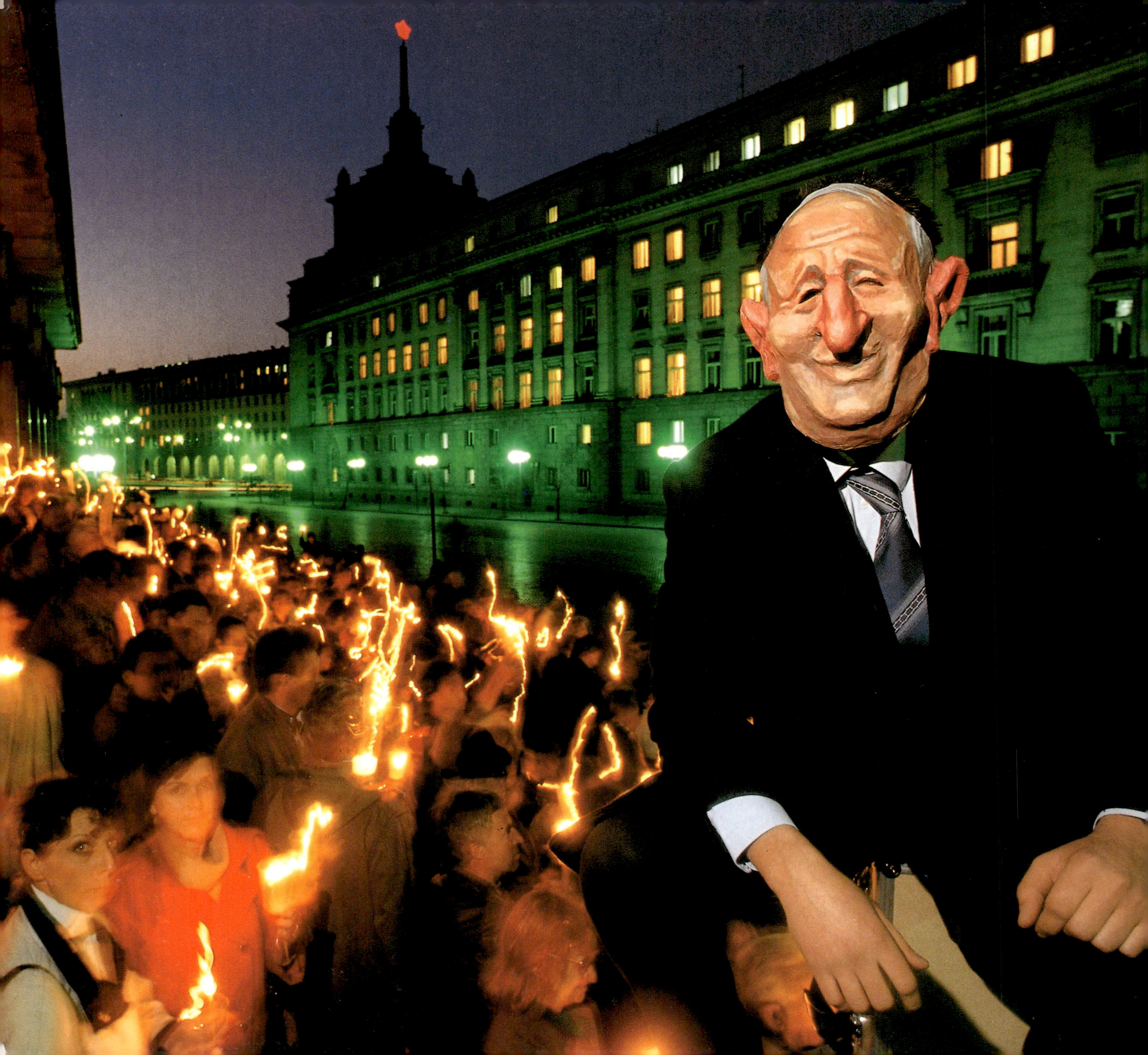

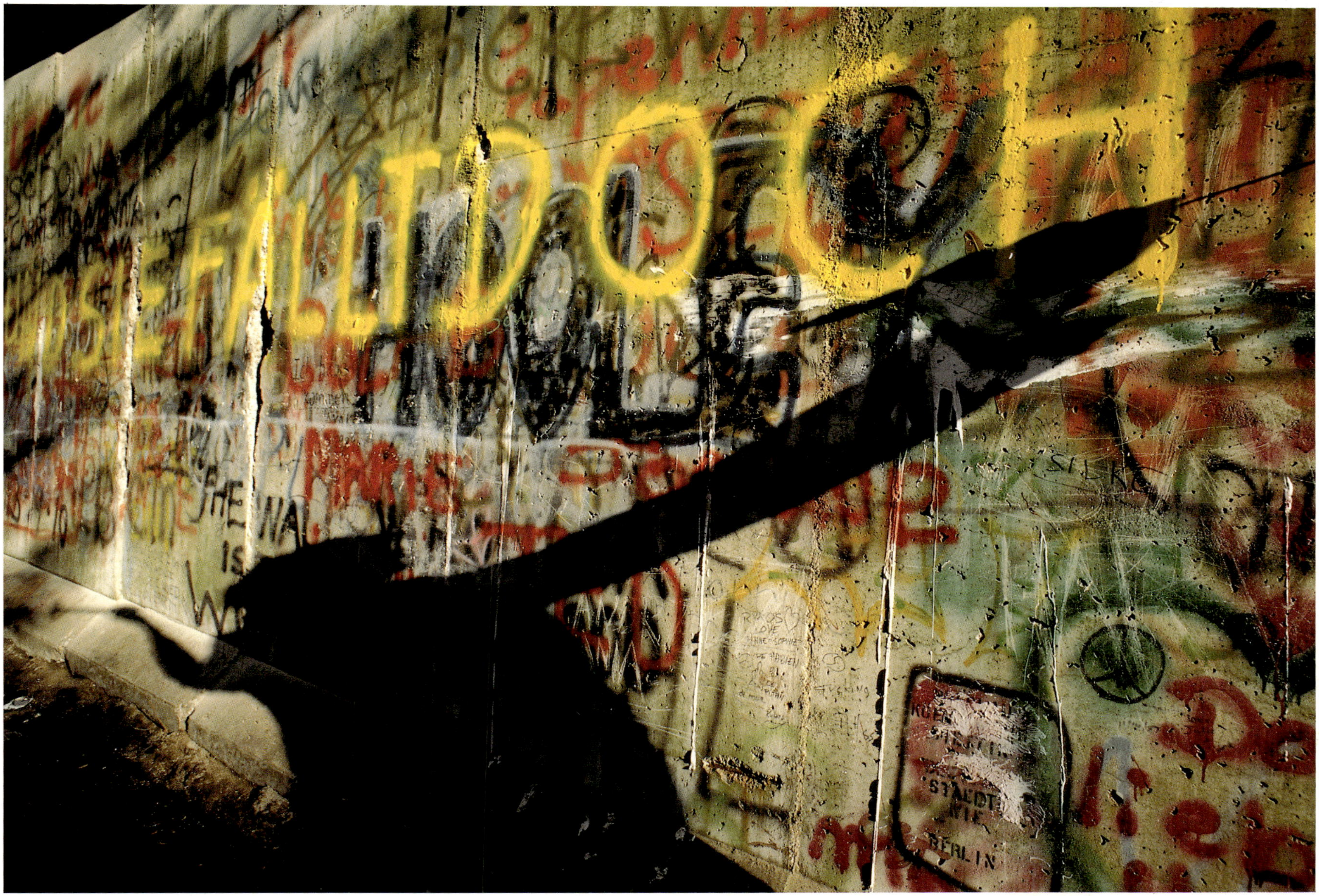

Facing page • The red star is still shining over the Party headquarters in Sofia. Here, in the early days of 1990, however, the ageing dictator Todor Zhivkov joins the procession of demonstrators only as a caricature, a mask from the past with a frozen grin. The all-powerful ruler of Bulgaria is suddenly just a puppet, borne aloft as a trophy by the people. The tragedy becomes a comedy, power a farce. (January 1990)

Above • '*Und sie fällt doch*' – 'But it will fall nevertheless'. A nonsensical piece of Wall graffiti is transformed overnight into a prophesy, even a warning: it *is* falling, despite head of state Erich Honecker's boast that his edifice would stand for 'another hundred years'. A few weeks later, the Wall fell prey to the souvenir-hungry 'Wallpeckers'. Galileo's proof was demonstrated in a new way: there is no wall, no dogma so firmly founded, that it may not be shaken one day. (November 1989)

AFTERWORD

Hanns Joachim Friedrichs

Bilderberg – the name of the group of photographers whose works compose this book – translates literally as 'picture mountain'. In choosing their name, however, I suspect they had something other in mind than a description of the dilemma which would face them as they selected photographs for a book about the Wild East and how it came about. But prophesies often come true simply because they have been uttered, and the people from Bilderberg were indeed confronted by a mountain of pictures, taken over a period of five years within an area comprising everything that was once the Eastern Bloc, and tracing a development which is still in its infancy, however dramatically the world may already seem to have changed. They were to compile more than simply a visual calendar, more than an illustrated chronicle of social upheavals in Eastern and Southeastern Europe in the second half of the eighties; rather, they were to search for the clues which would lead to the reasons which would in turn explain why the world of those Europeans living east of Aachen is suddenly no longer what it was. A better world, at least in prospect, say the politicians. A world at all events radically different, unpredictable, turbulent, wild.

It is said that without the invention of television, without the possibility of witnessing events which affect everyone, but which only a few actually experience at first hand, the revolution in Eastern Europe could not have happened. It may well be true. It was television – in doing no more than noting and passing on what had manifested itself as the wish and will of the people – which fostered the solidarity which led, in the end, to the collapse of the ruling cliques. First in Poland in 1980, with the founding of the Solidarność (Solidarity) union movement, which many people believe would never have happened had not the first Polish pope made the first papal visit to Poland one year earlier. It was still banned and living underground when Mikhail Gorbachev came to power five years later – the man to whose will for reform Solidarity owed its survival, and Germany its unification. In the mid-eighties, however, such a development was still out of the question; Poland aside, it was to be another four years before the cracks in the Soviet Communist empire became visible to the naked eye.

A first hint was given in early 1989 in pictures of East Berlin dissidents at a rally in memory of Rosa Luxemburg and Karl Liebknecht. After travelling around the world, these images returned to East Germany to bring millions the assurance that they were not

alone in their protest against a Party which permitted no other thinking than that prescribed by its dogma. Later came the candle-lit revolution, the demonstrations in Leipzig, Berlin and Dresden, fearfully hushed up by the regime but recorded and broadcast every evening by the class enemy in the West. Not staged by him, however, as propagandists from the Socialist Unity Party would repeatedly assert – being unable to conceive of any such thing as uncensored reporting.

It may well be that West Germany's ARD and ZDF television channels occasionally fell short of journalistic perfection – but neither corporation had to worry about its credibility in the eyes of its East German viewers. Life in Leipzig and Berlin in the autumn of 1989 appeared on the screen more or less as it was really lived. And what appeared on the screen clearly served as a rallying cry, an encouragement to all those still hesitating to take to the streets themselves, to demand a better German Democratic Republic and later a unified Germany. The message was plain: it was no longer lethally dangerous to stick your head above the parapet, to stand up and be counted.

Elsewhere, State television lent its own support to political change. The central broadcasting station in Bucharest became the focal point of Romanian resistance to Ceaușescu's tyranny. In Czechoslovakia, editors and engineers used the threat of strike action to force through live broadcasts showing Vaclav Havel, in a speech from the balcony of a Party building in Wenceslas Square, promising to bring a rapid end to the Husák regime.

During the period in which this book was being compiled, I had the undeserved good fortune to be working in a television news editorial department which was flooded daily with the latest momentous happenings from Eastern Europe. I, too, have my own mountain of pictures, compiled from the thousands of images which at the time I thought would be unforgettable. It proved otherwise, and I now need a prompt, a name, a place, a town, perhaps a book like this one or the latest instalment of a story from those turbulent weeks, in order to dredge up from my memory the fragmented recollections that remain. Some surface easily, often of their own accord.

There was the night the Wall came down, of course. I was sitting in the studio as the mist began to clear towards ten o'clock in the evening, and it may indeed have been from me that a few million East Germans learned how greatly their lives had changed on that night of 9 November 1989. Or four weeks earlier, with the Palace of the Republic surrounded by huge crowds on an evening supposedly celebrating the fortieth anniversary of the founding of the German Democratic Republic. Gorbachev was there, and the tens of thousands lining the banks of the Spree cried 'Gorby! Gorby!' – just as others up to their necks in water might cry for help.

Or 9 October in Leipzig, the day on which it seemed possible, if not probable, that the authorities would finally clamp down on the weekly Monday demonstrations it had previously – nervously – tolerated. I remember a telephone conversation I had early that evening, in which a young man from the Leipzig Campaign for Peace and Human Rights assured me that the local radio had just broadcast an appeal for non-violence by Gewandhaus conductor Kurt Masur, a cabaret artiste and three prominent representatives from the regional headquarters of the Socialist Unity Party. This was absolutely unprecedented and surely gave grounds for hope. That hope proved well-founded: no blood was shed on Karl-Marx-Platz that evening – the evening, as we now know, on which the Leipzigers dug the grave of the Party and its State. The burial took place just four weeks later.

The Czechs dealt more gently, more quietly, more ironically with their regime. When it finally ended in January 1991, the people in Prague's Wenceslas Square pulled out their bunches of keys and rang in the new age – a jangling funeral knell for the unlamented Czechoslovak Socialist Republic.

Seconds later, minutes at most, all of this had flitted across the screen. The price of the immediacy, the moving intensity of the media, is its fleetingness. History is condensed into the length of a news bulletin. Then the next story comes on and starts to erase the pictures which a moment before had seemed indelible. Only where we in television consider one angle to be particularly striking, only where we want to give the viewer time to consciously register details and perhaps decipher hidden meanings, do we hold it still, do we freeze the moving image – into nothing less than a photograph. It is something we do only rarely, it being judged inappropriate to the medium: the viewers' expectations run along different lines. We do not wish to change that (and nor can we). For alongside the specific unique example of television there exist many other forms of mass communication which are much better suited to the need for leisurely contemplation, the need for intense absorption in a text or picture. In that respect, the present book is an outstanding example of what photojournalists can do for the examination and presentation of world history.

But I am biased – by my own unrequited love for photography, by my own unfulfilled dream of becoming a photographer, a photojournalist. It was not to be. There dawned on me just in time the realization of my deplorable lack of talent, the recognition that the urge to communicate could be better satisfied in other ways – by working for television, for example. But my admiration for those who can tell a story without words has never left me. A few years ago I compiled a report on a well-known photojournalist for ZDF, the second German channel. For a whole week I stood directly behind or beside him as he took his pictures, and then photographed my own version of what he had just sighted and shot – using cameras no less expensive than those of the maestro himself. Everything you do, I told myself, do exactly as he does: choose your subject, adjust your f-stop and shutter speed, select your lens, film and filter. That way nothing can go wrong on the mechanical side. Nor did it. And when the films came back from the laboratory, it was even possible to recognize the occasional similarity between the person behind his camera and mine. But no more than that.

The story the maestro had told (about Hawaii) was beautiful. I had taken a few snapshots. But that's photography for you.

BILDERBERG

The Photographers' Archive

Rudolf Trefzer

Hamburg, as probably the most important media centre in the German-speaking world, is home to a large number of contributors of written and photographic material to publishing enterprises. One such 'supplier' is Bilderberg, a picture agency with a wholly original basic concept and approach to photography.

To be a freelance journalist working for high-quality magazines is no doubt the ultimate ambition of many a photographer. The reality of such a career, with the constant pressure of competition, is not all sunshine, however. What, then, could individual photographers do to strengthen their position in the media jungle, to shield themselves from the despotism of the 'big' publishers?

The answer, plainly, was to become stronger and more independent by joining forces with other photographers and making a common stand. It was a solution pioneered by the Magnum photographers, who formed their own agency in 1947. And although a number of similar ventures subsequently foundered, others were rewarded with success. One such is Bilderberg, which has been flourishing since its foundation in 1983.

After occupying several temporary addresses, 'Bilderberg – Archiv der Fotografen' (Bilderberg – The Photographers' Archive) is now permanently installed in former factory premises in Hoheluftchaussee, Hamburg. Inside, it is immediately clear that Bilderberg is no conventional photographic agency. For in addition to the expected equipment and furnishings, there is also a spacious common room with a kitchenette, and a seating area with black leather sofas and a large table. Although the days are gone when the photographers each worked in the archive themselves (twelve employees now carry out such tasks), the 'Bilderbergers' still meet together regularly to talk business and show each other their latest work.

The agency of today was, in spring 1982, still a dream. If you could start up your own photographic agency with a number of like-minded colleagues – so ran the thoughts of photographer Andrej Reiser – not only would all the profits go directly to the photographers, but it would be easier to control the use and whereabouts of the photographs themselves. Reiser turned his idea into action, and in February 1983 the dream became reality: fifteen photographers founded their own agency and gave it the ironically ambiguous name of 'Bilderberg' – 'Picture Mountain'.

For fifteen competitors to form a common front, and to ensure the success of the agency, certain issues needed to be discussed and clarified. Everyone involved first had to learn how to run a business, and to this end the Bilderberg photographers – whose ranks have since swelled to twenty-three – assemble at regular intervals to discuss current problems and exchange information.

In principle, each individual works for himself. After the first use of his pictures, however, all further sales are handled by Bilderberg for the benefit of the group as a whole.

But Bilderberg is more than just a commercial photographic agency. Like the celebrated French agency, Magnum, it sees itself as a professional alliance and a discussion forum.

'In the beginning', Andrej Reiser recalls, 'we all found it very difficult to overcome our individualistic, competitive natures. But after just two or three years it had become one hundred per cent clear to us all that the founding of Bilderberg had been a highly significant step that had changed the way we thought. Although we are still rivals in the market-place, antipathy has become solidarity and jealousy has become constructive competition.'

But that is not all. In founding their own agency, the 'Bilderbergers' have also created a counterbalance to the economic power of the media world and, at a personal level, prevented their being played off one against another.

Although Bilderberg photographers have no explicitly formulated philosophy or compulsory code, what they do all have in common are travel and the classic tradition of photo-reportage. They are specifically not news photographers – trigger-happy roving reporters who carry a camera, as others might a ball-point pen, just in case there should be something to snap.

There is no specific Bilderberg style, however; the individual photographers all have a different and distinctive signature, different preferences and areas of particular interest. What was taken by whom is thus something which can very likely be read directly from the works themselves.

Bilderberg is now well established on the international photographic scene. However, for the ease of decision-making, and to maintain the cohesion of the group, the 'Bilderbergers' themselves are determined to keep any possible future expansion under strict control.

BILDERBERG PHOTOGRAPHERS

Rainer Drexel
Georg Fischer
Klaus D. Francke
Michael Engler
Wolfgang Volz
Andrej Reiser
Renate von Forster
Eberhard Grames
Klaus Bossemeyer
Wolfgang Kunz
Joachim Ellerbrock
Gerhard Schafft
Hans Madej
Frieder Blickle
Karol Kallay
Milan Horacek
Till Leeser
Gert Wagner
Hans Jürgen Burkard
Walter Schmitz
Thomas Ernsting
Peter Ginter
Dorothea Schmid
Reinhard Wolf •

• Estate administered by Bilderberg

THE CONTRIBUTORS

PAVEL KOHOUT

Born 1928 in Prague, Czechoslovakia. After finishing school, he studied European literature at the Charles University in Prague. At the same time he worked as an editor of children's programmes for Czechoslovakian radio.

In 1948 he became a commentator for 'Mevro', the special broadcasting station set up on the occasion of the International Broadcasting Exhibition in Prague. From the middle of 1949, Pavel Kohout spent a year as assistant to the Czechoslovakian cultural attaché in the USSR; from 1951 to 1952 he was chief editor of the satirical weekly magazine *Dikobraz* (Porcupine), and during his military service from 1952 to 1955 reporter and author of the army arts journal *Československý Voják* (The Czechoslovakian Soldier). Then followed a year in the arts editorial department of the newly founded Czechoslovakian television corporation. From 1956 onwards he worked as a freelance writer and director, in particular for Prague's second-largest theatre, the Vinohradské Divadlo (Theatre in the Vineyards).

Pavel Kohout was politically active from a young age, and his first poems expressed the unalloyed optimism shared by the majority of Czechs and Slovaks during the post-war years. They earned him early fame and, later, correspondingly harsh criticism.

Having explored many fields of literature, it was Pavel Kohout's talent for play-writing, characterized by particular sensitivity in the portrayal of personal and social conflicts, which triumphed. He was one of the first Communist intellectuals to argue the rejection of Stalinism even before its official condemnation, for which he also had to suffer the initial censure of the authorities. His critical analysis of the Czechoslovakian youth association cost him his membership of the executive. His public activities were thus predominantly pursued under the umbrella of Czechoslovakia's writers' association.

His first plays soon brought him renewed popularity. He became the most-performed Czech dramatist, abroad as well as at home. Thus in the late fifties he headed the list of most frequently staged foreign dramatists in the USSR and GDR. The early sixties saw increasing numbers of performances of his plays in Western Europe, Asia, Africa and North and South America. In choosing his subject matter, Pavel Kohout regularly reworked the material of others, which – remaining true to the original yet independent at the same time – he made a central component of his dramatic oeuvre.

During the Prague Spring of 1968, in which the movement towards 'Socialism with a human face' reached its climax, Pavel Kohout, in his capacity as chairman of the Czechoslovakian Communist Party Organization of Czech Writers, was simultaneously the author of the famous petition to the State and Party leadership signed in July 1968 by two million citizens.

After the events of August 1968 – the invasion of Czechoslovakia by the nations of the Warsaw Pact – he was expelled from the Czechoslovakian Communist Party and banned from working, performing, publishing or travelling abroad. His works were removed from public libraries and largely destroyed. The discrimination, denunciations, arrests, trials, murder threats and other forms of harassment to which he was subjected, such as his eviction from his Prague apartment, were all deliberately aimed at persuading Pavel Kohout to leave the country – something he rigorously refused to do, however.

It was consequently only possible for his books to appear abroad and for his plays to be performed in foreign languages. His works were circulated in Czech in typed manuscript form, chiefly by the well-known Edice Petlice (Lock and Key Editions).

Over the following ten years, he was involved in every civil rights campaign and acted as co-founder and co-author of the internationally renowned 'Charter 77', whose ideas he continues to uphold.

In 1978 he was awarded the Grand Austrian State Prize for European Literature. At the invitation of the Austrian government, and with the authorization of the Czechoslovakian authorities, he was allowed to accept the award in Vienna in person. He was further granted permission to take up an advisory post at Vienna's Burgtheater.

On their way back to Prague in October 1979, Pavel Kohout and his wife Jelena were stopped by Czechoslovakian border officials. They were forcibly deported to Austria and, on no recognizable grounds, were stripped of their Czechoslovakian citizenship. Jelena and Pavel Kohout were subsequently offered Austrian citizenship, which they accepted, taking up residence in Vienna.

He turned down all the posts and functions offered him after the 'peaceful revolution' of November 1989 in order to devote himself fully to his artistic projects. The Kohouts have since had their Czechoslovakian citizenship restored and now live alternately in Vienna and Prague.

HANNS JOACHIM FRIEDRICHS

Born 1927, for many years chief editor and presenter of 'Tagesthemen', the daily news programme broadcast by ARD (Public Broadcasting Corporation of the Federal Republic of Germany). After studying in Berlin and London, he became a political editor for WDR (West German Broadcasting Corporation) in Cologne, followed by more than twenty years with ZDF (Second German Television Channel), as foreign correspondent in Washington, New York and Saigon and, as head of sport, presenter of 'Aktuelles Sportstudio'. Today lives with his wife, dog and a small Sony as a freelance journalist in Hamburg. His many awards include the Grimme Prize (1975 and 1990), the Eduard-Rhein-Stiftung Special Award (1987), the Telestar from ARD and ZDF (1990) and the Golden Camera (1987 and 1991).

ALEXANDER A. SMOLTCZYK

Born 1958 in Berlin. Studied economics and social sciences in Berlin and Montpellier. Numerous journalistic assignments in Eastern Europe. Since 1989, Alexander A. Smoltczyk has lived in Paris where, as correspondent and freelance contributor, he writes for *tageszeitung, GEO, Zeit-Magazin, Vogue* and other publications.

His book *Auf der Suche nach der verlorenen Revolution* (In Search of the Lost Revolution) appeared in 1989.

PHOTO CREDITS

Page	
17	Andrej Reiser
18	Andrej Reiser
19	Hans Madej
20	Karol Kallay
21	Hans Jürgen Burkard
22	Eberhard Grames
23	Andrej Reiser
24/25	Hans Jürgen Burkard
26	Andrej Reiser
27	Hans Jürgen Burkard
28/29	Hans Jürgen Burkard
30	Hans Jürgen Burkard
31	Hans Jürgen Burkard
32	Hans Madej
33	Andrej Reiser
34/35	Hans Madej
36	Rainer Drexel
37	Frieder Blickle
38	Rainer Drexel
39	Hans Jürgen Burkard
40	Karol Kallay
41	Frieder Blickle
42	Hans Madej
43	Walter Schmitz
44	Karol Kallay
45	Hans Madej
46	Hans Madej
47	Hans Madej
48	Hans Jürgen Burkard
49	Hans Jürgen Burkard
50	Milan Horacek
51	Hans Madej
52	Andrej Reiser
53	Hans Jürgen Burkard
54	Hans Madej
55	Hans Madej
56	Hans Madej
57	Andrej Reiser
58	Hans Jürgen Burkard
59	Andrej Reiser
60	Andrej Reiser
61	Ellerbrock & Schafft
62/63	Hans Jürgen Burkard
64	Walter Schmitz
65	Andrej Reiser
66	Eberhard Grames
67	Eberhard Grames
68	Eberhard Grames
69	Andrej Reiser
70	Hans Madej
71	Hans Jürgen Burkard
72/73	Hans Jürgen Burkard
74	Hans Madej
75	Hans Jürgen Burkard
76	Hans Jürgen Burkard
77	Hans Jürgen Burkard
78	Michael Engler
79	Andrej Reiser
80	Hans Madej
81	Andrej Reiser
82	Karol Kallay
83	Karol Kallay
84	Hans Madej
85	Hans Madej
86	Andrej Reiser
87	Hans Madej
88	Andrej Reiser
89	Hans Jürgen Burkard
90	Thomas Ernsting
91	Dorothea Schmid
92	Andrej Reiser
93	Andrej Reiser
94	Hans Jürgen Burkard
95	Hans Madej
96	Andrej Reiser
97	Andrej Reiser
98	Andrej Reiser
99	Hans Madej
100/101	Andrej Reiser
102	Andrej Reiser
103	Hans Jürgen Burkard
104	Andrej Reiser
105	Karol Kallay
106	Frieder Blickle
107	Frieder Blickle
108	Michael Engler
109	Michael Engler
110	Hans Madej
111	Thomas Ernsting

We would like to thank Rolf Gillhausen, whose experience and advice during the compilation of this book were invaluable.